Philip Lynott
Renegade

Alan Byrne

sonicbondpublishing.com

Sonicbond Publishing Limited
www.sonicbondpublishing.co.uk
Email: info@sonicbondpublishing.co.uk

First Published in the United Kingdom 2024
First Published in the United States 2024

British Library Cataloguing in Publication Data:
A Catalogue record for this book is available from the British Library

ISBN 978-1-78952-339-3

Typeset in ITC Garamond Std & ITC Avant Garde Gothic Pro
Printed and bound in England

Graphic design and typesetting: Full Moon Media

Follow us on social media:
Twitter: https://twitter.com/SonicbondP
Instagram: www.instagram.com/sonicbondpublishing_/
Facebook: www.facebook.com/SonicbondPublishing/

Linktree QR code:

Philip Lynott
Renegade

Alan Byrne

sonicbondpublishing.com

Acknowledgements

To those who ceaselessly supported me in my Lizzy research and that of Philip's solo adventures:

I've known Phil Osborne for over 25 years now – a real Lizzyhead. I have time and again deferred to his boundless knowledge. He has provided access to his extensive hard copy archive of cuttings and also offered editorial guidance over the course of my Lizzy books. I wanted to acknowledge Phil's contributions here. Gill, sorry for having him on loan for so many years!

To Adriano Di Ruscio for proofing, editorial and photographic support. Thank you Grandaddy! Dave 'click click' Manwering for being the photograph man. Frank Healy for always being a frank and supportive Lizzy demon. Ye're combined Lizzy affliction needs no dressing. To Nick Sharp, who contributed without fail in the original research phase – thank you.

For the kindness in giving me your time, for which I'll never not be monumentally grateful, I'd like to extend a massive Hola to everyone who spoke with me on the Lizzy research books charge:

Will Reid Dick, Brian Downey, Ted Carroll, Brian Robertson, Soren Lindberg, Jerome Rimson, Tony Visconti, Bryan Evans, Robin George, Paul Hardcastle, Eric Bell, Michael O'Flannagan, Brush Shiels, Shay Healy, David Heffernan, Gerry Gregg, Jim Fitzpatrick, Tim Booth, Freddie White, Laurence Archer, Marcus Connaughton, Philomena Lynott, Smiley Bolger, Robbie Brennan, Joe Staunton, Fiachra Trench, Andy Duncan, Junior Giscombe, Lawrie Dipple, Tex Read, Tim Hinkley, Mel Collins, Jeff Wayne, Chris Spedding, Peter Hince, John Helliwell, Jimmy Bain, Don Airey, Chris Tsangarides, Betty Wray, Clive Edwards, Maurice O'Callaghan, Philip Chevron, Roddie Cleere, Tim McStay, Sean O'Connor, Robin Smith, Jeremy Nagle, Charlie Morgan, Paul Gomersall, Denis O'Regan, Steve Johnson, Brendan Bonass, Damian Corless, Conor McAnally, Gus Isidore, Mark Stanway, Martin Giles, Clive Richardson, Bruce Gowers, Martin Adam, Kit Woolven, Maurice Mulligan, John Alcock, Paul Mauger, Pat Fenning, Peter Antony, Charlie McPherson, Andy Fox at GTFM and Stan Skora.

Looking back at the photographs: many thanks to Jan Koch, Dave Manwering, Dermott Hayes, Adriano Di Ruscio, Steve Claw, Anders Erkman (RIP), Kieron 'Diamaint' Loy, Michael O'Flanagan, Wolfgang Guerster, Martin Riordan, Alan Topping, Mitch Foley and Feekie O'Brien. To Monte Conner, Jim Cameron, Lennart Hedenstrom and Johnny Az Conlon for their Lizzyness. To Rene Aagaard for his Gary Moore Bible. Aileen McCauley & Irish Film Board for their assistance.

RIP Kit Woolven and Chris Tsangarides: I never met Kit or Chris in person but we skyped and phoned when I was researching the books. They both had great laughs, proper laughs. They were forthright, warm and often comedic in their recollections of working with the band. They both very affectionately spoke about the band members. They spoke of their frustrations at times but it never superseded their love of Lizzy's music and Philip's solo work. They were beyond great to chat with. 'Kids are great', Kit said to me after I told him about the arrival of my son, Rory... 'You can blame them for everything'. Both band and solo legacy are perpetually richer for your involvement. Salute to you both! X

Always the most supportive allies and eternal irritants: Regina and John Byrne and my sister, Sarah Paris France.

A bellow to an incredible talent: Bill Hicks! The great Amber Jennings: you're missed! Noinin 'clever bitch' Toibin, Penny 'window licker' Keane and Maeve the Cyclops.

My Thanks to Paul O'Connor, Shane Murphy, William Kelly, Dani Boy Melo, Reverend Joe Johnson, William Barbara Arnold, Dr. Thomas Keane, Christine 'Pristine' Keane, Niamh 'a book cover gonna come' Daly, Peter O'Neill Course Director at Juice FM Tramore Road Campus, Cork. Seamus Burkish Delight, Nan Khan, Kev 'Min' McLean, Stina 'Min' Orbell, Del Wilson and everyone else in Aberdeen, too. Aine, Conor and Fiadh Campion-Aloha! Eoin Keating – out there drinking Canada dry! To Dermot, Marie, Riona, Anna, Aidan and Rose for their welcoming to an unidentified office in the city. X

This book is for Sinéad, Rory and Siún. What a curious adventure this is ... Roxy, too, I guess. She doesn't bite – yeah right!

Foreword To The First Edition

When Alan Byrne asked me if I'd like to write a foreword for *Philip Lynott – Renegade Of Thin Lizzy*, I was hesitant. Although I produced the *Jailbreak* and *Johnny The Fox* albums, I hadn't spent a lot of time outside these recording sessions with Phil Lynott other than meetings and rehearsals. How would I write something about a man who was something of an enigma?

Alan's mad request started to make sense, though, once I'd begun reading the book. How much insight would it give to the reader on Phil's background and how his earlier life shaped this man who would become a poet, rocker, lyricist and driving force behind the pre-eminent Irish rock band? The answer was a lot. The first few chapters reveal details of his background and influences of which I had no clue. Great job, Alan.

When I first met Phil, he struck me as an interesting guy with a point of view. But despite his overt affability, there was always a feeling that there was much more to Phil than would be revealed quickly. His physical presence drew attention: after all, he was black, Irish Catholic and a rocker. Tall and thin, he was noticed wherever he went. He had a fondness for drink and drugs – not uncommon in the 1970s – and had a keen interest in women, to whom he was a romantic with an attractive and powerful charisma. He was a thinker, too. Obviously, his background and multicultural roots played a big role in this artistic direction, and as evidenced by his songwriting, he expressed his unique perspective on society in his words and music.

Phil was a charming man with a dry sense of humour. He was brooding, and the responsibility of getting Lizzy's direction focused obviously weighed on him. Thin Lizzy wasn't a democracy: Phil was the final arbiter on what Thin Lizzy would record, how they planned their touring and the image of the band. Of course, Scott Gorham and the two Brian's – Downey and Robertson – had their say, and their ideas were valuable, but there was no doubt that Phil was in control.

In my role as the album's producer, Phil's control could be problematic. Phil was quite stubborn, so I had to be sure to make suggestions and influence the sessions tactfully. This was not always successful; there were several occasions where we would butt heads, but ultimately, Phil was a reasonable man, and compromise, or course direction, went ahead if it made sense for the ultimate goal of the project.

Sometimes, I wonder what he would be doing now had he lived. I think perhaps he would have become a renaissance man, probably still writing poetry, playing music and being involved in fostering the careers of others. Maybe a figure similar to an Irish Leonard Cohen? But knowing Phil from my few short months with him in the 1970s, I'd bet that whatever Phil had chosen, it would have been an interesting path.

John Alcock

Philip Lynott
Renegade

Contents

Author's Note 11

Introduction: The Greatest Emerald Hero.............................13

Side A

    Chapter 1: Dublin Days 19

    Chapter 2: The Countdown To Lizzy.............................34

    Chapter 3: Rampant In Ramport 45

    Chapter 4: The Compass Points To Soho 67

    Chapter 5: Such A Very Fine Line 82

Side B

    Chapter 6: The Romance Is Over 101

    Chapter 7: Sometimes, Guilt Overcomes! 119

    Chapter 8: The Lady Loves To Dance............................127

    Chapter 9: Waiting Just To Catch Your Eye 133

    Chapter 10: Hard Times...151

Coda: Don't Talk Behind My Back 186

Skid Row – 1969, A Tribute To Philip Lynott.......................189

Further Notes And Sources 190

Author's Note

The original edition of this book, *Philip Lynott – Renegade Of Thin Lizzy*, was written between 2009 and 2012, with publication in the latter year by Mentor Books. Danny McCarthy was the owner of Mentor. He died unexpectedly in 2018 and I'd like to acknowledge his zest for the project, which was about 36 hours away from being shelved before his intervention. He took on a book about Philip and Lizzy in a harsh economic climate. He took the chance and I'll always be very grateful to him and the folks at Mentor for that, especially Una Whelan.

Here we are some years later with a brand new edition, remixed, reconfigured and rid of a ridiculously long subtitle. For this opportunity, I'd like to express enormous thanks to Stephen Lambe and everyone at Sonicbond for their contributions to this new book. It was a collaborative effort stemming from strong editorial advice from beginning to end. I hope you, as the reader, enjoy the variations that we were able to put into the book.

I've had immeasurable help over the years when it came to researching, from those in the band willing to sit down and give their time to those who worked with the band to help them achieve their aims in the studio and beyond. Time is a precious thing to give to anyone and I feel very fortunate to have been in receipt of that kindness. While I endeavoured to construct as full a picture as possible regarding Philip's work outside of Lizzy, the consistent thread of Lizzy's career trajectory is apparent throughout the text, as this was the bedrock upon which his solo expressions could be constructed and subsequently unleashed. To anyone that adopts the 'No Lynott, No Lizzy' refrain, most commonly used in tirades directed at ex-band members for reforming the group from time to time, then perhaps also consider 'No Lizzy, No 'Old Town' and No 'King's Call'. Philip was at his strongest within the context of the band but this strength also allowed him these other explorations, many of which you will read about in this book. I hope you like them and enjoy the aroma of the musical choices he offered in his lifetime. In other cases, you will read about recorded material that remains unpublished, much of which shows a different poet at play than the familiar one we know.

This book exists as an attempt to bring more of that light show glow to the work Philip did outside of the Thin Lizzy structure. When you look at the trajectory of his working life, once Thin Lizzy's commercial future was secured with the breakout albums of 1976, *Jailbreak* and *Johnny The Fox*, it was a matter of a few months before Philip began these bits on the side, contributing to Jeff Wayne's musical version of *The War Of The Worlds* in that same year. While there was no linear passage to his solo adventures, the workaholic threads are relatively easy to identify. If not working in the studio or on tour with Lizzy, he was documenting other songs or zipping back to Ireland to help local heroes and prospective challengers to the throne

I hope you enjoy the story of *Philip Lynott – Renegade* and the recollections of the people that helped Philip achieve his iconic status in Ireland and beyond.

Alan Byrne, October 2024.

Introduction: The Greatest Emerald Hero

Believe it or not, Philip Lynott led Thin Lizzy for 13 years, during which time they released 12 studio albums of original material and two live albums. Add to that, his two solo albums and a string of guest appearances across a variety of other projects. He also co-founded a new band in 1984 before going solo in 1985. His death in January 1986 put paid to any possibility of Thin Lizzy reuniting, although they have since reconvened from time to time under various guises.

Philip Lynott was a prolific songwriter in the context of Thin Lizzy and his solo work. He was also the writer of a considerable amount of unpublished material, the reasons for which are covered in various chapters of this book.

His output beyond Thin Lizzy never quite generated the same level of steam as the band he led, despite the high pedigree of songs such as 'King's Call' and 'Old Town'. His two solo projects – *Solo In Soho* and *The Philip Lynott Album* – were released while Thin Lizzy was a going concern. And while his main focus was to try to keep the band in the charts, these solo projects reveal a different road warrior, that was willing to stretch his musical ambitions with a variety of genres while embracing and using then-new technologies to record.

Philip's songs within Lizzy and beyond were often lyrically layered extravaganzas. He very carefully wrapped tales of his own life in song, using sentimental adornments, and perched them snugly in the architecture of strident arrangements worked out with fellow band members and producers or – as his confidence grew – by himself. Any song can be deconstructed and rearranged to fit a particular aesthetic. And perhaps, in some cases, songs on his solo albums could've been reconfigured and slotted into Thin Lizzy projects. The reverse was also possible and often did happen. 'Talk In '79' from his debut album *Solo In Soho* originated from the 1977 sessions that made up the *Bad Reputation* album, which Lizzy recorded in Toronto, Canada, with producer Tony Visconti. So, by default, an outtake from Thin Lizzy's *Bad Reputation* album ended up being the earliest known track that was worked on for Philip's debut solo effort. It was temporarily titled 'Talking' until Philip later re-worked the track for inclusion on his solo album, with Mark Nauseef taking on the drumming duties. The engineer on Lizzy's breakthrough albums *Jailbreak* and *Johnny The Fox* – Will Reid Dick – recorded the original drum track, while the song was brought to fruition by Kit Woolven, producer of *Solo*

In Soho, or 'the last man standing', as he was known to say. 'We used to listen to 'Talk In '79' quite a lot because of the way Will Reid recorded it with, I believe, just four mics', recalls Woolven. 'Usually, there might be a minimum of ten mics for a kit, so the fact that he got that drum sound using only four mics was fantastic. The performance was brilliant.'

When you consider Philip's Thin Lizzy output, as prolific as he was, what remains officially as his solo output amounts to roughly 80 minutes of his music throughout two albums. Not taking into account his various guest appearances but solely calculating his output under his moniker, it's not a hugely significant quantity of time. Nor is the entire content of that 80 minutes completely memorable. There are snapshots that signpost where his writing may have taken him across both albums had he lived a longer life. We see the romantic leading man in the promotional video for 'Old Town': for him, a step into the then unknown. The rambunctious character that led Thin Lizzy was seldom seen with the look of worry on his face. The facial expression Philip revealed after singing the first two lines of 'Old Town' on the Ha'Penny Bridge in Dublin reveals a new facet. Is he concerned or relieved at the state of the relationship being portrayed? This allegorical piece is likely the most considerable commitment to celluloid that he ever made. Unlike his final promotional video for the song 'Nineteen' made just weeks before his death, his browbeaten look is a return to Lizzy terrain – the macho man toughs it out with some bikers in the Californian desert. The director of this shoot – Clive Richardson – remembers:

Phil was no different in many ways from any other performer. He worried about how he would look. It was something we discussed. There was never going to be a situation that he was going to perform in the video without his guitar. This was his shield, I suppose, and what he needed to get into the character of the performer. He wouldn't have felt comfortable without it. Also, you couldn't really say he was acting. He was just himself and he was cool. As I said, he was concerned with perception, and we did have a conversation about the scene where he gets on the back of the bike and they ride off. He was asking, 'Is this naff?'. He needed reassurance on how it looked and how he looked.

Perhaps Phil's most significant achievement in his solo career was the selection of 'Yellow Pearl' (on *Solo In Soho*) as the theme music to *Top Of The Pops*. However, 1981 was also a confusing period in his career and that of Lizzy. Arguably beyond their peak, second-guessing the next commercial move was not without its challenges, as you'll come to read in these pages. 'Yellow Pearl' was also a collaboration with Ultravox frontman Midge Ure.

During 1981, Phil's visits home to Ireland increased in frequency. The previous 18 months had seen him set up his family home in Dublin's affluent suburb of Howth. The longevity that London alluded to in its promises of glory for musicians had led him to utilise the English capital as his primary base for the prior ten years. However, at 32 years of age, Philip was now a married man and father to three-year-old Sarah and one-year-old Cathleen. Around this time, he also had business interests in Ireland that required his attention, having gone into partnership with his mother, Philomena, in the hotel business near his Howth home. Together, they'd purchased the Asgard Hotel on Balscadden Road, a short distance from the harbour. Within 18 months of ownership, the hotel succumbed to a fire, and after being demolished, it was converted into apartments, which is what they remain to this day.

The early 1980s was a turbulent period for people like Phil and bands like Thin Lizzy. It was also the period in which he launched his side career as a solo performer. While Thin Lizzy was still a functioning unit and their most recent album, *Chinatown,* had been a top-ten hit in the UK charts, it hadn't sold anywhere near as many copies as its predecessor, *Black Rose.* His debut solo album, *Solo In Soho,* didn't meet the commercial expectations of all involved either, despite being tenanted with some strong and diverse material. In many ways, his mind was heavily burdened with a growing mistrust of an industry in which he was once the toast. His fear of being sidelined by new musical trends helped bring this distrust of those around him to the boil. He wasn't the type of young man to confess widely about his doubts. Much of the material he was writing around this time reflected a thirst for expressing himself in different ways – the type of songs that didn't quite fit within the context of Thin Lizzy. At the start of the year, what turned out to be his final sessions at Compass Point Studios in the Bahamas yielded only one song that would make it onto the next Thin Lizzy album. The remainder either featured on his second solo album or were never published at all during his lifetime, one such example being the work in progress, 'It Hit Me Like A Hammer'.

It was also a relatively quiet year on the road for Thin Lizzy, which allowed Philip to focus more on his solo material. His current writing was taking him in multiple directions, much to the discomfort of his management team and record label Phonogram. Philip was writing songs like 'Beat Of The Drum' – a contemporary song arranged in a traditional setting, though without the commercial cunning of 'Whiskey In The Jar', which it could've so easily been shacked-up with. In June, he worked on a track called 'Sweet Samantha', again devoid of the expected rough-and-tumble Lizzy style but showcasing his versatility as a writer. Philip loved to venture into new musical terrains. However, his record label perceived it as an unnecessary hindrance. Rockers sell records; poets need grants. His distrust was elevating.

One reported source of his discontent stemmed from a rumoured rejection of the original submission of his second solo album to the label. It's reported that he was requested to omit a few tracks and compose material with an upbeat flavour to help them market the album to a wider audience. The album's working title was *Fatalistic Attitudes*. Blue skies and wild smiles it was never going to be. Kit Woolven was the engineer and producer involved with Philip during this period and recalls the tale about the album being rejected as misleading: 'Certainly, Phil's solo stuff was a production deal. We could submit anything we wanted to, that Phil said he wanted to be on his solo album. The record company had no yay or nay about it. They had to accept what we gave them.'

These were chaotic times for Philip, and while it can't be disproven that record label feedback about the album in progress was less than favourable, the only guide to their true feelings has to be the absence of a promotional video for the album's lead single the following year. While 'Yellow Pearl' was accommodated with a video and directed by Midge Ure, at the time of its release, it wasn't one of the original tracks selected for inclusion on the second solo album. It's a telling action, and in a time when video was about to be utilised in completely new ways to advance the mainstream success of bands, it only served to heighten Phil's distrust.

His friend and artistic collaborator Jim Fitzpatrick frequently walked the Burrow Beach in Sutton near Howth. Often, they strolled along the beach together. Phil threw stones towards the sea to entertain his dog Gnasher, who was named after Dennis the Menace's canine companion in the kid's comic *The Beano*. When he stopped to light a cigarette, his squinting eyes strayed to the sea, perhaps hoping that the resolution to his predicament would unfold in the waves that lashed the shore. His search for answers and personal identity only oiled the weathered wings of his creative indecision. The elements of air, earth and water had coaxed his imagination wide open in years gone by, and now he appeared to need those elements more than ever to make sense of his true self and direction. Fitzpatrick recalls how Phil didn't hide his disappointment when discussing his record label and had an inkling that all was not well: 'I'm running on empty', Phil complained, 'and if they don't like what I'm producing, then I've nothing left to give. I'm tired and bored with being a macho heavy-metal stud.' This confession wasn't lost on Jim as they continued to walk the beach with Gnasher. Though the pair were moving, Phil's mind was at a standstill. There was more. His wife Caroline's inability to fully settle in Dublin with their young family, along with the guilt of being an absent father and husband due to his professional obligations, bore down heavily on his mind. Phil's thoughts – more lucid than muddy that day – spotlighted his growing desire as he was trying to come to terms with himself. He asked:

How can you explain the texture of a day? You can get a dry, sunny day, a moist, sunny day or a cloudy, sunny day. There's a change in the texture. I've noticed this now walking in Howth where I live, when I bring the dog for a walk along the beach. I see the texture of the sea, and it's amazing how it affects you as a person. Sometimes the sea is so rough, it's awe-inspiring; sometimes it's so calm it's picturesque. But the atmosphere can change the mood you're in when you walk that same stretch of beach.

He had been intermittently working on this new solo album since the release of his debut *Solo In Soho* just 18 months earlier. He must've known his fortunes were changing when his record label reacted to his latest offering with cut-throat precision. Philip had gone as far as asking Fitzpatrick to produce some artwork for it: 'I did the painting of Philip at the chessboard. It was originally titled *Fatalistic Attitudes* and was for the cover of a solo album of the same name. The album was cancelled by the record company, who also refused to pay for the artwork. It was around this time that I did my last work for Lizzy and Philip. I ended up being owed in the region of £9,000 for work I did.'

The pair kept walking until they settled down on some dunes, where Jim sensed a 'desperate sadness coming from somewhere deep inside him.' The indubitable contrast in Phil's demeanour compared to earlier that summer, when he and his family had posed for Jim, was alarming. Jim took a roll of photographs that day and made a painting from one of the shots, titling it 'The Lynott Family, Glen Corr, Summer '81'. It shows Philip tying his shoelace alongside Caroline as their two daughters playfully climb all over them. It remains 'one of my favourite and most emotive paintings I ever did of him', says Jim.

Soon, the pair ended their exercising and exorcising and made for home – though, all the way back, Jim knew the sense of desperation that was filling Philip like a cancer was bound for the surface someday soon.

On other occasions, the pair visited the small cottage that was once the home of poet William Butler Yeats. The dwelling's elevated position gave a majestic view of the small uninhabited island known as Ireland's Eye. It was certainly a place for solitary thought, where Philip could reflect on the storms of his past while trying to comprehend the blustery and dangerous winds in his present. The bevelled edge of mainstream success and its attendant mood swings always presented the greatest challenges to bands that have dined at the top table. But when do you come to realise you're no longer *at* the top table?

When he realised he was being marginalised and tried to come to terms with it, his only option was to feed on the scraps at the music industry's perimeter. Artistic freedom was out, and budget cuts were in. He may have been shunted down the path where corporate muscle was no longer available to him for promotional purposes, but he certainly wasn't going to cave in and give the record company an album that represented 'The Boys Are Back In Town' part 40. His studded guitar belt with the leathers lashed to his person, in many ways, represented the restrictions he placed on himself when looking to diversify musically. He had to sell the rocker imagery to create the space to be the performer of songs like 'Old Town' and 'A Child's Lullaby'. The die was loaded. He often wondered how he got into this position. It hadn't been easy starting, and it wasn't easy climbing up the musical ladder. In lighter moments, he could look at his achievements in an amusing and upbeat manner, which is exactly how friends and collaborators remember him as a youngster.

Side A

Chapter 1: Dublin Days

When Philip first arrived in Ireland in the mid-1950s, he was cared for by his grandparents, Frank and Sarah Lynott. He moved into the house where his mother, Philomena, had been raised. For a few years, Philip had lived in England with her, but she was soon unable to cope with the sustained pressure of being an unmarried white mother to a mixed-race infant. Her parents agreed to raise him, in what was a courageous move, but one that was also open to ridicule and frenzied local gossip. It mattered little, as Philip later described being black and growing up in Dublin as being 'no different to having cauliflower ears.'

Aside from introducing his ethnicity to the locale where he happily grew up, his fevered imagination – like any other youngster of his time – was hugely influenced by the local picture houses. The allure of the adventures presented on silver screens ignited his inner curiosity. It's not inconceivable that the medium of cinema perforated Lynott's incandescent creativity. As a pre-teen, when taken to the pictures by his then-teenage uncles Timmy or Peter, the adventures of Roy Rogers and Trigger, The Lone Ranger and Hopalong Cassidy were the types of fare that appealed to his growing sense of adventure. Dives like the Star Cinema (aka The Rats) located in Crumlin were a frequent destination where he found the sounds of Hollywood making sweet overtures to his pre-teenage ego. He and his friends watched many western flicks at The Star, The Rialto or The Leinster on Saturday afternoons. Many of these picture houses were affectionately referred to as 'flea pits'. It wasn't unheard of for eight or nine-year-olds to be left alone to develop nicotine habits in these places. Philip was fortunate to live in Dublin, as many of the biggest movies of the day premiered there before often taking months to appear across the rest of the country.

It was Saturday afternoons like these that funded his busy mind. When his family found that he might be drifting in his schooling, he dismissed their concerns. Simply, he was allowing himself to develop in a way he felt was a natural shift. As he constantly filled his notebooks with ideas for lyrics, stories and characters, he was acquiring an awareness of his nature. His own voice on paper allowed him to recruit the personality he felt was required to present these ideas when it came time to perform them onstage.

One of the more popular games in Ireland during Philip's youth was known as the pitch and toss, where you would place an object known as a jack and pitch pennies to it. However, it was his interest in music that ignited his imagination and cemented his future – much to the annoyance of his grandparents, but very much so supported by his mother Philomena, who remembers:

Thinking back to his school days, he wanted to be an architect. He was good at drawing, but leaving that aside, I don't know when you realise that your poetry could just maybe fit into the possibility of working around music. I don't really have any recollections of the fledgling poet in Philip because he was in Ireland. But, I was always getting notes from him with hints being dropped: 'Ma, could you send me more money? I love you.'

He was like many others of his time – captivated by the music he channelled from across the airwaves of stations such as Radio Luxembourg. The new generation in Ireland was transfixed by these bizarre sounds coming across the wire. It was a calculated move by the station owners, as they sought to explore and target a burgeoning teenage market with a strong emphasis on what was a relatively new phenomenon: popular music. Whether it was the silky smokin' sensuality of Sam Cooke, the asphyxiated azure tunes of Ray Charles, or the blessed righteousness of Little Richard, they all fed the fury of Philip's escalating thirst for musical enlightenment. Elvis Presley was an early mainstay for a host of the hopefuls, but it was other artists like the late Buddy Holly, who was writing and performing his own material, that kindled and set his heart towards burning his own immortal trail.

Though his teenage relationship with his mother was long-distance, the bond they shared was strong. Being relatively close in age allowed Philomena to relate to a young Philip a bit more easily than her parents could understand him. It is fair to say that other than staying out beyond the appointed curfew time, he didn't get into much trouble as a teenager. In truth, he was probably too afraid of confession on Saturday mornings to push the boundaries.

A first brush with mortality came in 1964 when his Grandad Frank Lynott died unexpectedly from a heart attack. The effect on Philip was immense – the only father figure he'd known was gone. When Philomena flew home for the funeral, she found Philip standing in the corner with tears in his eyes. He was devastated. It also left the family under severe financial pressure, but uncles Timmy and Peter took on the mantle and began to support the family as best they could. Philomena's cheques sent from Manchester also helped alleviate the circumstances as they all tried to come to terms with their grief.

'I first met him when he was about 16', says Tim Booth of the Irish folk group Dr. Strangely Strange. 'his afro hairstyle is something I recall in that it was going up rather than outwards as it did later on. Being a black guy in Dublin, with his accent, it was great! When people met him, they expected a Caribbean accent, which used to really throw people off. It was great, he was a sweetheart.'

A pub named Sinnotts on South King Street in Dublin's city centre housed one of the more eclectic evenings to be had in the old town in the 1960s. Sinnotts was a lovely old Victorian pub where poets Leland Bardwell and Pearse Hutchinson used to run poetry readings in a tiny room above the main bar. This was a session held on a Monday or Wednesday night called Poetry & Music. Booth says, 'It had no PA, was totally acoustic, and the worst part of the evening was manhandling our harmonium up, and then – after numerous pints – down the stairs again. I think we were paid ten shillings each, with a few pints thrown in. It was half a crown admission: cheap at half the price. The poetry was often excellent, and the music was greatly appreciated, mainly for its words.'

Other local performers – such as poet Peter Fallon and percussionist Eamon Carr from the group Tara Telephone – regularly attended a gig run by Mick Colbert in Slattery's Pub on Capel Street. They were very much open-mic sessions, with everyone and anyone invited to contribute as they saw fit. It was at these sessions that Philip – one of the few black men in Dublin – took his first tentative steps in performing material that would later appear as early Thin Lizzy recordings. Though Philip had been known around Dublin as a member of the popular group The Black Eagles, it was at these poetry readings that he took his next step in public performance. Eamon Carr remembers: 'Philip was hip to experimenting and was always consciously anxious to take in whatever stuff he could. It was something I admired in him.'

The rivalry in the Dublin music scene was laden with negative repercussions. It had all the ingredients to leave lifelong scars, such was the bustling competition for gigs. The musicians' greedy appetites to have their music heard frequently led to bands falling out with booking agents, in-house fighting, and general mayhem – all of which played out in melodramatic scenes with less-than-tasteful grace. Bands pinching players from other bands to form new bands was rife and caused serious grievances on the scene. Guitarist Brendan 'Brenny' Bonass can vouch for this:

> Well, musicians only played with one band back then and wouldn't dare play with another. The significance for me was that I was known as a group wrecker. I was very ambitious, and more importantly, poaching was a big thing in those days.

By the time Philip was 17, he already had three years of performing with the cult-ish group The Black Eagles under his belt. That group launched his arrival on the Dublin scene. They had their fair share of ups and downs, but in early 1966, they were met with another challenge that would threaten their very survival. Their lead guitarist, Frankie Smith, had reached the end of his tether, forcing the group into the unenviable situation of either replacing him or calling it quits altogether and losing solid bookings. Drummer Brian Downey and Philip met with the group's manager, Joe Smith (Frankie's father), to discuss their options. It had been a reasonably profitable enterprise over the last couple of years, and, keen to continue the endeavour, it was Downey who suggested a replacement in the shape of Alan Sinclair. It wasn't the first time a group member had called it a day, as Downey himself had taken over from Mick Higgins 12 months earlier. Sinclair made his way to Leighlin Road in Crumlin to audition for the group, whereupon he was asked to play Jerry Lordan's 'Apache' (made famous by The Shadows), which he was familiar with, luckily. He recalls: 'I knew it note-perfect. Thereafter, I was introduced to the other members of the band, and the vocalist was Philip Lynott. I was astonished by two things: his colour and his energy. His enthusiasm for music was unbounded.'

The crucial element of The Black Eagles' experience was Philip's introduction to Brian Downey. Before joining, Downey had been playing with a band that evolved into the Liffey Beats, who one night found themselves in a support slot for The Black Eagles. This initial introduction came by way of Robbie Walsh, who knew Philip from the gigs going on at Fr. Brown's in Dublin's Drimnagh suburb. Downey retells the story of their shared-bill experience:

> I didn't know Phil at this stage. I knew who he was from school, but I didn't know him personally. I had seen The Black Eagles perform in

Walkinstown a few times and thought they were a really good band. It was Robbie Walsh who recommended us for the gig to support them. When we got there, one of the things I noticed was how much older they looked. They had their stage gear on, but they just looked much older than us. I was definitely the youngest – in fact, the youngest in the whole fucking place. They used to wear these blue blazer jackets that would sparkle, and Phil would be wearing a single glove, and he always looked directly at the spotlight. He had all the shapes back then. Anyway, halfway through the set, our lead guitarist broke a string. Instead of re-stringing it, The Black Eagles manager went out to the car, got one of their guitars and gave it to him. So, on we went, and he broke a string on *that* guitar, too. Joe wasn't happy at all, but he said, 'Lads, ye were alright, but the next time, bring your own set of strings.' That was the last I heard of Joe Smith for a while. The thing about that gig was that it introduced me to Phil for the first time. He knew who I was then. There was nothing to suggest anything was going to happen in the future, but it gave me the confidence to go up to him in school and say 'Hi.' The next Monday in school, we nodded and chatted in the schoolyard.

Though neither of them knew it then, this was the beginning of a lifelong journey, both personally and professionally.

Downey was born in Dublin's Harold's Cross area, but his family moved to Crumlin nearby when he was about six months old, eventually settling less than a mile away from the Lynotts on Leighlin Road. Downey was drawn to the drums from an early age, as his dad and uncle were drummers in the Harold's Cross Pipe Band, as were other family members. Downey says:

When they'd finish a march or performance with the Pipe Band, a designated person would be given the drums to take home and store. So, maybe once every two weeks, my dad would come home with a bunch of snare drums, bass drums and kettle drums and stick them in the bedroom. For me, as a kid, it was heaven. So, I guess I was about seven when my dad agreed to send me for lessons, but with a different pipe band in Dublin that he felt was a better one. As I got a little older, my taste in music changed and I didn't want to just learn about pipe-band drumming. I used to listen to records by The Shadows that my cousin – who lived with us – bought, and this thing called rock 'n' roll was catching my ear and imagination.

In the meantime, Philip's fondness for wanting to play songs that weren't top-40 hits was always at odds with what the booking agents were looking for. In his misguided quest to make The Black Eagles a credible musical entity, his musical choices were often curious and to be approached with caution. He insisted on including a variety of unknown album tracks by his favourite artists rather than playing the more common chart hits. Even at this early stage, his keen thirst for building a setlist was far beyond the grasp of his group mates, as Alan Sinclair recalls: 'He was the one who haunted Dublin's record shops for albums from which the band could lift material. He was the one who persuaded the group not to do our bread-and-butter songs as a working pop band. Because he was coloured, he naturally leaned towards Negro soul artists, and for a while, a great deal of our repertoire consisted of American soul music.

Though the group gained much from Philip's presence, he extracted more from the experience than perhaps his bandmates ever knew, in much the same way that he siphoned machismo from his silver-screen heroes in the local picture houses of his native Crumlin.

During his tenure with The Black Eagles, he often touched base with people who were to play integral roles in his development over the coming years. As early as 1965, fellow Dubliner Ted Carroll and friends had started promoting weekly gigs called The Bastille Club, at Cliff Castle in Dalkey, County Dublin. Here, they presented prominent bands such as The Creatures, The Kult and The Greenbeats. But on one night, having booked a top Belfast group called The Madlads, Carroll discovered that – unlike Dublin groups – some bands only played a one-hour set, which necessitated recruiting a support act to fill some time. Carroll recalls: 'A guy who was driving The Creatures told us that he could get a support act for eight quid, and so we went ahead and booked them purely on his recommendation. It turned out that his son was the lead guitarist, and he was The Black Eagles' manager Joe Smith. That was the first night I met Phil Lynott.'

With teenage curiosity, Philip soon became embroiled in experimental sessions at the Five Club on Harcourt Street, which is where he took his first steps orienteering the obscure orbit of a Dublin renegade in the making, Brendan 'Brush' Shiels. Though Brush knew Philip was part of The Black Eagles, he hadn't seen them in performance. 'The Brush', as he became known, was on the cusp of a few bands before eventually partnering with Ted Carroll for The Uptown Band. It's been said that Barry Blackmore – road manager for The Uptown Band – afforded Shiels the nickname due to his long hair and moustache.

The positive impact that The Black Eagles experience had on Philip in his apprenticeship as a singer can't be overstated. As the focal point of the group, he had to allow his audience access to what drove him musically while backing up his allure through the use of echo boxes and stage attire. Man about Dublin town Smiley Bolger – who'd become friendly with Philip during The Black Eagles days – had this to say about his development:

With The Black Eagles, Philip was really good. The quality of his performance was improving all the time. They were playing at record hops, tennis club pavilions and basement clubs around the city. I saw Philip performing in folk clubs before I ever saw him at the Club a Go-Go. I always saw him hanging around town; he was hard to miss. But the one thing that always stood out apart from being black, was his dress sense. He was always perfectly turned out and there was grace in his performance.

Philip regularly attended venues all over Dublin in pursuit of his multi-faceted musical aspirations while continuing to perform with The Black Eagles. It was in the suburb of Phibsboro that Philip met Terry O'Neill, who was playing with his own band but would go on to manage the first incarnation of Thin Lizzy. 'It was at St Peter's Hall in Phibsboro that I first met Philip and Brian Downey', says O'Neill. 'The Black Eagles played there on Saturday nights, while I played Sunday nights with my band called The Visitors. Later on, I ended up being a roadie for the first incarnation of Skid Row.'

The new music scene emerging in Dublin as Philip entered the twilight of his teenage years coincided with his growing awareness as a writer and singer of his own words. His regular visits to Sinnotts, Slattery's and Neary's off Grafton Street – the hosts of his embryonic aspirations – were standing him in good stead, but he had yet to convey his future plans to any family members. Marcus Connaughton of Irish broadcaster RTÉ recalls:

Slattery's – to use an example – was very much an *in* place around this time. A lot of groups involved in the beat scene used to perform there. I regularly met Phil at gigs and got to know the people who knew him, like Frank Murray. The Black Eagles maintained a healthy following until the time came for Philip to pursue a new direction.

It's not outside the realm of reality that Philip's frequent attendance at these venues contributed heavily to his later decision to commit his lyrics to book form with collections such as *Songs For While I'm Away* and *Philip*.

For now, he continued to perform with The Black Eagles while acquiescing to family demands that he secure a trade. He started an apprenticeship as a fitter with Tonge & Taggarts in Crumlin. And while his heart was never in it, he persevered as long as he could before reasoning that he was making more money from gigging. So when Philip was 17, he had the unenviable task of leaking his plans to his family. However, it was a move his mother, Philomena, supported.

In the last months of 1966, Ted Carroll and Brush Shiels began building the foundation for the Uptown Band. The band rose from the ashes of a recently disbanded group called Rockhouse, coincidentally managed by Carroll. Rockhouse was fronted by a young Paul Brady, who, since failing his college exams, was forced to withdraw from the group to concentrate on his studies. Brenny Bonass – lead guitarist with Rockhouse – agreed to join the new Carroll/Shiels combo, The Uptown Band. Carroll says: 'Brush had actually suggested that we ask Philip to join The Uptown Band when it was being formed, but we couldn't get hold of him at that time, so we settled for rhythm-guitarist/vocalist Dick O'Leary.' Several months later as The Uptown Band started gathering momentum, there was a coup which saw Ted Carroll ousted and replaced with Larry Mooney as manager. Within a short period, Brush also left to reunite with Carroll to form a new band. So, as Brush and Ted Carroll were hatching a plan to launch a new group to allow the rebellious act of writing and performing their own material, The Black Eagles were reaching their necessary end. The dominance of the showband mentality of playing chart hits served as a brutal broadside to performing their own material.

Around this time, Philip was being courted by Carroll and Shiels to form a Dublin *supergroup,* but he wasn't immediately convinced. In the wake of his early retirement as a fitter and turner, Philip voluntarily left the family home in Crumlin to ease the distress that his choices had made. He moved to the opposite side of the city, settling in a flat in Clontarf. It was the first of many such moves over the next three years. Though he no doubt felt disapproval from the family, he knew with hand on heart that the path he'd chosen was the one most suitable for his mindset and verve.

In September 1967, the newly formed supergroup Skid Row commenced rehearsal as a three-piece, with Nollaig Bridgeman on drums, Brush on vocals/bass, and Bernard Cheevers on guitar. But things changed quite quickly. 'After many band meetings, we decided that we needed a singer', says Brush, 'and that's when we got Phil in the group. We set up an audition, and he sang 'Hey Joe', and it came out so well, I knew I had my man. We gave him the job.'

The end of The Black Eagles was a blow to drummer Brian Downey, who'd become very close to Philip. The pair initially met while at the Christian Brothers school in Crumlin and were firm pals after a short time, music being the initial spine of their friendship.

Back in the old town, it wasn't long before Skid Row became the hottest band around, with regular write-ups in the local and national press. Philip still maintained his excursions to the spoken-word scene. When not performing him*self*, he regularly attended as many events as funds would allow to enhance his understanding of the development of his own words and inner voice. His entanglement with experimental music grew enormously once he became aware of a house known as the Orphanage on Lower Mount Street. It was rented out by a woman named Annie Mohan, affectionately known as Orphan Annie. Tim Booth of Dr. Strangely Strange takes up the story:

I don't know how Phil heard about it, but he started to drop by. I didn't really live there myself; I was just kind of in and out. There was also a woman named Annie Christmas, who unfortunately died a few years back. Annie was the daughter of a guy called Harry Christmas, who worked for either HMV or EMI. He was the Irish CEO of one or the other. Anyway, one day, Annie was in the Orphanage with Phil, and I think he would've been a year or so younger than her at the time, but I think they were stepping out. I certainly like to think that they did 'cause Annie always had a thing for Phil.

The initial Skid Row lineup didn't last all that long, with Bernie Cheevers opting out for the security of an apprenticeship with Guinness and Nollaig Bridgeman leaving for Germany. Very quickly, the band secured the services of drummer Robbie Brennan while replacements for Cheevers were considered. Brennan says: 'I was studying engineering at Bolton Street at the time. We had a meeting at the Coffee Inn in Dublin just off Grafton Street, went for a rehearsal, and I started soon after.' Before getting the gig, Brennan had been looking out for slots on the showband circuit after the disintegration of his previous band, Chosen Few. In the end, he opted to finish his degree but couldn't resist the lure of Skid Row when the chance arose.

These were happening times for Philip in Dublin. He couldn't stay away from the city bustle. He hoarded his ambitions in the pubs and clubs and was never shy to introduce himself and welcome the flood of foreign students to the Irish capital. In an interview with Chris Salewicz of the *NME*, he confessed:

> During the hippy days, when I was starting to get into singing, we used to buy a five-bob bottle of wine and sit over there just getting wrecked. It's great here. When people ask me what kind of smoke I like, I always say Stephen's Green. You used to meet these tourist chicks all the time. You'd say, 'I'd love to show you around, but I've got no money', so they'd go, 'Oh, it's okay, I've got money.' So that was it; you were in. I wasn't a gigolo, but I was pretty fookin' close, he grinned.

However, the original Skid Row was the lineup that caught the imagination of the gig-going public at first. Within an extraordinarily short period, the band topped local polls as the next best-sliced-and-gobbled loaf. In late February 1968, Ted Carroll confirmed: 'They were that good, it only took three months to reach the summit.' Skid Row's eclectic style was geared towards deep thinkers. The writing and performing of their own material was also a reaction to the still-hardened grip the Ireland showbands had on major venues. If local bands such as Skid Row, Granny's Intentions and Dr. Strangely Strange were playing the club venues across the country, then the ballrooms were tied up with the showbands. It's a difficult argument to link the impact of the showband's success to the lack of opportunity presented to singer-songwriters during this time. What is definite is that they played completely different circuits. So, on one hand, it can be argued that one didn't interfere with the other, but the flip side is that the availability of the ballroom space was never in the offing for the innovators.

It wasn't just music in clubs that was the happening thing in Dublin, or even the spoken-word performance opportunities that had emerged. The equally important art scene was also flourishing in the capital city. Artist Jim Fitzpatrick became a familiar face on the local scene and also contributed to the beat group Tara Telephone. The band initially consisted of Eamon Carr, Peter Fallon, Declan Sinnott and Lucian Purcell, with various other people dropping in and out of the sessions. Fitzpatrick recollects:

It was probably between 1967 and 1969 that I was involved with Tara Telephone. In fact, I remember getting a phone call from a San Francisco radio station wanting to interview me because we were the only beat group performing outside of San Francisco. It was news to me! Though, really the great facilitator for this exposure was BP Fallon. He had connections with David Bowie, Marc Bolan and John Lennon, so when we were publishing *Capella*, he arranged for promotional shots to be done with Lennon and Yoko Ono holding our magazine aloft. *Capella* later became *Book Of Invasions*. It was generally a really cool period then, with a great art scene. In those days, Brown Thomas had an art gallery downstairs that allowed artists to showcase their work. In fact, that's where I sold my Che Guevara print.

Though Fitzpatrick and Philip were peddling their individual conceits in related social circles, the pair had yet to meet. By this stage, Fitzpatrick was married with a child and working every God-given hour to support his family, so his opportunities were a bit more limited compared to the nightlife enjoyed by Philip. Fitzpatrick says:

The very first time I saw Philip was walking down Grafton Street. We always nodded at each other, but it was only later I got to know him. I knew that The Black Eagles had been popular around Dublin. They did have a large female following, mainly due to Philip's presence. It was during this time that Philip met Carol Stephen, who later gave birth to his son Darragh. Anyway, it was the poet Peter Fallon who introduced me to Philip, very much so on purpose, in a pub called Neary's. I recall seeing him before this as well, as we were both getting photos done by Roy Esmonde at his studio. We only passed each other on the staircase and exchanged 'Howyas', but there ya go.

The emergence of a multitude of clubs on the Dublin scene did much to proliferate expanded choices for emerging audiences, both locally and countrywide. The Five Club on Harcourt Street, The Countdown Club, The Scene (Parnell Square), Moulin Rouge and so many others were essential in propelling this new intensity. Brush Shiels ran his own club night called The Ghetto, while BP Fallon ran Happenings. As this collective paraded their respective hopes, they dropped in and out of each other's slipstream in the months that followed.

There was a young guitar player named Gary Moore who'd started making waves in his hometown of Belfast, playing with The Method and gigging on occasional excursions to Dublin. On one particular occasion – as he was about to quit The Method – Moore was substituting for another guitarist in a band called The Few and playing a short distance from Skid Row, who were in the 72 Club on Middle Abbey Street. Brush takes up the story:

We had a very good guitar player – Bernie Cheevers – but he left to become an electrician with Guinness. I knew Gary was good as soon as I heard him, doing a lot of stuff off the *Blues Breakers* album. I offered him a job that night. He said, 'You'd have to talk to my father.' So I went up to Stormont to see his dad, Robert, and he just asked me to look after Gary. So I say, 'No problem.' I reckoned it wouldn't take longer than six months to get this band off the ground.

Once Moore relocated to Dublin, he was initially put up by members of Dr. Strangely Strange, as Tim Booth remembers:

When he came down from the north, we put him up in this other house which also became known as the Orphanage, because some people moved from the first house into the second house. It wasn't exactly a crash pad, but if we liked people and they had nowhere to stay, we'd put them up and look after them. I do remember Phil saying to me that Gary is down from the north, that he's a bit lost and could we keep an eye on him, so we did. It was lovely because the house was full of harmoniums, banjos, keyboards and mandolins. Gary was always playing these, and Phil would drop around to check up on him. At this point, Phil wasn't playing bass, but he was playing guitar, 'cause I can remember him playing me some of his songs on acoustic, and I would show him what I was working on.

Skid Row – having developed a great reputation within a short period – took advantage of the opportunities this presented. They played a memorable gig at Trinity College Dublin's Dixon Hall after barely six months together. Patrons saw them do a wide variety of covers, such as 'I Am The Walrus', 'Crying Time' and 'Watermelon Man', but they always added their twist with their interpretation of the song. Tim Booth: 'I saw them doing a version of 'I Am The Walrus' in Trinity College, Dublin, and was blown away by that, thinking 'How can you do that?'. How they knew what way to do it, I don't know because I knew how to play 12-bar stuff.'

Philip's tenure with Skid Row wasn't to last after a now-infamous and never-seen-since performance on RTÉ's television show *Like Now,* where he was singing grossly out of tune. Philip had been experimenting with balloons (nitrous oxide), which were doing untold damage to his vocal cords, so by the spring of 1969, his voice was shot. It's interesting to note that around this time, Skid Row recorded a few demos, which Brush Shiels confirms:

A guy called Tony Boland brought us into Eamonn Andrews' studio, where we did demos called 'New Places, Old Faces' and something else called 'Mervyn Aldridge', but maybe I'm wrong. In the meantime, Phil had gone over to Manchester to get his throat done – he had terrible trouble with his tonsils. But he wasn't even on the plane, and we were rehearsing without him, and we thought we sounded great. So when he came back, I let him go.

Though demoralised at the band's mutinous decision, Philip took it on the chin and went to work extending his repertoire by taking up bass guitar. Such was the strength of his friendship with Brush Shiels, it was he who took Philip in hand and gave him bass lessons on and off over the next six months. So, by the summer of 1969, having jutted in and out of a variety of pick-up bands to make a living, Philip eventually hooked up again with Brian Downey (who'd recently departed another short-lived outfit, Sugar Shack) and formed a new band called The Orphanage.

The Orphanage rhythm section of Philip and Downey was yet to be cemented, as Philip didn't feel competent enough on bass as yet. Therefore, the pair recruited Pat Quigley to play bass while a local named Joe Staunton handled lead guitar. From time to time, Phil joined in on rhythm guitar. But as the band gained momentum, it began adopting a protocol of welcoming a variety of musicians for one-off gigs: an almost circus-like affair. Though by no means a band that was seriously attempting to obtain a record deal, they were nevertheless proficient in their objective of including original material. Guitarist Joe Staunton has a vivid recollection of meeting Philip: 'I had always seen Phil play around with the Black Eagles and thought he was great. My first introduction to him is a great memory. It was up at the Teachers Club in Parnell Square in Dublin. It was a pretty warm first meeting because he was so friendly and I was dying of a cold that night, just completely blocked up. He was just one of the boys, really, and he never lost that.'

The band's set included Bob Dylan's 'Lay Lady Lay' and George Harrison's 'While My Guitar Gently Weeps', but soon they were inserting their own material such as 'St. Stephen's Green', 'The Friendly Ranger', 'Step In My Shoes' and 'You Fool, You!'. Though ventures to local studios like Avondale and Trend were sporadic, they gave the fledgling rock gods much-needed recording experience.

Philip frequently met up with Terry Woods on the local scene and later recorded an unreleased version of 'Dirty Old Town' with him and others in Dublin. He'd been playing the local circuit over the past few years (with his girlfriend and soon-to-be wife, Gay) with the group Steeleye Span. Throughout 1969, Woods had regularly joined Philip onstage for The Orphanage gigs and ended up being a regular house visitor. Woods recalls: 'I knew Phil from when he lived with his granny. He used to come and visit Gay and me in a flat we had in Harold's Cross, and he would play me the songs he was writing. I played with him on the night the Americans landed on the moon. We went down to the pub and watched a bit of it.'

At this stage in his career, Philip was mainly writing his songs on guitar, though soon he moved to bass, developing an unorthodox playing style, but one that worked for him. In between Orphanage gigs, he still regularly attended weekly gigs in Slattery's Pub on Capel Street, often accompanied by Gary Moore. Often, Moore ended up performing with Tim Booth as a duo, with Philip watching on in support. Tim Booth: 'On one occasion, I recall I had dropped a tab of acid, and then we did the gig. It was an amazing experience. I strummed the guitar and sang while Gary played guitar, and people seemed to be genuinely amazed by our performance. We thought we were brilliant, and I think we may well *have* been on the day. When I started to get a little ropey, Gary kept an eye on me.'

The Orphanage continued to play the local circuit throughout the summer and into the autumn, showcasing their eclectic influences and generally enjoying the freedom of various musicians joining them at different gigs. Though there was never quite a destination in place for their artistry, there was the intention of making music the way to make a living. Unfortunately, the group's short life span means that very little recorded material survives, though what little there *is* highlights an interesting insight into Philip's lyric journey. The lyrics he wrote around this time were to surface on recordings made 15 years later.

He adopted the attitude of never discarding any lyrics or ideas made by him or others and duly noted anything in his workbooks which could be utilised at any given time and for any given project. By this time, Philip Lynott was an artist on the scent.

Chapter 2: The Countdown To Lizzy

It's late November 1969 in Dublin city centre, where Philip Lynott, Brian Downey, Pat Quigley and Joe Staunton are marching through the first of their two planned sets for the evening. The venue is the Countdown Club, just off O'Connell Street. In the crowd of revellers are two guys who'd recently jacked in their commitment to the Irish showband music scene in their attempt to make inroads in writing and performing their own material. Their decision was largely affected by the music emerging across the water in London, where the blues had finally bled into the mainstream and where Jimi Hendrix was mapping psychedelic highways for this next generation of musicians to traipse.

The two young men were Eric Bell and Eric Wrixon, both hailing from Northern Ireland. They sauntered through the club in a comfortable daze, suitably oiled with cheap sherry, and sat on the floor to listen to the band. Under such influence, Bell foresaw a band in his brain even before he buried the corpse of his showband past. He was convinced that what he was witnessing was the road to travel, the next journey for his own creative evolution.

It was hot in the club that evening, and the band were creating good vibes with many of the audience in alternative states of ease. Wrixon had shared a tab of LSD with Bell earlier in the evening, and combined with the cheap sherry, the pair were tripping in more ways than plenty.

On stage, drummer Downey bewitched Bell with his persuasive, percussive movement. Downey's subtle style was suggestive as he drove the band forward. He just happened to be perfectly in sync with Bell's tripping. The reason for Bell's visit to these beat clubs was plain and simple – he was searching for a drummer and singer to form a new three-piece blues band inspired by Hendrix and Cream. It wasn't just the drummer who caught Bell's attention – the singer out front who occasionally played maracas also made an impression, though it was really Downey who dazzled with his drumming. Though Bell was frightfully aware that his condition might prohibit any solid conversation, he took his chance when the band finished their first set, going backstage to initiate a chat with the pair. Eric Bell remembers:

Before that night in the Countdown Club, I had asked what seemed like thousands of musicians to form a group with me, and nobody was interested, not one person. My hair was very short at the time, as was the look for the showband, which I'd just left. I started going into bars and clubs on my own and just approaching everyone. Meanwhile, all these guys were sitting about with hair way beyond their shoulders, wearing bell-bottom jeans and kaftan coats, and I was wearing a suit. They were looking at me as if I was from the drug squad or something. It went on for weeks and weeks, and then, one night, I ended up in the Countdown Club with Eric Wrixon.

When Bell presented his idea of forming a new band to Philip and Downey, he was met with a tepid response, to be filed with all of the others, he initially thought. As he started to leave, Philip announced that The Orphanage had been taken as far as it could go, so maybe Eric's idea to form a new band was the right way to go. Downey was initially reticent but eventually agreed to try out the idea. So, in the Countdown Club that winter night of 1969, a four-piece band was sired through the rich determination of Belfast boy Eric Bell. Wrixon – a keyboard player – joined the band, though his tenure was short, as Bell's initial vision for the band was as a three-piece. In later years, Wrixon commented: 'Phil was screwed up completely. He had a chip on his shoulder about being black in Ireland and not knowing who his father was. He then decided to learn bass, but he never in his life became a good bass player. I was eight years into my career and I didn't have the patience. I didn't want to spend my life waiting for Phil to learn to play bass.'

In retrospect, Wrixon's comments appear a little harsh, considering Philip was only starting to learn the bass and needed time to acclimatise to the requirements of playing and singing at the same time. His primary focus was always going to be singing. However, the 'chip' that Wrixon refers to is an equally debatable point, with many of Philip's closest friends and family maintaining that his ethnicity and familial circumstances were crucial in helping him construct his worldview. In an interview some years later, Philip was to comment on any prejudice he bore witness to: 'In some ways I was lucky. There are not many blacks in Ireland, so there is not too much racial prejudice. When I came to England, I never encountered any anti-Irish feelings because the English have never heard of a black Irishman.'

Journalist Bob Hart recalls a tour of Irish bars with Philip in New York City. The pair encountered two huge, red-faced New York cops who looked like comic-book Irishmen but spoke like New Yorkers: 'Phil lifted his pint and enquired politely, 'Are you Irish by any chance?' One of the cops replied, 'Of course we're Irish, born in Brooklyn, but Irish. And where might you be from?' to which Phil grinned and said, 'If I told you, you'd never believe me.'

Over the coming months, the group exchanged views on band goals, set up management, and went about their rehearsals. They had yet to decide on a name, but that could wait since they had to fill a set with material and make the brave choices of how to balance the inclusions with their own stuff. The proviso that Philip insisted on before this band could commence was that he wanted to play bass and include some of his own material. One of the earliest known songs he wrote was 'Chatting Today'. Band manager Terry O'Neill recalls their humble origins:

> The band rehearsed in Countdown almost every day for about six weeks. I agreed for the band to play a gig for expenses in Countdown in lieu of those rehearsals. When I left Ollie, we started to rehearse in various rooms in CYMS on North Frederick Street and in the Teacher's Club in Parnell Square. They also had acoustic rehearsals, mainly for original material, in 'Clontarf Castle' – the half that Phil, Eric Bell & Eric Wrixon shared with well-known band manager, the late Larry Mooney. Later I did a deal with Bill Fuller to rehearse in The Town & Country Club – a big underground ballroom in The Ambassador/Gate Theatre building on Parnell Square. In return, we did some Monday nights for a very small fee.

As the band continued to rehearse and get their material tight, a press release was drafted to announce their arrival on the scene. Of course, they still needed a name, and it eventually unfurled itself in Bell's imagination while reading the comic *The Dandy*. A *Dandy* character known as Tin Lizzie caught his attention, and with minor adjustments, the band agreed to the name Thin Lizzy. Though a rock legend was not yet born, yearnings of legendary status certainly filled their fevered minds.

It had been an emotional period for Philip over the last 18 months, from the time he was with The Black Eagles through to his brief sojourn with Skid Row to his entanglement with The Orphanage. A lot more besides had happened. It was while he was a teenager in The Black Eagles that he'd become involved with a girl named Carol Stephen, who had first seen him perform at a Sunday-afternoon disco. Before long, they were boyfriend and girlfriend, often meeching off school to spend time together. As their relationship developed, Philip invited her to gigs he was playing, much to the annoyance of Brush Shiels, who said the following: 'He was told not to bring his girlfriend along – a lovely girl, Carol. There were no girlfriends allowed at the gig or in the van. The idea was we go to the gig, look at the girls and piss off the blokes. And that worked.' What few people knew at the time, was that Carol became pregnant with Philip's child. In a 2011 interview with *Irish Independent*, Carol offered further insight into their relationship:

I was 17, we'd been together a while. I gave the whole thing over to my father. He looked after it and me very well. When I first discovered I was pregnant, Philip thought there was nothing left for us to do but run away and get married. He was dead keen on doing that. We hadn't a fiver between the two of us, so I had my parents at home and I knew they weren't going to judge me, and I just allowed my dad to take over the whole situation. My mum too, she was great.

During her second trimester, Carol went to a home for unmarried mothers in Castlepollard, Co. Westmeath, and remained there until she gave birth to her son Dara. Philip and Carol split -up before she went to the home in Co. Westmeath. They did, however, get back together briefly. Carol:

After all of that, and Dara had been given up for adoption, one day, I was walking down Grafton Street, and Philip was across the road. Philip came straight over and he was asking me how I had gotten on and everything, as he didn't have a telephone back then, and there had been no connection with him since before I left, and the two of us went up Grafton Street. We were wondering where to go, and at the top of Grafton Street, there was a cartoon cinema. So we sat in the back of the cinema, and he wanted to know all about the baby and being away, and I told him all about that. And the two of us stayed there in the cinema, because in those days you could sit in the cinema and watch films over and over, and we sat talking about Dara and sobbing until it was time to get the last bus home.

The inescapable truth of the matter is how much his life had mirrored that of his mother less than 20 years earlier. The irony of the circumstances couldn't have been lost on Philip. Such was the social climate of late-1960s Ireland that, in most cases, having a child out of wedlock dictated that the child was placed for adoption and the mother-to-be was placed in a home for unmarried expectant mothers. It seems that this huge emotional treadmill – for both Philip and Carol – led to the breakdown of their relationship. Dara and Carol were to meet again and establish a relationship later in Dara's adulthood.

Philip's childhood experiences were much the same as anyone else's, though not as conventional as most. Music, it appears, was the outlet he needed to expound any emotional fragility. He could create scenarios for the characters in his songs; he could use his first-hand experiences yet write in the third person to offset any insightful criticism.

Later on, Philip penned the delicate 'Little Girl In Bloom', where he wrote of a young girl who has discovered she's pregnant and is reluctant to confess to her father. The eerie irony is impossible to ignore:

Little Girl in bloom carries a secret
A child she carries in her womb
She feels something sacred
She's gonna be a mammy soon
When your daddy comes home
Don't tell him till alone
When your daddy comes back
Go tell him the facts
Just relax and see how he's gonna react

It's fair to say that the young woman in the song could so easily be a composite character – an adult Philip trying to comfort his mother in the past and – since he wrote the song a couple of years after his split from Carol – attempting to comfort her in his own past. If he couldn't deal with the current circumstances, Philip would time-and-time-again write down his feelings in notebooks, and try to come to terms with how his life was unfolding.

What is evident in the clutches of his first selection of songs is an emotionally naive, soulful and searching young man who yearned for a port to call his home but struggled to generate the endurance required to dock. He did, however, contribute to the creation of something which was to endure, and that was a band called Thin Lizzy.

Throughout 1970, Thin Lizzy travelled the main roads, the back roads and the yet-to-be-named roads of Ireland in their quest to build a solid reputation as a bookable act. From their official unveiling to the local press on 18 February 1970 when Terry O'Neill was managing the band, until an unlikely stroke of luck the following November, they played *any*where if it meant sharpening their armoury. Soon, O'Neill relinquished his interest in the band for £500. During O'Neill's tenure, to bolster funds, the band played during showband intervals, where the audiences were sure they were from outer space, visiting planet Earth to sample the nightlife, maybe even the good life.

It was when they were asked to back up a singer in the Joe Cocker mould named Ditch Cassidy at a Decca Records audition at the Zhivago Club in Dublin that they were accidentally noticed. The band had been together for roughly a year before a chance encounter with Decca A&R man Frank Rodgers. Rodgers was more taken with the backing band than he was with the singer he was there to see. Such was the impact the band made that he returned to London raving about them, trying to secure them a recording contract. He later recalled Philip as 'being so thin you could knit with him.' It was the Irish luck of the draw for the band, as Philip confirmed in a *Record Mirror* interview in 1977: 'This was a big thing for Ditch. We played half an hour with him and on our own before he came on. Frank freaked on us but was not too keen on Ditch. We weren't trying to stroke him, that was the way things worked out. So we signed to Decca and were brought over to London to make our first album.'

Within a year of playing and finding their feet, the band secured a record deal, though the chopping and changing of management during this time said much about the band's state of affairs. As early as February 1971, they welcomed Ted Carroll onboard as co-manager with Brian Tuite and Peter Bardon. However, before Carroll's introduction, the band had already begun recording their debut album. In a time when albums were recorded fairly speedily, the sessions at Decca flashed by like lightning had you the chance to catch that lightning amid the low-lying clouds of dope fug in the studio. In a foggy Decca studio, the band laid down some of their strongest material while suitably funked by the pot available to them. American Scott English produced the album, his pillowcase full of grass in tow.

From the time Thin Lizzy's self-titled debut was released in April 1971 until their last contractual Decca album in September 1973, they released three full studio albums, an EP and multiple singles – only one of which – 'Whiskey In The Jar' – endeared itself to the UK chart listings. At the time, it was the UK charts that mattered; therefore, the UK was the all-important destination for any commercial inclination the band might've had.

After the album's release, the band returned to Ireland to replenish the coffers and tighten their set before commencing a pub-and-club tour to promote the album. Eric Bell: 'We were so naïve in some ways that we thought the fact that Phil being a black Irishman and catholic, and me being from Northern Ireland and protestant, was another thing that would attract the people to the shows.' The short Irish tour concluded with a gig at St. Anthony's Little Theatre in Dublin on 16 March, supported by Ditch Cassidy, before the band's planned first UK gig at Sisters Club in North London. But that debut gig was cancelled when the band were unable to leave Ireland on time to make it to the venue.

In 1971, not all bands released singles, so the only way to promote songs was to break them on the road and build up word-of-mouth. *Thin Lizzy* was awash with good songs representative of their musical direction but perhaps lacked the edge the band needed to set them apart from their peers. The emerald tinge strewn across many of the tracks (particularly 'Diddy Levine', 'Eire' and 'Dublin') highlighted their appreciation of their roots, though the manner in which they went about sourcing this appreciation throughout the recording sessions – by drinking and drugging – was only further proof of their commitment.

Philip's awareness of the Celtic cast in his writing was an issue he addressed in multiple interviews, such as the one below with the late Harry Doherty of the *NME*:

To write modern Irish songs as opposed to traditional Irish songs, that was the thing, so that people could look back and say, 'Ah, well, there was a black Irish writer back in the '70s writing songs that went like this, that had strands of the Celtic thing but were also influenced by Western society.' That was how it came about.

Other songs on the album show an uncanny knack for writing in code. 'Look What the Wind Blew In' contained the curious line, 'Then somewhere from the north/This gale I knew, just flew in.' In the aftermath of his relationship with Carol, he met a girl named Gail Barber. Over the coming years, Gail went with him on his adventures with Thin Lizzy, even going as far as upping and leaving Dublin to live with him in London. Gail originally hailed from Belfast, Northern Ireland. She was the daughter of a dentist, was well-educated, and on one of several trips down to Dublin, she happened upon a 20-year-old Philip Lynott. His mother:

Gail and Philip were courting for about six years, and they were in love and very happy. After moving to London and following his career, time had an effect on their relationship, and they just drifted. In the business, all the women were throwing themselves at him, and it is my opinion that you really shouldn't have a lady friend; you shouldn't. Their lifestyles were at the opposite ends of the spectrum, and then fights would occur and she would be telling me about it. It was very sad, but on the other hand, they always remained friends, and she did visit him, and he would always love her in his own way, and that was about it.

His focus was always on the band. Though he and Gail were together for a relatively long period, his craving for success with his band put paid to any marriage plans. Starting a family was discussed, but as Philip took more and more time out of his personal life and injected this commitment into the band, it sealed the fate of the relationship.

Between 1971 and 1973, Thin Lizzy released *Thin Lizzy*, *New Day* (EP), *Shades Of A Blue Orphanage* and *Vagabonds Of The Western World*. The pinnacle of their success on Decca Records came with the release of 'Whiskey In The Jar' in November 1972. It took its time to make its way up the charts, but by the end of the following February, it had peaked at six in the UK.

Tim Booth of Dr. Strangely Strange had also moved to London at this point and was approached by Ted Carroll to do some promotional graphics for the release of 'Whiskey In The Jar'. Booth recalls: 'I used to hop around to see Ted Carroll, as he lived just down the road from me and he was managing them at the time. Ted asked, 'Would you do a feckin' logo for them?.' I dragged this logo out of my subconscious, along with a little comic strip for 'Whiskey In The Jar'. I also did a whiskey bottle strip, which was sent to all the DJs. I did some posters as well, which I didn't think were very good, but Ted liked them and the logo.'

Sending miniature bottles of whiskey to all the DJs contributed to the song becoming a big hit throughout Europe. It was an unexpected success but was welcomed by management, as the web-laden coffers needed replenishment. But sustaining the success, proved to be a larger obstacle. No matter what they tried, Thin Lizzy couldn't follow up 'Whiskey In The Jar' in England. Several singles were released ('Randolph's Tango', 'The Rocker' and 'Little Darling'), but none dented the UK charts, though they were minor hits in other European territories.

As each Decca album was released, the band found themselves playing the same clubs and universities, realising the lack of scope in their material was contributing to their problem of identity in the public eye. As they toured, Philip saw what the crowds in England wanted and realised he could write a much harder type of rock 'n' roll song. He understood this would go down well and that the slightly folkie type of thing they'd been playing was really for a niche audience. Philip discovered this a lot earlier than other bands. Tim Booth: 'Phil's penchant was much more performance. Whereas we were shoe-gazing, Phil was really out there, and he would deliver it full-strength to the back of the hall. He learned to be a thespian in that respect.'

Guitarist Eric Bell became very disenchanted as they trawled across Europe miming performances in promotion of 'Whiskey In The Jar'. He was also consuming large quantities of alcohol, which wasn't helping his fried emotional circuitry. Bell was the first of many guitarists to leave Thin Lizzy, and he did so in spectacular style by heaving his guitar into the air while on stage promoting *Vagabonds Of The Western World* on 31 December 1973. The impactful massage of time has muddled the memories of whether or not Bell returned to the stage that night. A meeting with management a few days later didn't resolve the issue, leaving the band on the brink of collapse. It left Philip and Downey in a precarious position, as tours had been booked and deposits accepted. So they quickly recruited guitarists Andy Gee and John Cann to fulfil commitments before convening a further meeting with management to discuss the future.

The unfortunate breakdown of the relationship between Bell and the band couldn't have come at a worse time. Their latest album, *Vagabonds Of The Western World,* was their strongest so far on the Decca label. The album also featured the band's debut collaboration with musician Fiachra Trench:

I remember that Nick Tauber was the producer, and I think I had already done some other work for Nick. I'm not sure if it was the Irish connection or if it was through Nick Tauber that I came to be involved. It was my choice to have a string group, and there's an oboe on the track as well.

Vagabonds Of The Western World was the album that established the incomparable artwork of Jim Fitzpatrick and the band. It remains an impressive cornerstone in an extensive body of work he undertook, but with a little help from Tim Booth:

I got a message from Jim asking for permission to use some aspects of the logo I had created, and I sent back an okay saying, 'Do what you wish with it.' He's since put up the original, my original, on his own website and afforded credit, which he always does. Jim did great graphics for Lizzy over the years, which also helped to build the image that they had. This was something that was similar to working with Fiachra – again, Jim struck a chord with working with Phil. Jim's work was much heavier and in your face at that time. He took my initial work of the logo and made it much better, so fair play to him.

In any case, Philip and Downey agreed to start over with a new imagining of the band. The exhaustive process of finding not one but two guitar players was upon them. They rented a country club in London as their base for auditions before some persistent cajoling and meddling by their roadie Big Charlie McClennan led to them allowing a 17-year-old named Brian Robertson to try out. He had been aware of Lizzy for some time, rehearsed their albums, and passed the audition after getting 'the nod from Downey', as he recalled.

At first, Philip was content with the Lizzy lineup as a three-piece. But following yet another management meeting, he was overruled, given the experience of coming up short if things didn't work out with Robertson. Plus, this was a new imagining of the band, so a second lead guitarist was required for this new vision.

A couple of weeks later, an American by the name of Scott Gorham arrived to audition. It had been a dull couple of weeks before his arrival, but having recorded the audition tapes and listened back to them later, the band found that his 'bizarre Californian style' blended perfectly with Robertson's, and thus the jigsaw was complete. Gorham's laid-back personality perfectly countered the firebrand within Robertson. The change to a four-piece in the spring of 1974 led to a period of examination for all the band members – an exploration of personalities, styles, and – most importantly – their collective musical intent.

Perception was a problem for many bands of the time, as musical trends changed so quickly, and Thin Lizzy were no exception. The Decca albums were at times hugely experimental in content – not as readily accessible as other bands of the day, such as Slade, whose sound was instantly recognisable. Over the next few months, Thin Lizzy hit the road with killer intent, keen to build on their existing fan base while attempting to harvest the fruits of this labour with new themes explored in the material they were developing. Their efforts were rewarded remarkably fast when they secured an initial three-album deal with Phonogram imprint Vertigo Records.

Being more confident on the bass and discovering what style worked best for him, Philip reacted positively to the aggressive demeanour that enveloped Robertson, both personally and professionally. It was Robertson's contribution to the arrangements of some of the new material that proved to be invaluable to the band's changing style.

It was also around this time that the relationship with Gail Barber began a downward spiral, sparking a torrential outpouring of emotional entries in his lyric books. He revisited these time and again over the coming years, much to her dismay. Being the inspiration for a song is one thing, but confessing in song what he could never say in words hit her marrow-deep.

However, as the band pushed to change the public's perception of them as a folk-rock act, they did themselves a disservice with their first offering on the Vertigo label. They released the 1974 album *Nightlife* to little fanfare. In truth, the record was a mixed bag, but it did contain the tortured classic 'Still In Love With You', inspired by the fragmentation of Philip and Gail's relationship. The album didn't make the charts, which was a major disappointment for the band. The cover sleeve was its most impressive feature, again designed by Jim Fitzpatrick: 'He (Philip) was getting heavily into black music. I was a real propagandist for black music and culture, and it's actually something we started on with the *Nightlife* album cover where the panther is gazing out over the city, not that we said anything like that at the time.'

The band followed up *Nightlife* with the more focused *Fighting* album, though, again, sales were short of record company expectations. The material was certainly stronger and was planted in one genre rather than the cocktail of styles on *Nightlife*. When it came to choosing a single, the band were again met with problems. The album tracks 'Rosalie' (a Bob Seger cover) and 'Wild One' were issued as singles but went nowhere. Thin Lizzy was a band that was hurting. Now – five albums in and under increasing financial pressure – they knew the final album of their Vertigo contract *had* to deliver. Losing the deal might've ended the band's creative life.

The band found themselves burdened with this pressure as the winter of 1975 approached. Queen's 'Bohemian Rhapsody' was terrifying chart compilers – not just in Britain, where Lizzy had been based for the last five years, but all over the globe. As Queen had done, Thin Lizzy needed to find a signature sound – a song, something the public could identify with. Philip's shoulders may have been on the verge of splintering from the strain, but what energy he had left, he used to create one of the most enduring collections of songs on a career-saving album. Next stop, Battersea!

Chapter 3: Rampant In Ramport

When Thin Lizzy met producer John Alcock during the final months of 1975, they knew the seriousness of their predicament – the last chance was smugly perched within their consciousness. Their record label Vertigo had anticipated commercial success that never materialised. The band's morale was strong because they'd been on the road virtually non-stop for the prior 18 months, learning each other's form, but they knew they had to come up with the goods if they were going to survive the next year.

By now, the band were managed by CMO – an agency headed by Christian Morrison. An agent named Chris O'Donnell was the band's point of contact and took care of their day-to-day affairs. The financial strain on the band was titanic, and under this duress, the Morrison/O'Donnell combo secured a meeting with the highly motivated and technically gifted producer John Alcock. Management arranged for Alcock to see the band on stage at first, and if he liked what he saw, another meeting was to be arranged. Alcock's second proviso was to hear some demos and discuss what the band wanted to achieve with their next record.

For any rock 'n' roll group at this time in Great Britain, radio airplay was the key to survival. It wasn't necessarily a hit single that the band needed, but something that could fit into playlists of stations such as Radio 1 or Capital, which gave that all-important exposure. The major problem for Thin Lizzy was in how they were perceived by the record-buying public. It took a lot of roadwork to rinse away the image they obtained because of 'Whiskey In The Jar', but washing it out of their minds and setlists was exactly what they did. *Nightlife* and *Fighting* had shown them without a strong producer at the helm, and any potential they had could easily fall asunder. A new approach was necessary if they were going to avoid being dropped by their record label.

Alcock went to one of Lizzy's live shows and liked what he saw, and soon enough, a meeting was arranged to meet Philip alone. Alcock was impressed with the tapes Philip played and also the ideas he played on acoustic guitar. In some songs, there was only a verse or two, and in others, just a chorus, but Alcock left the meeting secure in the knowledge that there was material in place that could be worked on and developed.

In light of the subdued reception of their recent two Phonogram offerings, the band put extensive efforts into demoing material. Prior to pre-production with John Alcock before Christmas, the band went to Free Range in Covent Garden, an 8-track studio built by engineers Lawrie Dipple and Simon

Tassano. On 26 November, the band arrived at the studio on Tavistock Street (minus Philip) to work on 'The Cowboy Song' and 'Jailbreak'. Lawrie Dipple, who was engineering the session. He remembers:

> Compared to many that came through the doors at Free Range, this was a real rock band. Their gear arrived with their roadies ... they had roadies! There was plenty of banter, and they clearly had confidence in their own abilities. They knew they had class. Scott and Robbo were really friendly and took a real interest in getting the sound together. Phil showed up in the evening, and the tracks came together quite quickly. The tracks had definitely been rehearsed to some extent beforehand. I was very impressed with how tight they were. There weren't many overdubs, mainly vocals by Phil – I can't recall the others singing at all – and some guitar parts. I didn't have the luxury of assistants in those days – no tape operators or anything like that. I did the whole thing and finished the mixes late that night.

Of the two songs, it was 'The Cowboy Song' that had evolved the most. Given that the band played early versions of it on their last tour, it was noticeable how it eclipsed 'Jailbreak'. In its demo form, 'The Cowboy Song' sounded rough, though its appeal lay mainly in its chugging and boisterous quality. The rough demo mix reveals an acoustic guitar track that never made it beyond this point. It's the attempts to find the right lyric, that amuses the most. His voice sounds quite youthful as he belts out the discarded couplet:

> I was friends with Jesus
> Oh, but what a cross
> I didn't make it home for Pentecost
> Just roll me over

The demo for 'Jailbreak' was just as curious. The chorus, as we later came to know it, was in place, but the arrangement and lyrics were still a work in progress:

> City fathers call us scum
> But I don't care what I have done
> You see, I'm only having fun
> C'mon and have yourself some

As the band began developing the arrangements of songs like 'Jailbreak' and 'Cowboy Song', Alcock's note-taking increased. It helped him gain a deeper understanding of the songs that needed specific work, those that needed a stronger direction and which ideas might be good but were going down a road that wasn't best suited to the band.

Alcock's recording experience was crucial in sieving the band's ideas. His encouragement of Philip's vision for the record was tantamount to the success of the sessions. The recording budget was small, so the production team knew the task at hand was fierce but achievable. The band had to adhere to the schedule, as they knew what failure of the record would mean. However, it was Alcock on whom considerable pressure lay: 'Well, they (CMO) made it very clear to me that they had to have at least a couple of tracks that would be suitable for airplay and please the record label. Although not specifically stated, the hint was that they might have trouble renewing their contract if this record didn't have some airplay and sales growth.'

In pre-production, the band were armed with the remnants of a lot of ideas, but the main responsibility at Alcock's feet was assessing the arsenal of ideas that had potential, and gently dismissing those that had zilch. It was a three-man team in the studio – Neil Hornby was the tape operator, Will Reid Dick handled the engineering, and Alcock led the control room charge. They were a very tightly-knit team and technically adept under Alcock's guidance.

The rehearsal environment varied wildly. It wasn't uncommon for rehearsals not to be a full band situation. Sometimes, there was only Brian Downey and Philip, and at other times, maybe Scott and Robbo were present working on their own ideas. During this period, the first stage was to figure out the backing tracks.

On 8 January 1976, Thin Lizzy settled in for an intense period of recording slightly off the beaten track in Ramport Studios in Battersea, South London. There, they discovered creative comfort, which gave the belief they had in themselves a chance to thrive. Once they got into the studio, they defined a routine fairly quickly: time for work and time for fun being the general rule. However, Philip hadn't quite worked out the lyrics for many of the songs. He preferred to continue working on lyrics as the basic tracks went down. 'The Boys Are Back In Town' is a perfect example of a song that was only partially complete before entering the studio. When Alcock first heard the song, it was just a groove with incomplete lyrics and the main riff missing. 'GI Joe Is Back' and 'The Kid Is Back' were both working titles for 'The Boys Are Back In Town', though nowhere in the band's recording archive is a recording titled 'GI Joe Is Back'. This title could've just been given as part of Philip's writing process and documented in his lyric books. With the real pressure of getting the backing tracks right, he was comfortable recording the music, leaving lyrics until much later in the process.

However, frequently, Philip would sing vocal cues and throw in the odd phrase, but there were never really any guide vocals. He spent much of his time writing, rewriting and honing lyrics in the control room with Alcock while work progressed on the musical arrangements.

Engineer Will Reid Dick seized the opportunity to work with the band. Prior to the sessions at Ramport, in-house engineer John Jansen returned to America, affording Reid Dick the unexpected opportunity of landing his first official engineering gig, on possibly Thin Lizzy's final record. Having worked as a tape operator at Ramport since 1973, Reid Dick had first seen Lizzy as a three-piece with Eric Bell and admitted he preferred a raunchier style of guitar playing more in the mould of Pete Townshend. He recalls: 'I do remember asking to get their back catalogue when I got the gig for *Jailbreak,* so I could get some feel for where the band was at. Certainly, with Scott and Robbo, it was a very different band from the one I had seen. So, for my preparation, their latest stuff was essential to me for the work ahead – in particular, the *Fighting* album: I was really impressed with it and played it constantly.'

When the backing tracks sounded solid, Philip would make changes, humming along to himself to make the parts and phrasing fit with what he'd planned or was still planning. Alcock says:

> My part during this phase was getting things recorded well, with feel and arrangements that actually worked. Mostly, that went quite well. Of course, there were always retakes until it was done. That really consisted of Phil and myself improving the tracks. Downey, Robbo and Scott would also suggest improvements or changes. For the most part, though, when everyone was happy, that was the take.

When it came to recording Downey's drum parts, the technical team employed a then-uncommon way to get the most out of his subtle and neat style. Reid Dick confirms:

> We would normally have four mics on the drums – two overhead, one on the bass drum and one on the snare. At the time, it wasn't the most

common technique, as multi-mic'ing had more popularity. We mic'd the drums like that to get a more open sound, a more live feeling. The problem we found, though – with Downey not being a particularly heavy hitter – was that sometimes the sound could come off as being a little soft.

The freedom that Alcock afforded his team encouraged input from Hornby and Reid Dick. Alcock's convivial approach helped Reid Dick's ability to flourish when mixing the guitars. He felt that the band's drive had to come from the guitars and Downey's solid, understated technique. Reid Dick continues: 'At the time of the recording, Phil was living in this flat with a guy who was a roadie for Genesis, who obviously had access to their guitars. So, for the *Jailbreak* sessions, Phil managed to borrow a few of their Les Pauls, and they ended up being used to get that sound for the album.'

It was Phil's flatmate Terence 'Tex' Read who got hold of the Genesis guitars. Affectionately referred to as Tex in the business, one of his tasks as a roadie was to make sure any repair work needed on the guitars was conducted by a specific technician in the northern reaches of England. Upon his regular returns to London, he dropped into Ramport Studios where the Lizzies helped themselves to the quality equipment. It's no coincidence that the guitar sounds on the new album *Jailbreak* were superior to previous albums.

When it came to recording guitarists Brian Robertson and Scott Gorham, different approaches were needed. Lizzy regularly double-tracked their guitars, solos and vocals.

> It could only really work with Scott because he worked his solos out, you know. Like once he knew where his solo was in the song, then he'd take a cassette away and go to work out the solo. Whereas, with Robbo, he'd just have a few drinks and whack it out and whatever came out came out. It might take a few goes, but he'd do it like that. With Scott, it was fairly easy to say, 'As you know exactly what you're going to be playing every time, can you double it?' Certainly, on a number of them, we'd have two tracks of his rhythm guitar. Whether we actually used them all the time, I'm not sure, but we certainly did it on some of them.

On the *Fighting* album, Lizzy showed great compositional style in places ('King's Vengeance' and 'Spirit Slips Away') and had even begun cultivating an image that was reflective of the changes in Philip's lyric writing. With about 30% of the album at a more advanced point by 19

January, gems in waiting like 'Emerald' and 'Warriors' were still very rough outlines. Alcock aimed to take these outlines and figure out how to cure their directional ailments. On the whole, the recording experience was upbeat but not without incident, the most famous being the recording of 'Running Back'. It was being primed for single release, much to Robertson's annoyance, as he refused to play on it. Keyboard player Tim Hinkley was dead bang in the middle of the maelstrom, as he confirms: 'It was Phil who wanted me to repeat the riff over and over on the keyboard, as he liked the vibe it gave the song. I was only talking to John Alcock about it recently, and he recalls the same story in that Robbo and Scott were not keen on it at all, but they were overruled, and my contribution to the sessions, stayed.'

Alcock normally used his own session players, and if the decision had come down to him, it could've been the late Nicky Hopkins employed to play the keyboard part. Alcock takes up the story: 'I'm guessing it was Phil's idea to call Tim. The keyboard part – as good as Tim was – isn't too demanding, and I recall that Robertson considered it really didn't need a keyboard player to come in – the part could've been played by him or someone else in the band. It wasn't an unreasonable comment, although it may have been Tim who came up with the part, which is very hooky.'

Several creative arguments occurred during their residency in Ramport, but in such a pressurised environment, the band knew the bigger issue at stake. The unravelling in the studio led to occasional visits to The Butchers Arms pub on Thessaly Road, a short stroll from the studio, in order to relieve tension. Alcock:

> If a band is good at what they do and each member has separate personalities and ideas, then creative differences invariably come into play. That kind of clashing can be good; people find compromise, and subsequently, the end result becomes better. Clashing like that can also be taken to another level, and that's when things get dangerous and destructive and when things just don't get done. I found that each Chris was generally helpful and supportive, visiting mostly later in the day to make sure there were no problems that required their attention.

A minor amount of overdubs were added to 'Running Back' by its completion on 6 February, and then the process began to find the album's lead single. If the band couldn't come up with a suitable single, the danger of being dropped from the label was a very indigestible reality. At the same time, all involved knew that the album was strong, and with careful planning, it might just be enough to save their musical lives. Reid Dick, in particular, fondly recalls the sessions:

Well, working with John Alcock was good, as he wasn't the type of producer who would ever tread on your toes. I think one of his key talents was that he was good at getting the musicians in the right frame of mind. He allowed me to do what I felt had to be done and left everyone to their own devices. He had enough confidence in me to do my job, and there's a special freedom in that. We were good mates at the time, and I've got a lot of respect for him because of that. Another factor was that we were never really bound by traditional working hours at Ramport. We were allowed to go about our work, we knew the task at hand, and as long as we did it well – as was expected of us – there was a lot of room for creativity to be expressed.

Artist Jim Fitzpatrick worked on the sleeve. The *Jailbreak* artwork – principally Philip and Jim's idea – was woven together as carefully and sublimely as any fretboard interplay that Robertson and Gorham put down on tape. Here, Fitzpatrick discusses his working relationship with Philip around this period:

We were both very influenced by H.G. Wells' *The War Of The Worlds* and American Marvel comics. Philip wanted something that reflected these influences, and together, we worked on the imaginary story of 'The Warrior' that Philip had in his mind, and I reworked the roughs to reflect this idea until it all held together. I was very lucky with Thin Lizzy because I was only dealing with one man. Normally, when you're dealing with bands, it's like dealing with the beast with five fingers because everyone has a say, and everyone wants to look perfect. They often have an image of themselves that doesn't tie in with reality, but you have to go along with it because they're paying the bills. Philip, however, was great because he gave me a free hand.

With the new album about to be pressed and distributed, Thin Lizzy knew that breaking through the system was within their grasp. The industry buzz around the album was palpable. But things didn't start too well when the album release date was revealed to be 26 March and a single had yet to be chosen. The band undertook a few minor dates in February before launching the UK leg of the *Jailbreak Tour* in March, with a US leg to follow in April, May and June.

It seems ridiculous that the first single from *Jailbreak* only made chart inroads as the band were nearly three months out on the road. After various radio stations in the US began to pick up on *Jailbreak*, 'The Boys Are Back In Town' received significant airplay and was soon issued as the lead single. The song raced up the *Billboard* chart, peaking at number 12, whereupon Phonogram decided to issue it as a single in the UK and found themselves with a top-ten hit. During the tour, Philip completed several interviews in support of the album and had this to say to *NME* reporter Chris Salewicz:

There's some guy here in LA who's written how I'm Bruce Springsteen. Now I have to spend half of my interviews saying, 'I'm not fookin' Bruce Springsteen' and that I appreciate him, but I don't try to imitate him. I take it as a compliment when we're compared, but I take it as an insult when it's said I imitate him. I mean, it rolls off my tongue now, that answer. But this guy here in LA worded it in such a way that all of a sudden, I'm on the defensive.

By the middle of June, the band's US tour was stopped in its tracks when Philip contracted hepatitis, just as 'The Boys Are Back In Town' was hitting the heights of the UK chart. The tour stopping was a tragic blow, given the tour reception they were enjoying and the recognition afforded by the British public. The negative impact was immense, with momentum lost for the promotion of the new album, which had followed the single high into the charts across Europe and the US.

The touring lifestyle hadn't helped Philip, and, as the focal point, he was involved in every promotional aspect. Here, he offers insight into the tour cancellation:

The reason I think I got so fucked up was because I was just going mad, doing it to death. You know what we're like on the road – we go berserk: wine, women and song. Course, I was doing my fair share of all, and I got run down, and it made me susceptible to hepatitis. I was in no position to think about my career. I was flat on my back; my eyes were yellow. I went into delirium when I was in hospital. When I say delirium, I mean I was lying flat on my back for a week, and I don't remember a thing about it.

The band returned home to the UK, heartbroken over the tour cancellation. With Philip obliged to rest and recuperate, he used the enforced downtime to begin work on outlines for the next recording sessions. With a holster full of hindsight, Lizzy should really have been put back out on the road in the US once Philip felt up to it. Instead, ambiguous pressure dictated that a new studio album be recorded, and the momentum that could've pushed *Jailbreak* to further stateside success was never recovered. John Alcock:

> Clearly, Lizzy should have lived on the road for a year after *Jailbreak* and only returned to the studio when they had a substantial pool of material, had a chance to evolve, and endured more rehearsals. But this was the 1970s when bands typically released LPs much more frequently than now. Who was at fault is difficult to say. I wasn't involved in any meetings with the label, and I have no way of knowing what financial or contractual influences were in play.

The new sessions with Alcock leading the charge again were booked to start on 3 August, leaving a very short time for prepping of material. Equally astonishing is how little time Philip had to recover from hepatitis, a debilitating and often fatal disease.

The band's public profile was considerably higher after the success of 'The Boys Are Back In Town', and they were finally making money. For tax reasons, they chose to record the new album outside the UK, at the infamous Musicland Studios, which was situated beneath the huge Arabella Hotel in Munich, Germany. It was a notorious suicide spot, no doubt in part due to its high-rise architecture. Reid Dick confirms about the weeks leading up to the sessions: 'I remember that the band really only had about two or three songs that were in some way complete.' The label brought the recording sessions forward so the album could be released before the treacherous Christmas novelty-song market.

After a couple of days, the band called a halt to the sessions and flew back to the UK on 6 August before returning to Ramport within a week. The short stay and experience in Munich could be seen as a true reflection of where each member was at personally and professionally. Robertson's escalating alcohol consumption affected his friendships with the other members, while Philip's abstinence from alcohol was a necessity but didn't hinder his recreational drug use. Even Reid Dick's patience in the studio was worn thin by the setup available. Reid Dick: 'Musicland – from my point of view – it's fair to say was a truly uninspiring place, certainly at the time. One thing in particular that I found amazing was when I asked the staff where the splicing block was, only to be told that they had none. They used scissors. It was by no means a great idea to go and record there – but for tax reasons, it had to be done.'

The best resolution for the Munich debacle was the return to Ramport, and the fact that the band were going to have to accept the wrath of the Labour-led UK government and acquiesce to its tax demands was now a minor issue given the limited time to get the album completed. Despite the recent bad luck, it couldn't be ignored that there was a sense of excitement in the run-up to the sessions because of the success that *Jailbreak* had generated. But, with that came an undercurrent of apprehension, as Alcock recalls: 'On the one hand, I wasn't going to refuse to work with Lizzy. On the other hand, I wasn't looking forward to it with the same sense of optimism. Between the amount of material and the wavering direction of some of the material, we also had time constraints. The problems in Musicland, along with personal issues, surfaced with some members. I anticipated that there would be problems, and there were.'

The decision to leave Munich was crucial. Luckily, Ramport was available for the block booking required to complete the album. Time was tight and tensions were high due to the failure of the Munich sessions, but things were about to get worse. The backing tracks were slowly coming together as the band worked around the clock to claw back some of the time lost in Germany. By the middle of August, Alcock confided in Philip:

Well, finally, we sat down in the control room for a chat. I voiced my opinions and told Phil that I was worried about how strong the record would be. He was quite abrasive, saying, 'I'm glad you finally noticed' and 'Can you write the fucking songs?'. It was clear he was frustrated, too – he realised that deadlines were looming, and I'm guessing he'd had conversations with each Chris, and he didn't see taking more time as a viable option. He was certainly under a great deal of pressure and was probably feeling the burden on his shoulders alone.

It was evident throughout the sessions that Robertson was having a hard time, and this came out through some of the music he was writing himself. The song 'Borderline' is a cut-glass example of his frame of mind during this period. Written as he was breaking up with his girlfriend, it highlights a sensitivity that belies the brash front that he often parlayed. The 'Jeanie' in the song is Jeanette Melbourne. She visited Philip at his flat after Robbo presented the song to the band along with the lyrics he'd written. Jeanette recalls the time:

> Though I don't remember specific words that I read that day, they were an outpouring of Brian's feelings. I don't think I heard the song before it came out on the album. I felt quite sad when I first heard it, and I felt very sorry that I hurt someone in that way and made someone feel like that. I was also very young at the time; we all were. I was heading toward a bad place in my life back then, and relationships weren't at the forefront of my mind. I wasn't showing the commitment needed, and the relationship just faded out … We all used to hang out and socialise quite a bit, so I got to know and become friendly with Frank Murray, and I also became friendly with Scott's girlfriend, Marie, for whom the song 'Sweet Marie' was written. I didn't really know or get to know Brian Downey all that well. We spoke, but I can't say I knew much about him. Someone else – I think his name was Tony – introduced me to Phil's flatmate Tex Read, who was a very colourful character. In fact, that's the one thing that stands out – there were so many great characters in London and around the band. Life just seemed full of fun. We laughed a lot.

Meanwhile, engineer Will Reid Dick was a happy man being back at Ramport. The studio was originally a church hall, which had been bought by The Who as a storage facility for their equipment. It was eventually converted into a studio, initially for them, and subsequently put out for hire. With a big live room and enough space for any band, it always had the best of gear, and the characters who ran it were instrumental in its appeal. Ramport was a one-room facility, so for the duration of their stay, no bookings were available for anyone else. The convenience of leaving their instruments set up from day to day was a major plus. Alcock had been part of the team that helped design Ramport. This came about through his close association with The Who. Such an environment – in the aftermath of the Musicland disaster – was very welcome, as was the presence of one Dave 'Python' Matthews, a Ramport stalwart and the *amusement* engineer, throughout the sessions. The Python's main itinerary was ensuring there was never a dull moment: a duty he fulfilled with jester-like aplomb.

'Fool's Gold' – which ended up on the album – presented Philip with several problems, principally the lyrics. Time after time, he would alter the lyric or switch the order of verses. In the end, he couldn't better the lyric that made the final cut, and so he ran with it. This was also one of the lyrics that Philip worked on right up to the point that he recorded his vocals. Alcock elaborates: 'Each time I hear the song, there are a couple of lines that stand out which I know I wasn't overly happy with. I know that Phil wasn't entirely sure about it either, but I have to emphasise that he was pleased with the final vocal. I just felt it was a bit uncomfortable, mainly to do with the phrasing.' Alcock refers to lines like 'How Sunday mornings they'd go down to the church on the corner' and 'Just near the part where the beautiful dancing tightrope ballerina ...'. He continues:

'I always felt that there was just too much, there were too many words. But the thing is, when you are producing something, it is tricky to tell a lyricist what he should or should not put into it, especially if it's personal. As a producer, you really aren't in a position to be able to do that, as lyrics can be so personal. For instance, I couldn't actually say, 'Rewrite it; I think it sucks' – if it's important to the artist, then you can't expect them to just throw it away. There are other ways to make these comments. I've always said that 70% of producing a record – or the sense of producing it – is that the producer is a shrink. The producer's sole purpose is to try and wring out the best of the band, whatever the issues may be. It's a walk-the-tightrope situation in that, as a producer, you can't be seen to be taking sides with musicians, especially in a situation when you have multiple personalities. My job was not just to make it work but to make sure it worked in the best possible way so that the end result validated the strife and effort invested.

As Philip was the cog in the wheel that allowed the band to keep churning out material, his ill health added to the trauma of recording the album. Engineer Reid Dick picks up the story: 'I think Phil did feel a strain and felt the pressure of success, but more so as the frontman of the band. Thin Lizzy revolved around him, and it has to be said that any other band member could've been replaced except him. As the focal point, he was burdened by this, and certainly, by the time the album was recorded, he was feeling various types of pressure.'

As the sessions progressed, it became clear to everyone that a track titled 'Don't Believe A Word' had strong commercial leanings. Initially brought to the band by Philip as a slow blues number, it was soon reworked by Downey and Robertson in the singer's absence, with Downey contributing the 12/8 shuffle and Robertson the middle eight. Much to their relief,

Philip was delighted with the new arrangement, as was Alcock: 'The lyrics resonate well with me; it's a very simple lyric. It's not overly poetic – the relationship with the girl, the guy messes up; he says he doesn't understand their relationship or why he messed it up, but for some reason, he still wants to be in the relationship'. In the end, the song was credited solely to Philip: 'As far as I'm concerned, that song should've been credited to the three of us', claims Robertson.

After three long weeks, things were becoming too intense. Personality clashes became more pronounced. During one particular session, the frustration within the band culminated in a real battle of egos between Philip and Robertson. Alcock recalls:

> Hours and hours would go by if you added them up when Robbo would tune his guitar and play something, and Phil would be in the control room and say, 'Go back, you're out of tune.' Robbo would adjust his strings and play it again. Once more, Phil would say, 'I can hear it and it's not in tune.' Robbo would take another slug from the bottle and play it again, and Phil would say the same thing again. Now, half the time, I couldn't make out what Phil was talking about, but he was the leader, and I couldn't say, 'Phil, you're deaf' because if I did, the argument became worse. This kind of thing happened a lot during the sessions. Now, if you really wanted to get down into the psychology of it, this type of interaction represented an erosion of their relationship and had little or nothing whatsoever to do with tuning a guitar.

The band returned for the last round of sessions from 30 August to 10 September. As was the case on *Jailbreak*, Philip did all the singing. By this point, that seemed to be a given, and most of his vocals were double-tracked. Reid Dick: 'Phil had a good voice, nice range, so it made sense that he would sing on everything.'

With the sessions at an advanced stage, it was impossible to ignore the disunity in the direction of the material: Alcock's worst fear. His misgivings aside, the well of inspiration beneath the writing showed that the chalice used to scoop the band's creative fuel was not corralled by anything other than their flagrant intent on artistic progression. Though the band could be hard to restrain, artistically, the album has its highlights in the vein of *Jailbreak*. Songs such as 'Johnny', 'Rocky', 'Don't Believe A Word' and 'Massacre' fell easily into their anticipated terrain. But the more experimental 'Johnny The Fox Meets Jimmy The Weed', 'Borderline' and 'Fool's Gold' showed alarming signs of a band not adhering to their previously-established winning formula. The remaining tracks 'Old Flame', 'Sweet Marie' and 'Boogie Woogie Dance' were another story entirely. John Alcock concludes:

I really can't understand how 'Sweet Marie' ended up on a Lizzy record, much the same as the way I feel about 'Romeo And The Lonely Girl" (from *Jailbreak*). 'Both always seemed more suited to a Phil solo record to me. 'Boogie Woogie Dance' was one of those songs that didn't do or say anything for the record. It was filler pure and simple. In those days, you had to be seen to have a running time for a record, and Lizzy were a track short, so that's really how it ended up on the album. The song might've worked in a live setting as an encore piece or even as an introduction to a show to get the crowd going.

The album was mixed throughout the remainder of September, with a release date planned for October. As the sessions evolved, the album title was still undecided. But late in the day, with Jim Fitzpatrick recruited once more for the sleeve, it finally emerged as *Johnny The Fox*. The album first appeared in the charts in November 1976, and the lead single 'Don't Believe A Word' surfaced in January 1977, peaking at 12 in the UK. Fitzpatrick discusses how the album sleeve came together:

Johnny The Fox was the craziest of them all. I had the artwork finished without a title, waiting to hear from Philip while the record company were screaming for the artwork. With only a few days left before the release date, Philip rang me and gave me the title. 'Eh Philip, there's no such title on the tracklist', I volunteered, pointing out the obvious. 'No one will notice, Jim. The album will be massive', he said. He was right. It was, and no one ever said a word. I thought I had better put the fox in after they rejected the idea of a cutout with the fox's head showing through. Echoes of the *Nightlife* panther are here too, but we always felt the central image reflected the idea of the *outsider* – something that appealed to both of us. The original design had a neo-Celtic metallic border with a warrior figure in the centre. Philip just loved the border and was determined to use it, so I got the go-ahead to proceed to the final artwork. It took ages, but it was worth it. He wanted something very Irish and Celtic without any twee *diddly Oi* connotations. There is just enough Celtic knotwork in there to do the trick, while the rest of the border is sheer madness. I enjoyed every moment of its creation.

Aside from the strife that creating the album entailed, it revealed strong moments in many ways, despite the occasional clashing over the direction of the material that eventually made the final cut. John Alcock had this to say:

> Phil was a very smart and creative guy. In his more lighthearted moments, he was also highly entertaining and very funny, but in a dry, quiet way. I always sensed that there were things going on in his head that I didn't fully understand and that he was driven by a creative direction that wasn't always easy to identify – so maybe my interpretation of Phil's ideas wasn't always accurate. But I think Downey *got* Phil much more than anyone, and it shows. Any great rock band gets its soul from bass and drums. Phil wasn't a flashy bass player, tending to be more simple and solid. Downey added *movement* and dynamics more, and the two of them worked really well together. I think Downey did a great job and really helped with setting the tone of the tracks to suit Phil's ideas. Phil – for whatever reason – had some difficulty with explaining his vision of how things should work. This wasn't often, but there was sometimes a sense of frustration in Phil when he couldn't get songs worked out to 100% of what he heard internally. I don't want to overstate this – it was not common, but it did exist. I think the records would've been vastly different had Downey not been involved. His role and influence was very much more than playing drums. His opinion on other parts that made up the songs was very valuable.

During October and November, Thin Lizzy toured Sweden, Germany, Holland, France and the UK in support of the new album before another visit to the USA in late November. This US tour was to make up for the aborted dates the previous summer and re-establish the band as great pretenders to the perpetually-spinning rock 'n' roll throne. But with typical Lizzy luck, the tour had to be abandoned on the night prior to leaving for it when guitarist Brian Robertson's hand was sliced open during a fight at London's Speakeasy bar, slashing the tendons. Band and management were furious, and Robertson was to live out the rest of his Lizzy career on thin ice. The band was once more left in the traps.

It had been a roller coaster year for the band and all of those involved behind the scenes. As those scenes unravelled, Philip made his first forays into working outside of the Thin Lizzy framework. With commercial chart success came opportunity. With financial success, he researched, and within 18 months, he built his first home studio, where he could document the avalanche of ideas that coursed through his creative veins.

However, his first adventure outside of Thin Lizzy on a mainstream project was, if anything, unexpected.

The project was to be a musical version of the H. G. Wells classic *The War Of The Worlds*, written by American Jeff Wayne. He went to see several London Thin Lizzy shows on the *Johnny The Fox* tour. The whole purpose of the exercise was to spend some time socially and discuss what was required for the part Philip was asked to play: that of Parson Nathaniel. There was an eerie sense of fate about this proposal, as for many years, Philip and Jim Fitzpatrick frequently engaged in conversational marathons about the work of H. G. Wells, Marvel comics and the present-day artists that Wells had influenced, such as Roger Dean. Wayne's vision of the album began long before any cast members were involved.

However, Philip was not the first choice for the role of Parson Nathaniel. Wayne initially had former Free singer Paul Rodgers in mind. Rodgers had expressed interest in the part and had gone down to Advision Studios in London to record some vocals. But Wayne was looking for more than just a musical performance for the role, as it also required some acting. Wayne: 'He couldn't see himself beyond the musical performance and soon withdrew from the project, at which point the hunt began all over again for the role to be filled.'

On a tour with his good friend and frequent collaborator David Essex, Wayne often found himself with a lot of downtime. Reminding him about those 'big scores I always talked about doing', his dad had given him a handful of books, including *20,000 Leagues Under The Sea*, *The Day Of The Triffids* and *The War Of The Worlds*. Wayne confirms the project's origins: 'My dad first suggested that perhaps some of these books might be open to a musical interpretation, and how I should consider producing something in this vein. With *The War Of The Worlds*, it really was the one I could feel in terms of movement and sound.'

Wayne continues: 'They got Phil to come down to Advision, and he listened to some of the demos we had done and agreed to take on the part. It was a big turning point for me. I heard the track 'Fool's Gold', where Phil does that spoken introduction, and that played a big part in my desire to have him for the project. He was very soulful.'

Philip took away some of the demos for consideration so he could formulate some of his own ideas. It would also allow him to do his homework and make the most of the limited time he had, given the busy period on Lizzy's horizon. With a new album due for release and the associated touring itinerary to promote, time was not on his side.

Philip excitedly reported back to Jim Fitzpatrick in Dublin about this latest project within which he'd become embroiled. The pair spoke at length about his participation. Fitzpatrick:

> He was very excited by the idea of stepping outside of his own life to do this. Wayne was very dedicated and thorough in the way he went about constructing the album, which is brilliant. I think he was also excited by the company he was keeping; it was very English company. They were top guys of their trade in England, and I think he enjoyed being the outsider in the middle of all that. Even the role he played was a guy who was on the margins, mentally at least.

He was suffering dreadful fatigue when he arrived at Advision Studios in South London in November 1976. It was just two months since he'd finished the *Johnny The Fox* sessions and a mere six since his diagnosis with hepatitis. His gruelling schedule wasn't about to get any easier. Philip was contracted for seven to ten days, though much of the first sessions couldn't be used due to a bout of flu. The first few days were a struggle, as can be heard on the available album outtakes. Though the role of Parson Nathaniel was emotionally demanding, the acting side of the performance was an exotic departure for Philip. Here, he tells Rosalind Russell of *Record Mirror* about the allure of the role:

> There were one or two things I was offered at the same time. They were so different to what I was doing with Lizzy that I decided to do them. Besides, it's the first time someone has asked me to do anything on my own merit. I also heard that Richard Burton was going to be on the album, and I'm on a real star trip. I was also offered Radio 1 jingles – don't hold it against me. I thought no one would know it was me, so I did them for a laugh.

In preparation for and during the recordings, Wayne's father, Jerry, worked closely with Phil on his part's characterisation. In the Wells story, Nathaniel is referred to as a curate. But for scripting reasons, it was deemed necessary to amend it to that of a parson. Further amendments were made in the form of the parson's wife, Beth, played by Julie Covington. Wayne invented the character for dramatic purposes and thus created another point of view for the listener. He'd written a piece titled 'Parson Nathaniel' as a duet for Philip and Julie, but it was discarded in the end, as Wayne felt it didn't feel or sound like it was driven by the excitement that was required for that particular passage in the story. So he set to the task of writing an alternative, which became 'The Spirit Of Man'. Philip continues:

> With *The War Of The Worlds*, I got a copy of the tape and listened to the singing, but I didn't know I had to do much talking. I sing with a slight American accent – well, maybe not such a slight American accent – but I had to talk in this very correct accent. It was difficult because I couldn't even speak English. I found it interesting. It was well worth it to work under someone else. I'm so used to getting my own way with Lizzy; I'm a spoilt brat.

The album was recorded out of sequence, with everyone doing their parts individually – not that anyone could tell, as it was so exquisitely assembled. Philip had been unable to complete his part in November, but the Lizzy US tour, which was due to commence before Christmas, was shelved when a hand injury sustained by Brian Robertson made the tour impossible to fulfil. Lizzy were to convene as the special guest act with Queen in January of the following year to try to convince America that Thin Lizzy was what it needed. This allowed Philip to return to Advision in December to finish recording his parts. In all, the experience proved to be fruitful, as Jerry Wayne and Philip spent many evenings laughing in the studio over various unusable takes due to Philip's vocal gaffes. Jeff Wayne concludes:

> Aside from that, Phil really responded to my father in a very positive way, and we were delighted with the results of his efforts. He always managed to turn his failures when recording into a good laugh. He was always prepared to go back time-and-time-again until he got it just the way we needed it.

Philip would have to wait another 18 months before these efforts made their way into the public domain, as the recording and editing process was extensive. The record was a groundbreaking piece of work, and to this date, it has sold in the region of 15,000,000 copies. Wayne, on whose shoulders lay the unenviable task of bringing such a project to fruition, succeeded.

Philip's work on *The War Of The Worlds* had opened his eyes to other music-related avenues that could become available to him, and it was from this point forward that his dalliances outside the framework of Thin Lizzy began in earnest. Such was the experience's impact on Philip that he readily agreed to work on a similar type of album with Jim Fitzpatrick: *Erin Saga*. Though the pair talked about it on numerous occasions, there was never a contribution from Philip on that record. It eventually appeared a few years after Philip's death and is now a collector's item. Fitzpatrick recalls:

> The idea was to get a major producer on board, actually someone like Jeff Wayne. In fact, we ended up getting quite the opposite of a major producer, whose name I won't mention. We put a very strong demo of the album together and gave it to Warners, who then gave us the money to do the album. Warners were very interested in the demo, but ultimately, when we submitted the finished album, they stiffed us. If I had done the album with Philip, he would've got me on board with the right people, people he had worked with, producers like Visconti, for example; for all of his faults, at least he was honest.

The New Year found Thin Lizzy in deep rehearsals, with Gary Moore stepping back into the fold on an *ad hoc* basis to fill the void left by Robertson's temporary absence due to the injury. They set off on the US tour and received some good notices in their supporting slot to Queen. Freddie Mercury's roadie Peter Hince: 'I think they were impressed by Queen's professionalism and discipline insofar as they incorporated a few ideas they'd picked up from Queen into their own set.'

Towards the end of March 1977, Thin Lizzy returned to London. It wasn't long before Philip flew across to Ireland, having previously agreed to get involved in sessions with his old pal Brush Shiels for an Irish label called Hawk Records, which was the brainchild of Tom Costello and Brian Molloy. Two tracks were cut ('Fight Your Heart Out' and 'Love At Love Bleed') over a couple of days at Lombard Sound Studios in Dublin. Costello was the proprietor of Lombard, which had been launched the previous year. Philip used the studio regularly, be it for tour rehearsals or recording, until its closure in 1984. It reopened in 1985 as Westland Studio, but Philip never recorded there.

Irish labels such as Hawk, Stiff, Scoff and Release Records came out of Lombard Sound. Director Tom Costello developed local talent by releasing one-off singles to get exposure for them. Though they were small labels by international standards, they served as an inroad for local bands to release records. Brush Shiels was contracted by Hawk Records to record a few singles. If the releases were successful, the normal progression was to produce an album. Marcus Connaughton – label manager for Polydor in Ireland – discusses Philip's involvement:

If Thin Lizzy were bringing out an album, my job was to ensure that the artwork for the album arrived on time, and making sure that everything that was required to produce the album was in place. For myself, on a personal basis, those were fun times, especially when the launch of the *Jailbreak* album came up a couple of years later. It was the kind of thing whereby a relationship existed before it actually happened. Even then, the thought of bringing someone in as a producer was a real luxury.

This trend of popping over to Ireland to help friends and local bands continued for the rest of Philip's life. Such was the blossoming popularity of Thin Lizzy in Europe that they were once again contracted to deliver a new album in the autumn of 1977. As soon as his work was concluded with Hawk Records, he was back in London rehearsing with Scott Gorham and Brian Downey. Though Gary Moore had agreed to cover the gap left by Robertson, it didn't mean he was interested in joining the band full-time. Moore fulfilled his obligations, then left Lizzy to return to his ongoing project with drummer Jon Hiseman. So, Lizzy was – once more – a three-piece.

It was as a three-piece that the band met a new producer named Tony Visconti, most famous for his work with David Bowie and Marc Bolan. With a contract agreed, the band went to Canada to record a new album, settling into Toronto Sound for the duration of May and June 1977. The early rhythm tracks sorely miss the fire-heart ingredient that was Brian Robertson. Though Robertson was eventually invited to participate, the vibe was less than electric, as Philip was still disgusted with him for his lack of professionalism by getting involved in the fracas at the Speakeasy the previous November. It was the dynamic that Robertson thrust on the band that added to their visceral ferocity, and this ingredient was essential to continue the evolution of the Lizzy sound.

Assisting Tony Visconti for the *Bad Reputation* sessions was Ken Morris, a Dubliner, as the band soon discovered: 'I knew Phil from the Dublin Club scene, but only as someone who had been in the front row of as many Skid Row performances as I could find. Skid Row was the dog's bollocks to us young musicians in Dublin at the time, along with Rory and a few others. The first few days were very informal, spent getting to know each other and showing where the *craic* was in Toronto: typical rock-band stuff.'

By the time Thin Lizzy's *Bad Reputation* was released in September, they were getting ready to tour America. The new album had brought considerable acclaim from the music press in the UK. The material on it was strong and varied in ways like the previous album, *Johnny The Fox*, with its softer material, but it was a much more cohesive product overall.

Only one single was released in the UK: 'Dancing In The Moonlight' – an outrageous slice of slick popular music and a very odd departure for the band in light of their previous choices for singles. The song's sax solo was nearly as famous as the one in Gerry Rafferty's 'Baker Street'. 'Dancing In The Moonlight' was a re-imagining of Philip's childhood exploits of staying out beyond the time appointed by his granny, of his adventures with girls in the cinemas of Dublin and much more – all told from the industrious plain of his subconscious, which he was readily tapping into. The saxophone player was John Helliwell from Supertramp, who happened to be playing in a big hockey arena in Toronto on 1 and 2 June. On 3 June, Helliwell went to record with Lizzy on his night off. (Supertramp drummer Bob Siebenberg was married to Scott Gorham's sister.) Helliwell remembers:

When I arrived in the studio, Scott, Phil, Tony and a very attractive girl called Mary Hopkin were there. It was actually the first time I ever met Phil. There was a nice atmosphere when I arrived, and it quickly became apparent that they knew what they wanted to do in the studio. The band was very adept at achieving their collective aims for the recording process. Phil seemed to have a really tight grip on where he wanted to take the material for this album. Tony was a very professional guy, not at all in a cold way, either. He was really on the ball for the duration of time I was there. Of course, having Mary Hopkin in the background was also nice. Overall, I guess it was just one of those friendly things that you do. I may even have been paid for the work that night. Later on, Scott came and worked on one of the Supertramp albums as a favour. It was really just me helping out, and if it didn't work and none of what I did was used, then that was okay, too. It turns out that they kept it, and 'Dancing In The Moonlight' ended up being a hit single, which was great for them.

This was the US tour that saw Lizzy in its ultimate guise: Downey, Gorham, Lynott and Robertson. However, the US tour wasn't without its drama, as boys will be boys. Brian Robertson categorises their rambunctious personalities: 'Lizzy was an intense band all the way down the line, even though Scott was a septic tank' (rhyming slang for yank): 'He'd be the last one in a fight. Phil and I would dive in, but Downey would need a few pints, and then he'd be off.'

It was around this time that Philip met a young woman who was to become a very important influence on the course his life was about to take. Her name was Caroline Crowther: daughter of the famous UK television personality Leslie. Caroline worked in the public relations office of one of rock 'n' roll's most infamous lip-service providers: Tony Brainsby. Thin Lizzy happened to be a client of Brainsby's when he threw an office party, whereupon Phil and Caroline met. When interviewed by Shay Healy for *The Rocker, Portrait Of Phil Lynott* documentary, she had this to say: 'I remember him standing in the corner of the room, flanked by all these guys who I later learned were always with him. He was really charismatic and exuded his sexuality.'

Over the coming months, their relationship developed. His flatmate Tex Read recalls: 'When he did tell me about her, he mentioned that she was Leslie Crowther's daughter. She was a really lovely-looking girl, and I just had to ask Phil if she had any sisters.' Though the pair were dating by Christmas 1977, no one outside Phil's inner circle really knew about the relationship. He took immense care with the press, being coy and throwing out the standard ambiguous answers when pressed about his personal life. Given his background, Philip always erred on the side of caution with the media, never really giving anything up other than the persona that his younger self had dreamt up and written in his teenage notebooks.

The band had worked hard for their commercial success. From day one, Thin Lizzy were a band with a precarious balance. Often reckless and frequently crisped by their indulgences, as band leader in the pursuit of worldwide renown, Philip's grip was going to be difficult to dislodge.

Now, with the gang back together and a new hit single and album, Thin Lizzy were – as the year drew to a close – dancing under the megawatt moonlight.

Chapter 4: The Compass Points To Soho

The band struck upon the idea of releasing a live album. It certainly helped in that it allowed more time to develop the skeletal material already demoed. However, this wasn't the only benefit. Constructing a live album from the available recordings from the *Johnny The Fox* and *Bad Reputation* tours would allow the band to tour the album, raising their profile further while satiating demand for more product. The idea for a live album was borne from circumstances beyond the band's control: their preferred producer, Tony Visconti, had other commitments to David Bowie.

Lizzy had been recording their live shows consistently over the last few years, and given Visconti's time restrictions, it made sense to revisit those recordings to see if an album could be assembled. The spring of 1978 was spent choosing the tracks and overdubbing some guitar and vocals. In late 1976, engineer Will Reid Dick went as far as creating his own live Lizzy album when Philip handed him tapes of three consecutive nights played at the Hammersmith Odeon at the time. These have since been released on the deluxe-edition re-issue. Though Visconti had control of the new sessions, Reid Dick's earlier version isn't easily ignored. He chose to include rousing versions of 'Johnny' and 'It's Only Money', and the recordings spotlight his attempt to keep a very organic feel to the proceedings. Visconti's highly-polished version that appeared a few months later bypassed all of that. Of course, the 'How much is live?' question that has followed the album since its release continues to pepper conversation about it. The deluxe edition, at the very least, confirms just how dynamic the band was in this period.

This latest Lizzy project was also the first for engineer Kit Woolven, who was initially tasked with sorting the tape transfers. At the time Lizzy was recording live, two tape machines would be running at various points in time, so if one ran out in the middle of a song, there would still be another running, so you could splice things together later on. Woolven recalled: 'You end up with an awful lot of tapes. It was a big job just to try to make out what was going to make up the bare bones of the album.'

Towards the end of April, the first live Thin Lizzy album was completed and slated for release on 2 June. However, the overdubbing and mixing took longer than expected as Visconti was in the USA as sound engineer on David Bowie's tour.

Record company commitments and Thin Lizzy weren't the only things swirling through Philip's mind, as it was around this time that he discovered that his girlfriend Caroline was pregnant. Though they'd been together for a relatively short time, he welcomed the news and soon phoned his mother. Philomena, in her book *My Boy*, recalls: 'I met Caroline personally for the first time in the house on Anson Road in the Cricklewood part of London. I could not help wondering to myself whether or not Gail still hankered after Philip, and if she would be hurt by the latest turn of events. But with Caroline expecting their first child, I realised there was no foreseeable way back into his life for the long-term girlfriend towards whom I felt a deep loyalty.'

With a schedule packed to the brim with recording and touring commitments, he intended to enjoy the break in Compass Point with friends who would guest on various tracks. Though billed as a working holiday, it was a more relaxed affair than expected. Engineer Will Reid Dick recalls accompanying the musicians who flew out on 23 April:

> I couldn't honestly say that what we did out there was work. I flew out with Phil, Scott and Mick (Lawford). I do remember that Huey Lewis flew in for a few days' work. We'd start at around six in the evening and do a few hours of work, and then around ten, we'd go to the Playboy Club. During the day, we'd spend most of our time on the beach. We brought out the recordings with us rather than actually starting on anything new out there. 'Jamaican Rum' and 'Tattoo' were a couple of things we did there. I really thought that the solo stuff Phil had come up with had a great contrast, which reflected his many influences, I think.

Much of the backing tracks taken to Compass Point Studios eventually surfaced on a new Lizzy album the following year, but there was also a variety of other solo material done. There was even some work done on Brush Shiels material that Philip had brought with him. In all, over the ten days, 15 songs were given some kind of treatment. The majority had Huey Lewis playing the harmonica. It certainly aided some of the tracks, such as 'Tattoo', 'Black & Blue', 'Blues Boy' and 'Cold Black Night'. However, little of what Lewis added made it to the finished versions. In fact, some of the material never surfaced at all. A song tentatively titled 'Christmas' eventually morphed into another song called 'Catholic Charm', though it too was never actually finished.

The working holiday vibe was very much the approach that Philip was taking with this other material he was writing and recording, which was, at this point, truly a work in progress with no finishing line determined for the experimentation going on. The song 'Tattoo', for example, was a song

Philip had been working on long before the Compass Point sessions. It was a lightweight number in its original demo form. Throughout working on the demo, Philip's lyric ideas were already firmly in place, but it was the arrangement that seemed to be causing most of the frustration. Gorham laced a scratchy and addictive guitar lick across the already-established rhythm pattern, giving a more solid direction.

Anxious to avoid the comparison of Lizzy's patented twin lead guitar sound, the solo material relentlessly pursued the opposite end of the musical spectrum. As he grew as a person, so did his tastes and the direction in which he wanted to journey. But convincing his record company and supporters didn't come easily. At times, his path seems over-indulgent, even misguided, yet it would be reprehensible to ignore the chameleon-like instinct that drove him musically. Of all the numbers worked on at Compass Point, the skeletal 'Jamaican Rum' and 'Tattoo' are standouts, with Gorham's unobtrusive style perfectly administering the musical medicine appropriate to the latter song's zenith. Frustratingly, his contribution was mixed way down on the final version released two years later.

Upon his return to London, Philip wasn't waiting around long as he continued working on the songs for their next album. They retired to Konk Studios, again with Will Reid Dick engineering. They spent 8, 9 and 21 May at Konk before overdubbing began on a show recorded at the Rainbow Theatre in Finsbury Park, North London that March. The gig was filmed for commercial release, albeit a heavily edited version of the live set, to coincide with the upcoming live record, which was now titled *Live And Dangerous*.

In preparation for the album release, Thin Lizzy played across Germany, Holland, Belgium and France before returning to the UK. Such was the workload that it left precious little time for anything else. Though Philip's personal life had taken a positive turn, his work commitments were such that much of the early stages of his relationship with Caroline were conducted through telephone conversations. Because he was always either coming off stage or exiting a recording studio, he was frequently too fired up to just slink off home and relax with a cup of tea. More often than not, he was out in the clubs, keeping in touch with new trends. His work never ended. And if an opportunity arose for session work outside of Thin Lizzy, he readily accepted it. An old friend from Dublin – BP Fallon – got him involved with sessions for the new Johnny (New York Dolls) Thunders solo album *So Alone*. Fallon says: 'I asked Phil to play bass guitar and sing on the LP we were making. At first, he was reluctant, but Caroline talked him into it, and Phil appeared at the Polygram Marble Arch Studios with a most impressive lump of hash. I was on the phone in the lobby when Phil emerged from the studio. He was concerned about Johnny's health: 'He's too out of it, knowwaramean?'. Thunders was a known addict who frequently fell asleep standing upright while trying to record his parts. Philip was to mirror Thunders' studio demeanour some years later when he was so blitzed he too couldn't get it together to record for any reasonable length of time.

Upon release of the *Live And Dangerous* album in June, Thin Lizzy's label pulled out all the stops with a promotional TV and radio campaign. The album peaked at number two in the UK and stayed in the charts for well over a year. The band chose to release a live version of the Bob Seger song 'Rosalie' as a single, which went into the top 20. In the years that have passed, the song has so become associated with the band, that many continue to believe they wrote it.

A week after *Live And Dangerous* was released, *Jeff Wayne's Musical Version Of The War Of The Worlds* finally made its debut, nearly a year after the recording was completed. That album was even more successful, entering the chart at 24 on 1 July, eventually peaking at number five. It stayed in the UK charts until November 1984, remaining in the top 100 for six years. Prior to the album's release, Wayne spent nearly two months working on the creation of a laser show for the album launch, which was due to be held at the (now defunct) London Planetarium on Marylebone Road. Wayne: 'Back then, it was very basic in terms of coordination, as it was all being done live. It turned into a major media launch, and at one point I was introduced on stage, and my recollection of it is that I was slightly embarrassed to be up there. All the cast were there bar David Essex, as he was committed to some theatre work at the time.'

During a selection of June UK dates in support of *Live And Dangerous*, Philip met bass player Jimmy Bain, who'd been sharing a Pimlico flat with Robbo since the previous year, which is when the initial seeds were planted for their own project: a band called Wild Horses. Bain says:

I got to be friends with Phil when I went on the road with Lizzy for the UK *Live And Dangerous* tour. I think that this period was possibly the best I've ever heard Lizzy play. Every show was an event, and they really captured the whole essence of rock 'n' roll as far as I was concerned. I was loving life at this time, hanging out with Thin Lizzy. I think the fact that we were both bass players helped a lot. We had similar styles in that we both played with a pick as opposed to fingerpicking, and we happened to actually like each other.

Philip's main focus during this period was promoting *Live And Dangerous*. The aim was to close a chapter in Lizzy's career, to conclude essentially what was now a greatest hits setlist for the band in concert. However, a large part of 1978 was spent writing and recording with a variety of artists, such as Johnny Thunders, Brush Shiels, Gary Moore and others. Before the promotional tour for the live album, Philip helped to record Moore's debut solo album, *Back On The Streets*. Though some of the songs were strong, the album sorely needed a commercial element. Philip's contribution, aided by Moore's direction in the material stakes, allowed this commercial element to flourish. A young producer named Chris Tsangarides was at the helm for *Back On The Streets* in Morgan Studios in London. Tsangarides says: 'It was in the middle of the sessions for Gary's album that I first met Phil. I liked him a lot, as he was such a great laugh. There were about three tracks left to finish when he arrived, and as I remember, they just busked their way through it.' Don Airey played keyboards on several tracks and remembers: 'I wasn't in the studio at the same time as Phil, unfortunately. The backing tracks were done live, with most of the guitar solos done in about five days, with a young Simon Phillips on drums. It was very exciting.'

As Philip continued to duck and dive between sessions for Lizzy, other artists and his solo album, the lines became blurred as to where his focus actually lay. Though he had to remain fully committed to Lizzy and its targets, it appears that his urgent need to keep in touch with ground-level bands and trends was equally intense. He began writing more aggressive songs, in no small part due to the company he was keeping on London's nightlife scene. He allowed punk bands such as the Sex Pistols, The Clash and The Ruts to etch hollows in his subconscious. The 'fuck everything and everyone' attitude that the punks portrayed drew him in to such a degree that he started incorporating their loosely-spiritual aggression into his own music at a faster pace. This eventually surfaced in his lyrics for songs such as 'Hate', 'Get Out Of Here' and 'Do Anything You Want To'. In much the same way that his writing started to change dramatically when Lizzy became a four-piece, he now willingly dove into the trenches of these new trends to explore what he could siphon for his own use. Perhaps out of fear and for a sense of belonging, he welcomed all experiences, and soon his songs were tinged with confessional despair ('Got To Give It Up'), reflection ('It's Getting Dangerous') and regret ('Didn't I').

Philip's allegiance to the punk movement was divisive, with some colleagues asking why someone of his talent would be bothered with the association, while others thought quite the opposite, such as Jim Fitzpatrick:

The music world had changed – hard rock, progressive rock, the whole fucking lot. The public wanted something new, and along came the Sex Pistols and changed everything. Lizzy was very lucky in that they were embraced by that movement, and could've stayed in that group happily. It suited him; they were all rebels, and so was he. Philip liked the fact he was recognised as a rebel by these people. These were the kind of guys that would stand up at an awards ceremony and shout abuse at these stadium-rocker types. It was a changing era. I've said it many times, my ideal band equals The Greedies – Thin Lizzy and the Sex Pistols together: unbeatable. It was a tragedy for me that it never became something more permanent.

By the conclusion of the short UK leg of the tour, Robbo's tenure in Thin Lizzy had come to an end. Too many arguments between him and Philip led to an untenable relationship. As Philip had the responsibility of leading the band, it was Robbo who had to leave. Jim Fitzpatrick says of this time: 'Robbo fitted into that punk mould: disruptive and crazy. Though I love Robbo, he certainly didn't help the cause at the time. The tour that he fucked up his hand, that was the one I feel that they would've broken through without a shadow of a doubt' (in America).

Aside from knocking heads with Philip, Robbo had his own plans. He hadn't been overly impressed with all of the new material, even though some of it was very embryonic, and the direction Philip was moving in wasn't the direction Robbo wanted to follow. With Jimmy Bain waiting in the wings following his ejection from Rainbow, the time was just about right to carve out fresh avenues. Robbo: 'As far as I was concerned, it was over. The arguing between Phil and me was getting worse every day, and I couldn't wait to start Wild Horses with Jimmy Bain. Personally, I think the band peaked with *Jailbreak* and *Johnny The Fox*. I told the boys that I was leaving after the Wembley gigs, and to be honest, I was just being smart, as I knew that I was going to get kicked out sooner or later.'

With Lizzy again reduced to a three-piece, a call was made to Gary Moore for the upcoming dates in America in August and September. Moore no doubt saw the pros of getting involved with Lizzy again, given the peaks they'd scaled since his departure in 1974.

Philip wasn't contracted to deliver his solo album for a while yet, so for now, all efforts were concentrated on preparing for the trail in America. He did a favour for his old pal Frankie Murray before leaving for the American tour by convening an assorted crew – including Paul Cook, Steve Jones, Chris Spedding, Scott Gorham, Brian Downey and Jimmy Bain – to perform as 'The Greedy Bastards' to open the new Electric Ballroom venue, previously known as the Carousel, which Murray had taken over. The fairly relaxed gig was even captured on film, though it's never been considered for commercial release. Bill Fuller, the club owner, was rumoured to have inspired the band name due to their demands for 75% of the door sales on the night of the gig. 'What a crowd of greedy bastards', he remarked. Nevertheless, they performed and would occasionally convene for more gigs, culminating in a Christmas single release the following year before putting the side project to bed.

The American stage of the tour was almost undone when Brian Downey decided he was unfit to travel. Exhausted by life on the road and the clashes within the band, he opted out. Once more, Lizzy's romance with America was in turmoil. Kit Woolven:

> Brian never wanted to go out to Compass Point because it was a bit like a party gone wrong. There was meant to be work going on, but it was a bit tough. We flew to Nassau and had the next day off. On Monday, the band were legless and recorded demos. On Tuesday, the band were legless or not present, with more work on demos, Phil's single, plus Gary's single. Wednesday, I got legless and the drums arrived. So, obviously, until then, we had no drums. By Thursday we actually got some stuff done. So, we'd been there five days then, and we actually got something done and things began to settle down. It was hard work. You can see why Downey would say, 'I'll work in the studio on a proper Lizzy album, I'll go out and do a proper Lizzy tour, but sod going off for jollies in the Bahamas and mucking about. Maybe this will be a solo job; maybe it'll be a Thin Lizzy thing.' Basically, he was being very professional.

Instead of recruiting a drummer in London, the band flew to Los Angeles to audition drummers and complete their rhythm section in time for the tour. Mark Nauseef subbed for Downey for these important shows. Nauseef and Downey were very different drummers technically. With only about three days to learn the set, Nauseef was under pressure to get it right, but he acquitted himself well.

Once the band completed their US obligations, they made their way to Australia to complete a series of dates that culminated in a now-famous performance on the steps of the Sydney Opera House. Crowd estimates vary widely, but what's not in doubt was Philip's charismatic performance. He toyed with the crowd, using his playful banter to draw them in whenever requesting some participation. The performance was filmed in its entirety and finally edited and released more than 40 years later. It serves as an important visual account of the band, which, for Thin Lizzy, are few and far between.

Returning to London at the start of November, the band was back working at Good Earth Studios, trying to finish material planned for the new album due the following spring. Gary Moore was now a fully-fledged member. A few hectic weeks in the studio were followed by some fun gigs in the lead-up to Christmas.

But for Philip, there was one more major event to finish off the year. On 19 December 1978, his girlfriend Caroline gave birth, and Phil became a father to Sarah Philomena Lynott.

When you came in my life
You changed my world
My Sarah
Everything seemed so right, my baby girl
My Sarah

With Caroline over in Dublin (Philip insisted the child be born in Ireland), he received the call that her time had come. Tex Read recollects: 'I was with him when he got the news that Sarah was born. We were in London working, but as soon as the call came – which it did about three in the morning – a flight was booked and I went with him to Dublin. I also remember him playing me both songs acoustically – the ones he wrote for both his daughters. Anyway, when we got to Dublin and he saw Sarah the night she was born, it was a magical time, though I have to say the fresh air in Dublin nearly killed me.'

Over the next couple of days, Philip took time out to play a few relaxed gigs with The Greedy Bastards, and within days of Sarah's birth, he was jotting down lyric ideas. December 1978 was the first Christmas he experienced with his own family – Philip had co-founded another three-piece. In time, this would change in much the same way as the band. But for now, the manic responsibility of trying to take care of his new family was all-consuming. It was a task he experienced mixed success with. Too much commitment to work and so little to himself was to be a pivotal error as he celebrated his 30th year.

The times were certainly changing, as was the company Philip was keeping in his social life. His growing drug habit was an attempt to escape the responsibilities that encircled him. It is interesting to note that the period leading up to Sarah's birth is the accepted period in which Philip started to lose control. When responsibility came knocking, he frequently chose not to answer the door; such was the lifestyle he'd become accustomed to. His guilt fermented in other ways, and through song, his confessions became all the more frightening and ritualistic. It was as if he gave in to the powers of duplicity, decay and ruin just when he should've been turning away from that lifestyle, given his personal circumstances. To this day, friends understand little about why he chose the path that drove him simply because he offered so little of his real self. Tex Read muses: 'Though he had kids and he wrote those love songs, they didn't altogether reflect his real life. He was a wild man. His songs were always about someone or something; there was depth to his work. It was almost like a schizophrenic existence because he was the rock star, but also a lot of other things: a father and family member. He came through the era of excess in the '70s. He wrote and played throughout this time, which is what he loved, and he was one of the lucky ones that got well-paid for it.'

The new year began with the same pressures as the previous eight, trying to combine time in the studio while finishing the latest Lizzy album alongside time with his new family. The recording schedule was finely tuned, and earlier parts of the new album were recorded in Paris, while the final stages were done at producer Tony Visconti's London studio. Philip's introduction to the extreme division of drugs had begun a couple of years earlier. He was already a habitual user of heroin by the time of the *Black Rose: A Rock Legend* sessions. In a documentary made years after Philip's death, his one-time manager, Chris O'Donnell, suggested Philip had picked up a bug which led to the hepatitis that resulted in the cancellation of the *Jailbreak* tour in America. To say he was being coy is an understatement, as Philip himself had confirmed in the press that he was overdoing it in all areas. The manipulation of the truth was maintained long after his death.

Philip's actions had caused the cancellation of a major promotional tour, but the lesson that could've been learned was discarded. Though management can't be held directly responsible for his choices, their reaction to sending the band back into the studio so soon was certainly questionable. This was also the management team that had yet to convince Philip to sit down and make a last will. Given they were all too aware of his escalating drug use, it's difficult to fathom why they couldn't at least have convinced him to address this issue. The management team had their own problems, such as that managing Philip and Thin Lizzy wasn't exactly at the top of their agenda. Soon, other bands recommended by Philip would tickle Morrison's fancy to such a degree that he prioritised them. In effect, Philip ended up trying to manage Thin Lizzy himself, with disastrous consequences.

Though the band had a reputation for hard living, the recording sessions in Paris were littered with references to their regular recreational dalliances with hard drugs. Just a few short years earlier, Jim Morrison of The Doors had died in Paris in what is now widely accepted as a heroin overdose. The ludicrous web of deceit enacted to protect not Morrison but those around him at the time only served to highlight the heroin problem that the city had during this period. Drug death has, of course, never stalled people from trawling its domain.

As a location to record in, Paris was certainly not a good choice for Thin Lizzy during this period. Excess in moderation is always recommended, but recess from the perceived pleasures that rock 'n' roll offered was seldom the road travelled. Excess was the street in which Thin Lizzy prowled. A hungry band – hungry for success, wealth, experience and, who knows, maybe even rebirth. The bottom line was the fact that as the 1970s was about to make way for the 1980s, Thin Lizzy – like any other band of their era – needed hits to remain solvent and push their artistic perimeters.

The recording of what became *Black Rose: A Rock Legend* reflected the band's splintered existence. Due to Philip's increasing unreliability, the album was conjured by way of several recording sessions in France and England, with an open-ended destination for many of the tracks written. This was the first and maybe only cohesive Thin Lizzy album which survived that work ethic. It's also interesting to note that the post-*Live And Dangerous* period was the most hostile in terms of musical direction. It's without any doubt that the Thin Lizzy that recorded and released *Live And Dangerous* was the band at its hulking best. What followed had to be triumphant and a new level from which the band could project and evolve.

In his efforts to breathe even more soul into the well of Celtic mythology from which he drank, Philip further lost himself through his commitment to his music. The leather-clad lynchpin of Thin Lizzy was losing sight of himself, laundering more inspiration than was needed from his public persona. *Black Rose* marked the end of Philip Lynott's prolific writing period. The Philip that followed was the image that the record company sold the public, the image that Philip had dreamt up and went on the ride for until it became an emotional penitentiary. It was going to take a lot more than hard living and bad-boy antics in the music press to consolidate the future.

The early signs of things being frantic were obvious in the material that was being written and recorded. But it's hindsight that brings the frightening realisation that writing and singing from such grimy trenches can only be correctly done by being in them. Philip sang about giving it up: that bad stuff. In 'With Love', he finally honed lyrics that had been in his notebooks for years – a song of farewell, Philip as Rick Blaine against Gail Barber's Ilsa Lund, to use a *Casablanca* analogy. The song's overtures of doom blatantly point to Philip's relationship failures or highlight his unwillingness to commit to such relationships. Given his upbringing, perhaps his understanding of commitment was in keeping with his own experiences. More would be lost than discovered, but, in song at least, Philip continued his search for belonging. His nature was that of a searcher, an adventurer. His upbringing was not conventional; therefore, neither was his approach to adult life. Utter curiosity was the wind which fuelled his sail. Philip siphoned lyrical and tonal shards from the early unreleased Lizzy song 'Leaving Town' for 'With Love', to tremendous effect.

On the new Lizzy material, he sang of degenerates, hopeless fools and Romeos that leapt from one bad circumstance to the next. He sang about hope through the eyes of someone – maybe even himself – yet, in reality, he cosied himself with a cloak of self-destruction. His tale of wanton waste is all in the writing, from day one at Decca until his final fling with Polydor in 1985. But that's not all it was about.

Black Rose: A Rock Legend contained some powerful material ('Waiting For An Alibi' and 'Do Anything You Want To'), but beneath the surface veneer, this once-great band appeared to be succumbing to musical trends and personal problems way beyond their control. It is also relevant to point out how complacency wormed its way into the band, particularly Philip. It had been a long struggle to achieve success on a global level, and the pressure of maintaining that success was more immense than the original battle. Pills, powders and potions provided temporary relief.

The return of Jim Fitzpatrick to the Lizzy fold was welcomed as Philip looked to continue their collaboration on the new album sleeve. Fitzpatrick was curiously absent from the previous album, *Bad Reputation*, though he did do some rough outlines for it. Fitzpatrick:

> I did a couple of different roughs that were fucking crazy. One was a dinosaur with a spaceship coming by. You see, there was no title at that point, and I wanted to do something wild. I could come up with a million ideas, but when they settled on *Bad Rep* as a title, it was hard to take dinosaurs and spaceships and make them work in that context. I remember, when I saw the final cover for *Bad Rep*, I didn't like it. We were on a run of doing some beautiful covers, and *Bad Rep* was just out of step with the work we had done previously. So *Black Rose* was one of the few albums where Philip had a fairly clear idea of what he wanted for the sleeve. It was very nice to have a title.

Philip and the band were scheduled for a long series of live performances with six weeks in the USA over February and March, followed by the UK leg of the tour promoting *Black Rose*, before returning to the USA for shows in June, July and August. Philip was also committed to completing his first solo album once the tour was finished.

It was while on tour in July that Gary Moore left the band for the third and final time. Unhappy with the performance levels of the group, he left the band high and dry in the middle of the tour just as the album was making chart inroads. Though Philip and Gary knocked heads nearly as often as Philip and Robbo had, this fallout was to last for several years. Tex Read explains: 'Now, Phil loved Gary. He was a strong personality, but he was also a frontman so that presented a source of friction. They were both stubborn types and often I remember Phil would arrive back home after a night out and say that he really wanted to get into a studio with him again. He was really down over the falling-out they had.'

On Moore's departure, drummer Brian Downey had this to say: 'He walked out when he knew the band and the album were moving, and after that, it slumped. The record took a nosedive, but we kept going. There's no way you can just stop when you commit yourself to the States. But I think the record company lost interest in it.'

Again, Lizzy's luck with touring the States had hit a snag, so in his attempt to save the tour, Philip called his friend Midge Ure to come and finish the dates by touring with the band temporarily. Ure continued to play with the band until the following year before joining Ultravox.

The band played a short tour of Japan in September, where they became aware of the latest in Japanese technology: the Walkman. By the time they got back to London in October, Philip had been away on tour for the majority of the year and was keen to rejoin his family. He also had a pressing engagement to uphold – the self-styled wild man of rock had proposed to Caroline Crowther earlier in the year, even going as far as asking her father for her hand in marriage. However, before he could look forward to some time off early in the new year, he had to get down to the rather serious work of completing the solo album for which he'd already received an advance. The roller-coaster ride of rock 'n' roll that Philip so craved was now in full swing, but conducting the ride was another matter entirely.

It was at Good Earth Studios in London's Soho that Philip bedded down and welcomed a variety of session musicians to overdub their parts on tracks. Time was tight, but he was comfortable with the schedule ahead of him and the co-production liaison with Kit Woolven, an understudy of Tony Visconti's. Though Visconti had produced the previous three Lizzy albums, he was too busy to take on the role for Philip's solo album, instead choosing to work with Zaine Griff for Nick Mobbs' Automatic label up the road at Scorpio Studios. Visconti's decision to not work with Philip, related to his experience recording the commercially successful *Black Rose: A Rock Legend*: 'Black Rose was the beginning of the end. Things were going really, really well, but there was a certain point in the album where Phil thought he could relax a little bit. He was drinking a lot and chopping out copious amounts of cocaine. I knew then, after that, I couldn't work with him anymore, it was too hurtful for me. I would just feel that I can't watch this guy kill himself. He was killing himself.'

Though these sentiments were not relayed to Philip, he happily worked alongside Woolven, who'd been the engineer on a multitude of sessions leading up to this period.

As the cigarette smoke cascaded down the control room walls, Philip was languishing on the settee, unashamedly incapable of tweaking a muscle, having made time earlier in the day to partake in one of his favourite pastimes. As the session men arrived, he readied himself mentally for another late-night session in a bid to bring the final curtain of structure to a project he'd been working on intermittently for nearly 18 months. The stop-start nature of the recording didn't hamper his desire for perfection, nor did it lead to the neglect of the finer details. In fact, Philip was very receptive to any suggestions made by people around him. Though the mixing of the album was several weeks away, the first six months of 1980 would be littered with personal and professional obligations, so perfecting the dexterous touches at this stage was all-important. Andy Duncan – the go-to percussion man at Good Earth – dropped by to play on a track called 'A Child's Lullaby'. Duncan: 'There was no preparation whatsoever for the sessions to begin with. Kit would just put up a song, and we all had a listen and would take it from there. Although it might seem strange, this was very much the way people worked. I'm used to adapting myself as the situation demands and thinking on my feet. Phil was also happy to entertain any suggestions'.

Philip had completed many of the backing tracks and was at this stage looking to sweeten some of the songs with overdubs, be it strings, percussion or even a horn section. It was during the session for 'A Child's Lullaby' that Duncan was asked to add a shaker:

> I just went in, and once we had got a sound, I played along with the track to demonstrate the effect. Everyone looked at Phil and waited for him to give the nod. I felt a bit like a Roman gladiator waiting for the Emperor to give me the thumbs up or down. Phil was very subdued, though, in this particular session. In fact, I don't remember him actually moving once from his position on the couch in the control room. It turned out he was playing soccer earlier in the day, and the reason he wasn't moving was simply because he couldn't. He seized up. Personally, I would've paid good money to see him in a pair of shorts chasing a ball around, not that I would have fancied going in for a 50/50 with him.

When interviewed about the song later, Philip said, 'Caroline and I had a daughter, and I wrote a song for her just two days after her birth. Then she started crying a bit, so I thought I would write her a song that made her sleep instead – kind of a lullaby. It's a cute little song that is also very sentimental. It's got an orchestral sound that I like. The arrangement is by Fiachra Trench and is very good. It was him conducting all the strings and horns on the album.'

Philip had included 'Sarah' on the recent *Black Rose* album, unfortunately, because for certain it would've made a great lead single for this solo enterprise. In any case, the bad boy of rock 'n' roll revealed the many tricks up his sleeve on this solo album. He also made time to promote the album, announcing its title, among other things, in the lead-up to Christmas in an interview with Trevor Dann for the BBC Radio 1 show

Rock On: 'The album is called *Solo In Soho*. I've really tried to go for different things – there are some reggae bits, some computerised stuff, and the slushy love songs, which everyone expects me to do. I'm playing a lot of instruments I don't normally play on this album.'

Fiachra Trench was a long-time collaborator of Philip's and was the man responsible for a variety of sweetening on Lizzy records. As the decade wore on, he contributed even more to Philip's work outside of the band. Though admitting that their 'relationship was cordial', he found Philip to be a 'very warm person to be in company with': 'I love that song 'A Child's Lullaby' – such a sweet song. Phil was definitely there for that recording session in Tony Visconti's place, Good Earth. There was even an ethnic flute on that, which was an unusual addition for a Phil Lynott song.'

Philip rounded out the decade with the first and only official single release from the Lizzy Sex Pistols amalgam The Greedies: 'A Merry Jingle'. A slew of television appearances followed to promote the song, helping it to peak in the top 30 in England. It was throwaway stuff, intended as fun, and it achieved its aim. That the supergroup didn't work toward something more substantial is perhaps one of rock 'n' roll's great misses. 'We were just in the studio having a laugh basically, mucking about, you know. We wish you a merry jingle. It was terrible', says a laughing Woolven. Kid Jensen said, 'Not only is this a great Christmas record, but a record that will stand the test of time.' He must have been on acid or something – stand the test of time? It didn't stand the test of Christmas.

The wider public would have to wait another few months before hearing the results of his solo debut completed in late 1979, as his focus turned to Lizzy and then family, for the first couple of months of 1980.

Chapter 5: Such A Very Fine Line

Lizzy entered Good Earth Studio on Saturday 12 January 1980 to begin work on their new album. Kit Woolven's recording diary shows him working with them until 3 February, before they called a halt to the proceedings. As a follow-on from the multitude of *Black Rose* sessions, the band was now in full flow, working on material for which nobody really knew the final destination. Some tracks would never see the light of dawn at all. Woolven: 'I went to the cutting sessions for a single on 4 February 1980, which was for 'Dear Miss Lonely Hearts' at Utopia Studios. Again, I was at Utopia with Ian Cooper on 5 Feb as well. So we were probably still doing bits and pieces on the solo album during the official first sessions for *Chinatown*.'

A gripe long since attributed to their yet-to-be-announced new guitarist was also really a band gripe which had begun back when the solo album sessions commenced in 1978. Everything was muddy and disorganised, and ultimately, this never changed for the remainder of their career. However, taking nothing away from Philip as he strove to achieve, his old friend Robbo offered this insight into his processes:

There are periods when you write a song about a person, or a certain situation, background or a certain influence, and it comes out, and sometimes it can be really brilliant because of that. Sometimes it can be really shite because of that, just nonsense. I find that nine times out of ten with people like Phil, there isn't any exact place where they are getting it from. It's the lyric; it means a certain thing. It doesn't matter what you say or sing; does it go with the music? Does it work? At the end of the song, he might turn around and say 'That's about her', but it's also about her as well as her mother. That's what girls thought about some of Phil's songs, convinced that he had written the song about them. Unless he wrote 'Sarah' – which he did write obviously about his daughter – his writing reflected what he wanted it to reflect. There wasn't any reality in what he wrote about sometimes.' 'Vagabonds Of The Western World', for example. Well, maybe some of the later songs reflected some things, like 'Got To Give It Up'. Those later songs, what he was doing on them is usually what happens when a songwriter is getting into trouble and the one where he's talking about his Mum ('Sisters Of Mercy').

In life away from the stage and free from the shackles of studs, stage sweat and exhaling tough talk, Philip was about to rush headlong into a union with Caroline. His tryst with her had now entered its third year, and she was pregnant with their second child. They had also acquired a lovely house called Glen Corr in Dublin's north-side suburb of Howth. Philip had wanted to lay down some roots, and now, with the money he'd earned from hit records over the past few years, he attempted to settle into some semblance of family life. He already owned a house on Kew Road in Richmond, which was used as his all-important London base, and his family would divide their time between both properties. He was also considering going into business with his mother. But for now, the focus was on his nuptials.

For all the bravado Phil projected, it was a curious choice to get married at the height of his fame. His marriage was regular fodder for tabloid headlines, given Caroline's profile as the daughter of TV show host the late Leslie Crowther. This was also around the time the music press began to turn on both the band and the image of its leader. Unfortunately for Philip, the 'leather-clad hero with a roving eye for the ladies' wasn't quite as in-vogue as he'd been just a few years earlier. Numerous stories were regularly fed to the media, which infuriated anyone close to the inner circle. Philip's aunt Betty Wray had this to say: 'The media portrayed him as the hard man of rock. That rubbish was fed to the media to keep Thin Lizzy in the public eye.' It's also hard to ignore how difficult it became for Philip to separate the man from the public persona, as his friend Tex Read says: 'Phil was no different to any other rock star of his time. They have a persona and they must keep it up. All he had to do was step outside his front door, and he'd have to be a different person. These kinds of pressures are the ones that can be very unhealthy.'

Under such duress, and with a solo album in the offing, Philip married Caroline Crowther on Valentine's Day 1980 in St Elizabeth of Portugal Catholic Church in Richmond, Surrey, with a reception at the Kensington Hilton afterwards. Philip certainly played the part, wearing tails, his wedding attire topped off with cowboy boots. The Thin Lizzy roadies were to pull their own stunt. Aunt Betty: 'At the church, we were all very surprised when the roadies arrived for the service. Philip only ever saw them in t-shirts and jeans, so they decided to surprise him by wearing grey morning suits and top hats. It was a lovely gesture'.

Philip asked his friends to take on certain roles at the wedding. Scott Gorham was his best man; Tex was looking after Leslie and Jean Crowther, while Philip organised everything for the family on his side. Many of his family stayed at the Kew Road residence the night before. In the morning, they were ferried to where Caroline's parents were staying, where they enjoyed a champagne and orange juice breakfast.

Andy Duncan – who'd worked with Philip on his solo sessions – was surprised to receive an invitation to the wedding. It was, in his words, 'a gesture of remarkable generosity. My relationship with Phil was cordial but relatively distant. As such, he was always friendly enough, but I'm probably not the first person to point out that he didn't seem like the sort of guy that you wanted to get on the wrong side of. So, I couldn't honestly say that I ever felt completely relaxed in his company. He did invite me to his wedding. I was genuinely surprised and touched when it arrived since I felt I hardly knew him. So there you have the paradox of the man, perfectly encapsulated.'

The wedding went off without a hitch, with many retiring to Philip's house after the reception. The young couple honeymooned in Rio de Janeiro for a couple of weeks, taking in the sights and sounds around Carnival time.

Family members admit Philip was only occasionally in touch, but he always welcomed the extended family to Lizzy concerts if they were playing locally. In fact, while in Japan just a few months prior to his wedding, his considerate nature reared its head when he bought a gift for his Aunt Betty's son Paul: 'He gave Paul an Olympus camera that he had bought for him on tour. It was a very expensive gift. Philip knew that Paul was to do a photography course at college. Paul was very pleased with his gift, and he still has it to this day. When Philip played at Leeds a few years earlier, Paul went with some school friends. We stood nearby. After Philip had sung a couple of songs, he said he wanted to say hello to his cousin Paul in the audience, and he dedicated the next song to him. The look on Paul's face was wonderful.' The Philip that revealed himself away from the stage was certainly a galaxy away from the tough and brash front he portrayed in press interviews. He'd been known on occasion to get into fairly intense situations with the press if he felt he was being judged unfairly. The *NME,* in particular, was the source of much ire when *Solo In Soho* was released. In reaction to a poor review, Philip was immediately on the defensive:

He had it in for me, y'know? – because certain people had said I was the acceptable face of hard rock as far as the new wave was concerned. Now, I never fucking gave myself that title. I've never been scared of the unknown. There was a time when punk was the unknown and people went, 'Well, the guys can't play, he's not singing in tune, they're shit', and I went, 'No, I like 'em.' There's nobody playing around, they've got energy which half the bands around today haven't got, they're playing short tight numbers and they shock you into thinking, and that appealed to me, but I wasn't jumping onto any bandwagon. Now this asshole, for some reason, seems to think, right, he must think he's the fucking prophet here. I'll get him. Now, maybe I'm being totally wrong in my criticism of him; maybe I'm getting him arse-about-tit. But when he went for my album, there was more on his mind than what he was listening to 'cause I read between the lines and the guy was a total fuckin' arse-hole. If he had said that to my *face*, I would've stuck him out there and then, simply because an insult is an insult, not criticism.

It was a pity that 'Sarah' had been routed to the recent Lizzy album, and equally regrettable that 'Jamaican Rum' didn't surface as a single instead of 'Dear Miss Lonely Hearts'. That song was written with Jimmy Bain, who was still trying to get Wild Horses off the ground with Robbo. In fact, Bain had recently become his neighbour, moving to Twickenham, a short drive from Kew Gardens. Bain recalls:

Phil's house was a magnet for musicians and beautiful women. When the beautiful women left, we would jam a bit. It was a gradual thing as I became more at ease. I mean, Phil was the total rock star and a big guy as well. What I could not fathom was how neither Scott nor Brian came by to write with Phil. I could almost feel the guitarists' discomfort at the thought of hanging out with the man socially. One of the first tracks we wrote was 'Dear Miss Lonely Hearts'. I had these chord changes on the guitar that were the same in the verse and chorus. He didn't come up with the 'Dear Miss Lonely Hearts' angle right away, but when he did, the song went to another level. The demo was slower, so we rocked it up a bit more on the record. When I first played it for him, he had no words but made something up to check out melodies. Phil could pick up quickly if I came up with a commercial idea. He just had a good feel for hearing it before most other people.

Woolven says: 'I personally thought 'Dear Miss Lonely Hearts' was a bit weird because it was the nearest track on there to being a Lizzy track, and probably should've been. I don't know; it was a bit like a grey-area Lizzy track. It wouldn't have been a great Lizzy track, but it was… I think the thing was, 'Well, we know Lizzy's tracks work; this is the first solo album, so let's stick something out that people know anyway', which I think was totally wrong. In fact, 'Jamaican Rum' would've been a great choice for a first single. It would've been a fantastic choice because it's so different.'

Jim Fitzpatrick: 'Out of nowhere, he'd just make these things up. Very fast as well.' Unfortunately, Fitzpatrick didn't participate in the solo album sleeve. 'With *Solo In Soho*, I think that the record company wanted a complete break in not wanting a Lizzy vibe to the sleeve. They wanted a photographic approach, which John Swannell eventually did. Philip thought the record company had the blinkers on, as he felt that if he could make the transition to release solo material that sounded different to Lizzy, then I could also make this type of transition in that I could stop doing Lizzy artwork and do something completely different. He wanted me to be involved because he believed in me and believed that I could produce something artistically brilliant. He liked the collaboration between the two of us, and I shared his opinion.' Though the collaboration was not to be on this occasion, it wouldn't be long until Fitzpatrick was back in the mix.

Though the 'Dear Miss Lonely Hearts' single made the top 40 in the UK, the album just managed to slide into the top 30. The commercial wobble certainly caused concern behind the scenes. The album was such a distinct departure from Thin Lizzy that it wasn't quite strong enough to attract a new audience, while sales suggested that the existing fan base was somewhat bewildered. It certainly didn't help watching the promotional video for 'Dear Miss Lonely Hearts', which featured the new Thin Lizzy lineup. Philip's debut solo single was somewhat misleading or perhaps downright confusing for people. The whole purpose of doing the album had backfired it seemed, but it *did* contain attractive material. Andy Duncan discusses its commercial shortcomings:

I think that the modest success of the album reflected the harsh reality that Phil's fans liked him for what he did in the context of the band. He had created a winning image of himself as the dangerous rocker, and they loved him for it. In the same way that actors become typecast once they've succeeded in a particular role and only get offered more of the same, so in reverse did Lizzy fans want more of what they had already decided that they liked from Phil.

The second single – and arguably one of his most significant solo efforts – 'King's Call' featured Mark Knopfler of Dire Straits, whom Philip had recently jammed with on the pre-Christmas tour a few months earlier. Mark's brother David Knopfler recalls the song:

I knew Phil initially because we were on the same label in the '70s. He made some generous comments to me about my playing, which was very characteristic of him; enormous generosity of spirit. Then I heard a demo he'd made of 'King's Call', which I'd very much liked, and so was able to return compliments. He guested on a Dire Straits concert at the Rainbow in 1979, where he was terrific despite being fortified with enough cocaine to kill most mortals. As I recall it, he laid out five lines. We all politely declined, so he was delighted to take five lines to himself. I think Phil would probably have liked the William Blake quote 'The road to excess leads to the palace of wisdom.'

It was an exceptionally difficult reality that Philip faced, though he seldom had time to dwell on such things. He hadn't confessed to expecting solo success, but neither had he anticipated the lacklustre response the album received. Artistically, it was a success on some levels, as it highlighted different musical influences and how he could adapt his writing to different musical styles. He could effortlessly access top-drawer commercial melodies and present them really well. The album certainly indicated an artist that was evolving, but the necessity for the fan base to evolve with the artist was all-important.

There were no plans to promote the album other than through the conventional means of videos, two of which he made for singles. Though the album proved to be divisive for supporters and critics alike, his colleagues found much to appreciate. Tim Hinkley – the man Philip introduced to Jack Daniels and Coke – explains:

I think, deep down, Phil had aspirations as a solo artist and maybe didn't quite like the demographic of having to compromise with the other Lizzy members. Phil was a leader, and I think he hid behind the comfort of the success of Thin Lizzy a little. Certainly, *Solo In Soho* was an enormous step for him. He was very much an individual artist. I can recall being with him on some German tour he was doing, and I think he really had a hankering to get on with his own stuff on a solo basis. He compromised a lot by being in a band, which you have to do, and it wasn't something he was very fond of. As with all great artists, he had tunnel vision when it came to it. Had he had more time on his side with the solo work, I think he would've gone a little bit more for the romantic side of things, the more melodic end of things with his writing.

The lack of approval from the record-buying public did little to deter Philip. While working with Lizzy, he continued to lay down various ideas that might not fit their format. Before long, the focus was back on the band bellowing about the new guitar player Snowy White, who'd filled the void left by Gary Moore. White had actually contributed to *Solo In Soho*. The band were holed up at Good Earth again, and soon another Lizzy single was in the offing, although the new album was far from complete.

A video promo was made for their new single 'Chinatown', and it peaked at a respectable 21 in the UK. The band spent April, May and June on the road in Ireland and the UK in support of 'Chinatown'. Instead of refining the material in the studio, the band were breaking in the new guitar player and a new keyboard player who was kept in the wings while the band were onstage. His name was Darren Wharton. The introduction of a keyboard player wasn't entirely new, as Midge Ure had handled this position on the tours of America and Japan the previous year before Snowy White took over on guitar. It certainly wasn't met with great enthusiasm by supporters, but at this stage, the position of keyboard player wasn't clearly identified by Philip or the band. Wharton was then just 17 years old and obviously in awe of the good luck that befallen him, as he told the press at the time: 'It's fabulous to be playing on songs like 'Rosalie', 'Jailbreak' and 'The Boys Are Back In Town' with the guys who made them the classics they are.'

Bassist Jerome Rimson, who played on Philip's solo album, had this to say about having a keyboard player in the band: 'I think that Phil really appreciated the rhythmic side of things, and also 'cause of Darren's involvement, he was getting into the synth thing and trying to reinvent himself to bring Lizzy forward, 'cause the band had run a course.' Philip himself admitted as much to the press when Lizzy was again a new band:

You forget, truly forget, the genuine enthusiasm and excitement about touring and doing gigs. Then Darren comes along, and Jesus, he's hardly been in London in his life, never mind being up on stage in Tokyo or Sydney. I could look over my shoulder and see that he was as excited as I used to get. Then I realised, here we are; this is Thin Lizzy taking on the world tour again, and we're a new band. It's all working; we've cleared the decks, and away we go.

Though he was speaking in positive overtones about this new incarnation of the band and trying to talk the whole band up in the music press, the material he was writing was really beginning to show signs of wear and tear. The poet was, in some respects, losing his touch with the pulse of the street. From this point forward, lyrical high-water marks were only evident occasionally. His choice of drug wares was monumentally beginning to affect his judgement. The once-visceral stage presence was little by little beginning to unravel.

The band needed a strong album to enhance their appeal to the 1980s audiences. Not even half the new album had been recorded before the tour. It wasn't until July that they managed to reconvene at Good Earth to continue working on the ideas that had been demoed earlier in the year. There were new songs, but they struggled for direction. Tracks such as 'The Story Of My Life' and 'Didn't I' were attractive pieces, but where would they fit best? On 'Didn't I', he recruited Fiachra Trench for string overdubs: 'Phil used to refer to it as 'Diddle I'. That song could've gone either way, Lizzy or solo.'

It was around this time that the confusion over which tracks suited which project really began to kindle the band's self-harming flames. Jerome Rimson:

> I watched him record most of the *Chinatown* album, standing at a microphone and making up the words as he was standing there. There were maybe 15 or 20 people in the control room having a party while he was out there trying to rescue the album. When I assess the psyche of Phil Lynott, I think he was driven to be a star because he didn't like who he was without being one. I would say that about a lot of stars. I have never yet seen in my life anyone who worked as hard as him.

It was during the epic sessions for *Chinatown* that Philip became a father again. His second daughter – Cathleen – arrived on 29 July 1980. Like her sister, she was born in Dublin. His determination that his children would have their Irish roots instilled strongly and at an early age, was all apparent. He was intensely proud of his Irishness, which he used to his advantage for many a romantic encounter, fleeting or otherwise, as Tex Read recalls: 'Phil was a very amiable guy. He was very Irish and did very Irish things. We really had some great laughs over the years.'

Though Philip's family home was essentially in Dublin, due to work commitments, much of the family's time was divided between Glen Corr and his London property. Having never learned to drive, he turned the garage into a home recording studio so he could document any flashes of inspiration as quickly as possible. Many of the songs he wrote were tested there before being presented to the band. Endless jam sessions with friends were put to tape, as Clive Edwards confirms: 'I did do a few things with Phil and Jimmy Bain, normally very late at night and a bit boozy to say the least.' Edwards had met Philip several years before, but it was only with Edwards' emergence as drummer in Brian Robertson's breakaway band Wild Horses that he became quite friendly with Philip, going as far as to regularly drop into his solo recording sessions at Good Earth. They were both playing in rock 'n' roll bands, frequenting the same scene and clubs, and shared a management team in CMO, so it was inevitable they would meet. Edwards recalls one of their many nights out: 'I remember standing talking to Glenn Hughes, and Phil walked in. He stopped for a quick chat, and after he left, Glenn said, 'That man makes me feel totally inferior, not so much as a singer, but by his lyrics and expression.' Now, when Glenn says *that*, it's worthy praise indeed. Phil was not just a lyricist; he was a storyteller, too. Lots of people can sing and write lyrics – look at David Coverdale – but Phil could tell a story with just a few words'.

Philip's work ethic was about to take a turn, as was the luck of his band. When they released 'Killer On The Loose' as a single – for which they recorded the video during the same week as the 'Chinatown' promo – the general media reaction was cool amid accusations of bad taste given the recent spate of murders later attributed to Peter Sutcliffe. The licentious lyric lacerates the listener's ear, while the driving riff coerces and commands attention. The unfortunate outcome for the highest charting single on the album was its removal from their live set. It was only periodically performed live over the following two years.

In an interview with *Aardschok Metal Hammer* in 1988, Scott Gorham recalled the reaction to the song:

> The song was banned from all UK radio stations and several other European countries. It was a sensitive issue for some people. Looking back, it was somewhat tasteless from us, but no one in the band thought it would cause such a row. Phil admitted afterwards it was wrong to release it, but he thought it had a good guitar riff. After a while, we stopped playing the song live.

The song was strong – as strongly backboned as any of their recent material – but the media backed Philip, in particular, into a corner, him being the public face of the band. His public image – often misinterpreted as chauvinistic – did little to help the situation. But in conversation, he reasoned quite well what the message in the song was really all about: 'It was written as a warning song, but I knew I'd be criticised for it. I suppose, with the past image of the macho, studded character, then that's understandable, to a point.' The single quickly shot up the charts, perhaps in part due to the press reaction. But then, upon reaching into the top ten, it stalled. The record label Vertigo had underestimated the song's appeal and committed the ultimate *faux pas*. Jim Fitzpatrick – who had discussed the lyric with Philip before its release – had this to say:

It went straight into the charts, and I remember talking to Philip that week and we were on a high because I had done a beautiful cover for the single. It wasn't meant to be a contemporary song and wasn't supposed to be about anybody at all. It got associated with the old Jack the Ripper, and then the video didn't help. It was very London the way it was decked out, very Whitechapel, with shifting-shadows stuff. I remember Chris Morrison and Philip distinctly telling me that the record company had completely fucked-up because they hadn't pressed enough copies and they underestimated that it would go straight into the charts, and they had no second supply stream. In other words, once it went into the shops, it sold out, and they couldn't get more stock for a week or two. By that stage, the impetus had gone. There may have been more to it than that, but it also got a huge amount of negative publicity, and, like I said, the video certainly didn't help.

Even before the single was released, Philip spoke to Kit Woolven about the choice, expressing concerns:

Phil did say to me about this song: 'Do you think we're going too far?'. I didn't particularly think so. I thought we needed to get something out that was much more edgy. The subject matter was very dodgy, obviously, but essentially, it was a protest song. It could be read two ways. It was saying there's a killer on the loose, and somebody better find him. There was a bit of a backlash, but then there's this belief as no such thing as bad press. Phil was very good at making sure he was in the papers virtually every week. He knew how to do something to get him or Lizzy into the press. I never had so much press myself. Phil would boost me up in the press, saying I was his soundman. Boosting up everyone around him helped perpetuate everything.

There was precious little time to breathe after the single was issued, as the release of the new album was followed by another tour in the lead-up to Christmas. The sleeve for *Chinatown* was again a collaboration between Philip and Jim Fitzpatrick. It was an ideal follow-up to the creatively successful *Black Rose* album sleeve and highlighted more than most what set Philip apart from his peers. Incorporating someone of Fitzpatrick's talent certainly added a dimension to the perception of both the band and Philip. Fitzpatrick was paid around £3,000 for his work on the *Chinatown* cover. Tim Booth – creator of the original Thin Lizzy logo – restated the importance of cover art:

> Phil was the main man, obviously, when it came to input for the album sleeves. The record company had a hand in it because they were picking up the tab. If Phil didn't like something, I don't think it would've appeared. There was a huge thing, however, for cover art in the '70s. I think the covers of their time were great, and they were so big – they were great to use for rolling spliffs, it was great for that. You can't really roll much of a spliff on a CD. Album covers were a bit like a comic strip – highly regarded at the time. I would say 60% of those who were buying the album also appreciated the artwork. When you think of Peter Blake's *Sgt. Pepper* cover, this was probably another aspect of how Phil's mind was working – as in, let's get some good artists in to reflect the work that's being done, as opposed to allowing the record company to pick out an artist that didn't reflect the work that the band was actually producing. After all this time, I think all the work that was done reflects a lot on the personality and interests of Phil and, of course, Jim. There are quite a few other images of Phil, but few match up to the iconic images that Phil and Jim created together.

Though the reviews for the album were lacklustre, it did make seven in the UK top ten. The reaction to this within the band – and Philip as its creative visionary – was not the cue to hit the panic button. Years later, Brian Downey considered it a 'fairly good album, and a lot better than people consider it to be.' However, like the previous album, the fragmented nature of the recording sessions showed on many tracks. 'We Will Be Strong' was staggeringly overlooked for consideration as a single in Britain, yet it contained that patented Lizzy guitar sound, while at the opposite end of the scale, a song like 'Having A Good Time' was included: a song in the 'Baby Drives Me Crazy' bracket. Yes, it was throwaway, fun, and a workout. But in the scheme of the album, what did it add? The outtakes from *Chinatown* certainly fit better within the context of the themes displayed on the eventual release.

On 'We Will Be Strong', Philip sang of his marriage and the time spent away from home, insisting that he and Caroline could be strong enough to get through the tough terrain of his absenteeism when touring or in studios all over the country. His recording habits were those of a night owl, which led to multiple problems when trying to reconcile the vows he had made. His wife was in her early 20s and was left to fend for herself, raising two children in a place that she could never really call home. Idyllic as it may have been in theory, she was still a young woman without the nearby support of her own family.

It was at this time that Philip tried to convince his mother to move back to Ireland, with an eye on having her available to help and support Caroline. He arrived in Manchester to propose an idea to her. He wanted to buy his mother a house in Ireland for her 50th birthday so she could be near Caroline and Sarah. Philomena had been living in Manchester for over 30 years and managing the Clifton Grange Hotel with her partner, Dennis Keely. Philip's proposal was a two-part deal in that once the Manchester hotel was sold, he suggested they go into partnership and buy a local hotel when she got settled in Dublin. Philomena discussed these idea with Dennis, and they agreed. Their first choice – The Royal Marine Hotel in Howth – wasn't available, so they turned their attention to The Asgard Hotel and successfully secured it. Philomena and Dennis turned the hotel's fortunes around in a relatively short period. Philip regularly stopped by, and his appearance did much to attract people, even if it was just for a drink at the bar. On more than one occasion, when the hotel was catering for a wedding, Philip reluctantly agreed to dance with the bride. Knowing this could help build the hotel's reputation, he shyly played his part.

Though the year was a mixed bag of success for Thin Lizzy, they could still sell concert tickets, and with Philip's first solo album torn from the ether and presented to the public, it boded well that at least the efforts committed to tape could enjoy some sort of lifespan once the furore of 'Killer On the Loose' had died down. But other band members had begun to look curiously at their trajectory, the band's goals and what the future may hold as ever-changing musical trends threatened their supporter base. Philip had weathered the punk storm, was intrigued by the latest synth technology being employed by bands such as Ultravox, and was even more curious about the talent emerging from Ireland. He'd taken to recommending a variety of acts – such as The Radiators from Space, The Lookalikes, and a host of others – to engineers and producers who had worked with him on Lizzy projects, even going as far as giving them support slots on Thin Lizzy tours. In time, he also flew back to Ireland to produce bands, such as Auto Da Fé, without ever charging for his work. Philip Chevron of The Radiators from Space and later The Pogues recalls Philip providing the Radiators with a platform by giving them support slots on various tours:

> Only age and experience have taught me just what a great thing Phil did for us. Bands today don't really get these kinds of opportunities. We never quite won over the Lizzy audience to the point where we got an encore, but they definitely paid attention. Also, Phil and the other guys treated us with benign fondness, like their younger brothers. When we once complained that we weren't getting enough attention from the crew at the soundcheck, Philip personally supervised that soundcheck, making sure we had everything we wanted. He did not upbraid his own crew, but in leading by example, I think he embarrassed them. We were never again given short shrift on that tour.

Philip's last visit to Compass Point Studios occurred with Kit Woolven in early January before Lizzy was again on the road across Europe. The constant cycle of album/tour/album/tour certainly did the band little favours creatively.

There was little direction with some of the new songs, and whether they'd go towards a solo Phil or Thin Lizzy project was open to speculation. He controlled more-or-less everything within the mechanics of the band, and members like Snowy White became more frustrated as keeping appointments was low on Philip's list of priorities. If the band were supposed to rendezvous at 2:00 in the afternoon, Philip might turn up at midnight and expect the band to work around his socialising. On the archive recording, Philip sounds very much the worse for wear as he tries to sing 'For Always'. It was a recipe for disaster, but that's how the last few years of the band unfolded. Multiple versions of the song exist in the archive, including a version adorned with Fiachra Trench's string arrangement. It would be *his* last contribution toward the Lizzy/Lynott legacy.

Philip became so unreliable and unmanageable that, on many occasions, his record label showed its hand by refusing to bankroll his ideas, be it for an album sleeve or even a music video. It just so happened that his unreliability also coincided with a serious downturn in the industry. The profit margins were never out of focus, and it was becoming harder and harder to sustain acts like Lizzy as new trends and tastes emerged in the 1980s. Sleeve designer Andrew Prewett:

> Certainly, there were many underlying things happening in the boardrooms of the record companies – the heady mix of the success of many top-line bands like Lizzy, they could not come to terms with declining sales and continued to make some demands. So many were still getting fan adoration and were blissfully unaware of the traumas of companies shaving profit margins and, at the same time, trying to adjust to the increasing production costs. Bands and managers were inflexible, and not in the real world of adjusting to this changing environment as I saw it. You cannot force a radio station to play your product.

In all the confusion over what direction the band should take, the record label issued the best-of collection, *The Adventures Of Thin Lizzy*. It was a commercial success but only served to mask the increasing band tensions. Philip tried to enlist the services of Jim Fitzpatrick for the album sleeve, but it didn't quite come together: 'I was dropped from the project because I refused to do storyboards. The record company got a comic book artist in to do the storyboard, and eventually, he did the cover as well. I had a much better idea for it, but that's another story.'

Philip had become an even heavier user of a wider variety of drugs – uppers, downers: you name 'em, he took 'em – and his ability to write was severely affected. Where dabbling had once been a source of insight, as the early 1980s toiled on, it became a lot more tricky to entice his muse. The fuel that he'd mined from Ireland had run dry, and in his attempts to bring Lizzy into the 1980s, he also brought an alarming reliance on heavy drugs. The band continued to write and record, but the direction of the material was getting muddier still. Songs like 'Hollywood', 'Leave This Town' and 'It's Getting Dangerous' emerged, with only the latter shining through as showing that there might be something left in the Lynott engine yet.

It was also around this period when Kit Woolven and Lizzy parted ways. Having recorded the majority of the new album, he handed the reins over to Chris Tsangarides to finish it while Kit continued to work on the solo material: 'At some point, we were up at Morgan Studios, which turned into Battery Studios, and we were all in the bar waiting for the studio to clear, for us to go in. I was having a few personal problems at the time, and Phil was saying to me, 'Buck your ideas up.' I just said I wished we could stick to one project and stop hopping around.'

That conversation concluded Woolven's input on the new Lizzy project. Their new producer was Chris Tsangarides, who was young, and bringing him in was an interesting move, considering that Philip's best work was done under the direction of someone older and more experienced: an authority figure. The label was unwilling to finance a bigger name producer, so Tsangarides was in:

When the time came to do the *Renegade* album, I was actually meant to be getting ready to produce the new Wild Horses album. I got a call not long before we were due in the studio from Chris O'Donnell, and he told me that the Horses sessions had been called off and would I consider the option of producing the new Lizzy album. I was only about 22 or 23 at the time and, of course, more than happy to oblige. I had been a fan of Lizzy and was delighted by the prospects of working with them. They had already worked on most of the tracks by the time I came to the studios. The feeling of confusion was in the air in that sometimes nobody knew if they were working on a Phil solo record or a Lizzy album.

Philip initially got to know Tsangarides when he was contributing to Gary Moore's *Back On The Streets* album. Tsangarides reflects:

I have Phil to thank for a lot. He saw what I did with Gary during the *Back On The Streets* sessions, and I considered it an honour for me to work on an album with Lizzy. I approached it from the perspective of a fan. I would work doubly hard to achieve everything I possibly could to make the album successful. They did struggle to find a single on the album, and I struggled to see one, but I think we felt that 'Hollywood' was the closest, and even then, I wasn't quite too sure how it might do.

Philip's lifestyle had started to affect his voice as much as his physical health. The energetic performances heard on *Jailbreak*, *Johnny The Fox* and *Bad Reputation* were nowhere to be found in the sessions for the next Thin Lizzy album. If the mood took him, he sometimes wouldn't work on the Lizzy material at all, preferring to develop some solo work. His writing had changed, as had his outlook and a preoccupation with the grimmer side of life began to emerge in his work. On multiple occasions,

Above: Philip at the Atlantic Hotel, Aarhus in Denmark, 1982. (*Jan Koch*)

Left: Philip with Gary Moore, Robbie Brennan and the Brush during the Skid Row days. (*Michael O'Flanagan*)

Right: Not a plectrum in sight in this early shot of Lizzy on the road in England. (*Dave Manwering*)

Below: Philip and Brian Downey keeping the rhythm at the Tivoli Ballroom, Buckley, on 3 May 1972. (*Dave Manwering*)

Right: Eric Bell intricately teasing his ray gun. (*Dave Manwering*)

Above: Brian Downey is more Decca than decadent in Cromer. (*Dave Manwering*)

Right: Eric Bell onstage with Lizzy during the Decca days. (*Martin Riordan*)

Left: The debut *Vagbonds Of The Western World* Sleeve. (*Deram*)

Right: The breakthrough *Jailbreak* album sleeve. (*Vertigo*)

Left: The *Bad Reputation* album, which included the hit 'Dancing In The Moonlight'. (*Vertigo*)

Right: The iconic *Live And Dangerous* album. (*Vertigo*)

Left: Jeff Wayne's ever-popular *The War Of The Worlds* album, which featured Philip. (*Sony*)

Right: The *Black Rose* sleeve, designed by Jim Fitzpatrick. (*Vertigo*)

Above: The fireheart Brian Robertson at Manchester Free Trade Hall in March 1976. (*Dave Manwering*)

Below: Gary Moore, Philip and Scott Gorham. Music was their passport. (*Alamy*)

Above: Philip on the mic, recording with DE Dannan in Windmill Lane, Dublin in 1982. (*Adriano Di Ruscio Private Collection*)

Below: Philip, Brian Downey, Jackie Daly and Johnny Ringo recording at Windmill Lane in Dublin, 1982. (*Adriano Di Ruscio Private Collection*)

Above: The Saville Row Model rock 'n' roller in 1983. (*Alamy*)

Above: Philip near his home on the Burrow beach in Sutton, Co. Dublin. (*Adriano Di Ruscio Private Collection*)

Left: Gus Curtis and Philip: friends and adventurers. (*Alamy*)

Above: Studded and ready for the road: Philip Lynott – renegade. (*Alamy*)

Right: Approaching the edge on tour with Lizzy in 1982. (*Jan Koch*)

Left: Philip with supporter Phil Osborne at the Manchester Apollo on 16 November 1981. (*Phil Osborne*)

Right: Between takes on the 'Old Town' video shoot in September 1982. (*Adriano Di Ruscio Private Collection*)

Left: Darren Wharton and Scott Gorham backstage in Sweden in 1982. (*Jan Koch*)

Right: Philip onstage at the final Thin Lizzy gig in Germany in September 1983. (*Wolfgang Guerster*)

Treading the boards all solo in Sweden in 1982. (*Steve Claw*)

Above: Philip footballing on tour in Sweden in 1983 with the Three Musketeers. (*Anders Erkman*)

Left: Philip handles both rhythm guitar and bass at the Lisdoonvarna Festival in July 1982. (*Mitch Foley & Feekie O'Brien*)

Left: Philip holding Sarah's space gun backstage with Grand Slam in 1984. (*Kieron Loy*)

Right: Grand Slam on tour during 1984. From left to right: Doishe Nagle, Philip and Laurence Archer. Mark Stanway is at the back. (*Alamy*)

Left: Gary Moore and Philip in promotional garb for their final collaboration, 'Out In The Fields', in 1985. (*Alamy*)

Right: Outside the Bailey Bar in Dublin with photographer Paddy Moynihan and Dermott Hayes during August 1985. (*Dermott Hayes*)

Left: Philip with Huey Lewis and his daughter at Record Plant Sausalito, California, recording 'Still Alive' and 'Can't Get Away' in January 1985. (*Adriano Di Ruscio Private Collection*)

Right: Behind the scenes on Philip's last video shoot for his final single, 'Nineteen', in California, November 1985. (*Clive Richardson*)

Left: *Solo In Soho* (1980), Philip's debut solo album, is awash with commercially viable material but was only a modest success. (*Vertigo*)

Right: The statue of Philip was unveiled in August 2005 on Harry Street in Dublin City Centre. (*Alan Topping*)

Left: *The Philip Lynott Album* (1982), his second and final solo offering, proved to be an unsuccessful adventure in experimentation. (*Vertigo*)

he'd taken the 'loner' theme and worked it up to such a level of success that it was easy to visualise his adventures. But by the early 1980s, songs like 'Renegade', 'Somebody Else's Dream' and 'I Hear You Call' gave way to a more melancholy insight. He wrote songs about fatherhood – loosely based on his own experience – such as 'Growing Up' and a ditty for his second daughter: 'Cathleen'. He also began collaborating with Gus Isidore, who he met through bassist Jerome Rimson, and the pair worked on the monster track 'Someone Out To Get Ya', which, disappointingly, has never emerged. Philip was certainly spreading himself thinly, but in an appearance later in the year on RTÉ's *The Late Late Show*, he confessed that he felt there was more life left in the band and that while it was still going for him, he would continue to work.

Though the songs written had a cynical feel, Philip seldom came across in interviews as having a fatalistic attitude. His image was built on him being a winner, so when he tried to come up with some deeper introspective answers, he wasn't really taken all that seriously. Jim Fitzpatrick explains:

We regularly talked about the speeches of Martin Luther King. He ended up using various spoken-word segments in some of the cuts on his solo album. I sent him a lot of black music – I'm talking about some serious soul-based stuff. I honestly think that the record company was terrified that he was going to move musically in that direction. Though Philip had a very Republican outlook, I was – and still am – a pacifist. I did try to get him to focus on injecting his opinions on these subjects, into his music. The solo albums strongly reflect where he was in his life – writing about his children rather than rock 'n' roll, and there was more to come. He did say to me that the last thing he wanted to be doing at the age of 50 was standing in tight-fitting trousers and spreading his legs on stage.

Philip could've never confessed such things to the press. Killing the golden goose was never really an option for him. The one way he could show the public he had something else to offer was through his solo work. Even when he was meant to be concentrating on his own work, he readily accepted other gigs, such as production work with Wild Horses, or offering songs such as 'Blackmail' or 'Fanatical Fascists' to Gary Moore.

Enamoured with synth technology through Midge Ure, Phil worked on a song called 'Yellow Pearl', which ended up being used as the theme music for *Top Of The Pops*. It was to become his highest-charting solo single, settling at 14 in the UK.

As his personal conflicts were nearing a critical point, it wasn't difficult to understand the strain that was put on his marriage. He had spent most of the 18 months after his wedding either on the road or in the studio. Though he tried to return as often as his workload would allow, his commitments meant that he couldn't contribute to the development of his marriage and family as much as he would've liked. The precious little snapshots he *could* give offered little consolation as he peppered his social existence with a potent mixture of doubt and a combination of untaxed substances. The man who returned from a tour with his band or a session in the recording studio became a frustrated figure. The well from which he drew his inspiration was drying up, while his attempts at reinvention through his solo work went unnoticed, apart from minor commercial successes.

The sessions for the new Lizzy album – again splattered across a variety of UK studios – helped little in his search for creative redemption. The new song 'Somebody Else's Dream' was a telling indication of his confusion both personally and professionally – as he told Radiators from Space member Phil Chevron in an interview for Ireland's *Hot Press* magazine:

At first, when I wrote that song – it was the day John Lennon was shot – I'd actually just finished the lyric when I heard the news, and at first, I thought I was just talking about the problems of being popular. While people are asking you for your autograph, they're actually saying to you, 'You must get really pissed off with people always asking you for your autograph.' Now, I remember I used to see Rod Stewart say things like that, and I'd go, aaaah pity the poor millionaire, you know? So I could see lots of critics going, 'Who cares about this person's life?'. But the more I used the phrase, the more I thought about it, I realised that ... the woman who turns around to her husband and says 'Not tonight, I've got a headache', she could say 'Listen, I'm tired of living out your fantasies.' Or *Cool Hand Luke* – I saw it on the telly the other night – the great line when he goes, 'Stop feeding off me, live your own life.' So it became more than the problems of being a pop star. I think the song will defeat the purpose of what it's about, actually, because everyone who listens will say, 'Oh, I feel like that sometimes', so they're actually sharing more of my dreams.

As the focal point in the band, the expectation for the success of Thin Lizzy burdened Philip. The media was drawn to him by the image he, for too long, had helped perpetuate. He was promoted as the poet by his management and released three books of poetry. He had a lot to live up to and a lot more to lose if he couldn't come up with the goods time and again. In fact, a couple of years later he was to sing about these pressures much more openly. When he was free from the leathers and poses required in the Thin Lizzy setup, he frequently came up with some of his most honest material. The unreleased track he sang with Junior Giscombe – 'Time And Again' is strong evidence of this:

> Time, again and again
> I will fall, and I need you to stand up
> Time, again and again
> I will fall

The sessions that made up the new Lizzy album became a cross to bear. Guitarist Snowy White began to lose interest, and the recognised Lizzy musical formula was becoming harder to recognise. In his absence, the other members took to singing on demos, something they'd never previously done. Confirmations of Philip's dismay cannot be substantiated, but strong rumours suggest that when he eventually surfaced in the studio, he wiped the multi-tracks containing days of work. His tendency to control everything when *he* was uncontrollable was a succinct reminder to everyone in the band that the Philip Lynott show required the presence of the one guy who failed to turn up on time throughout 1981.

He wasn't so far gone that he couldn't see the folly of his ways. In a good mood, all concerned confirm Philip to be a pleasure to work with; in a bad mood, it's better left unsaid. Too much gear too often let loose his inner ogre, but there were still glimpses of the poet at work, as Clive Edwards confirms: 'That's one of the things that disappointed me over the last few years of Lizzy. He was still a cut above the rest lyrically but never quite as sharp as you knew he could be. He was the best by miles in the '70s, and I blame the bad behaviour for dulling the man down, but he still had a rapier wit.'

Distance was the decision brokered to cater for the release of the second solo album and the upcoming Lizzy release. Lizzy had some obligatory promotional dates in the closing months of 1981, but the bulk of their touring commitments were penned in for early 1982. In August, the highlight for Philip was the headline spot at the inaugural Slane Castle gig, playing support to a young-hopeful outfit called U2, fronted by Paul

'Bono' Hewson. Singer Hazel O'Connor was also on the bill. Lizzy arrived by helicopter with the pilot swooping low enough during U2's set for the audience to get a glimpse of Philip's chin-heaving smile. Photos by Andy Spearman show Philip disembarking the helicopter with his daughter Sarah in his arms, sporting some very-1980s Nike boots, with the obligatory painted-on black jeans. The audience was nearly 20,000 strong that day, and they subsequently went ballistic. There was no doubt whatsoever who the real star of the day was, although Lizzy's performance wasn't quite as top-notch as is audible on the available bootlegs. Clive Edwards: 'They started to think they only have to turn up and it's brilliant. Unfortunately, they are still good and kinda get away with it. But it's never as good as when they were properly focused and hungry. That's what happens when the partying becomes as important as the music.'

It wasn't just Philip who was partying hard; it was everyone within the band's organisation. With Philip as the creative spark, he directly felt the blunt blade of the press. Though bruised, the people behind the scenes never quite felt the same impact. Alcohol and other drugs helped to cushion the criticism for a while, but soon enough, it would all be too much to take.

Philip turned his energies to the completion of the new Lizzy album, now scheduled for release in November. Curiously enough, the band were in the same boat as they'd been for *Jailbreak* when no single was chosen before the album release to announce its impending availability. Once more, they were caught in a marketing nightmare.

Though admirable when it came to songwriting and personal growth, these dalliances outside the band were having a severely negative effect on the group, which he proclaimed was always his number-one priority. His actions pointed in an altogether different direction. His personal ambitions may just have begun to outweigh his ambitions for the band.

Side B

Chapter 6: The Romance Is Over

Some good was to come later in the year, but the illness within the band was deeply rooted in the early months of 1982. The recent Lizzy album *Renegade* was a chart nightmare, stumbling in and out of the charts at lightning speed. Though the album could hardly be called catastrophic, it rendered the band catatonic. Phil's marriage was just two years old, and his home life was in disarray. He justified the loner lifestyle he gravitated to on songs such as the title track and 'It's Getting Dangerous' – the former being an autobiographical allegory on the lack of balance and stability in his personal and professional life: 'He's just a boy that has lost his way/ He's a rebel that has fallen down.'

The long periods spent away from home on the road or in the studio were curiously present, even when Thin Lizzy was quiet. Ever the fixer, Philip was always trying to fill in time to keep himself busy. He could justify it by saying he wanted to support his family, but he already had enough money in the bank and really didn't need to consider road-testing his solo material across Europe. He could've lain low, come back to Dublin and escaped the vicious underbelly that was prevalent in big cities like London – not that Dublin was a refuge from easy drug access. He had family support in Dublin. But he was drawn to the danger, amused by the invites, and seldom passed up the opportunity for a free night out on the town. It was one of the perks he'd enjoyed for years on the road, at home, or off on a wild one. His friends frequently admitted that he really wanted to be a family man and be in one corner with them when it suited him. But because he was the rock 'n' roll star, he also wanted to be in another corner enjoying the illicit fruits of his environment. He'd baked his pie but invited all of the wrong people into his inner circle to sample the taste. Those he kept locked out were the people who could point him in the right direction. Too many drugs had fried his circuits, and his behavioural patterns had all but terminated his record company's goodwill. Long-time collaborator and friend Jim Fitzpatrick offers this in respect of Philip's decline:

I'm not talking about heroin, not talking about cocaine; I'm not even talking about alcohol. It was the speed and shit like that – the pills that did a huge amount of damage to him. It stopped his neurons from connecting. He couldn't make those instant connections with words and lyrics. It was total burnout with him. The last conversation I had with him, we talked about it a little. He said he was running on empty. You don't need to say more than that, and that was toward the end.

Under such pressure internally, Thin Lizzy's touring commitments were completed by the first week of May, cutting their losses due to the diabolical album sales results. They were under financial pressure as a result of the album's commercial failure, which had cost in the region of £60,000 (over £230,000 today): a sizeable sum. The record company was running out of patience and refused to finance any videos to help promote the album. The dire knock-on effect for the band was that they never again made a video for the label, making do with appearances on a variety of TV shows. The label was teaching the band a lesson and, more importantly, trying to give Philip a wake-up call.

It's interesting to note that his efforts to align Thin Lizzy with new musical trends never quite bore the fruit that was expected. The consistent quality of a few years earlier had lessened to an extent, as he failed to capture and imprison the depth of his storytelling of that time. Stealing melodies from his imagination was no longer a cinch; his passionate sincerity was dulled by bad habits. Some say he had had his time; others suggest there was more to come. But certainly, the aftermath of *Renegade* was a low personal period for Philip. His pal Tex Read had this to say about his predicament: 'By the early-'80s, it's easy to say that his writing wasn't good enough. But for me, it (*Renegade*) didn't have that sound that they had coined years earlier. Having said that, they were a lot more soulful than any of the bands that followed them.'

Turning to his family for support wasn't an option for Philip. His refusal to relax and spend time with them was borne from his fear of being forgotten, of being musically irrelevant, at a time when bands like Wham! and Spandau Ballet were beginning to emerge as the new fad. With these anxious thoughts, he turned to his solo work, putting in a few requests to friends to join him on a variety of sessions recorded in Ireland and England before taking an outfit on the road across Ireland. It must've filled him with copious measures of trepidation, but he was no doubt relieved that he could keep the leather-clad, blooming Irish, mad Johnny-the-Fox identity at bay so he could present the audience with a more restrained and emotionally available character onstage. Stripping away the twin-guitar frenzies that pimpled the landscape of Lizzy, was crucial for the tour. Invoking the inner poet was something long overdue.

The band rehearsed at Lombard Studio, Dublin, over a period of days, with Tim Martin overseeing the desk. The in-studio live recordings are refreshing, and Philip appears jovial throughout the period. Whether he's messing with the count-in, trying to throw the band off, or fooling around with different lyrics on songs such as 'Old Town', 'Girls' and 'Solo In Soho'. As a recording, the rehearsals for the solo tour would fit nicely into a box set featuring Philip's solo work.

Quietly setting out on his first solo tour in Ireland in June 1982 seemed like a remarkably good idea. Road-testing material, which had yet to be parlayed for commercial release, was an age-old tool used to gauge reaction to new directions and, often, revisited inspirations. Brandishing a backing group which kept the sets tight and accessible, Philip tried to engage an audience that was primarily there to see and hear some Lizzy shenanigans. At various gigs, his confusion and hurt were audible. But for the most part, he relished the challenge of putting something new before existing supporters and attempting perhaps to convert those who were not yet overly committed to his storytelling as a solo artist.

Though relaxed, the band put together a fairly impressive overview of the solo material, which had been written though not necessarily recorded over the previous three to four years. They opened each gig with the then-current *Top Of The Pops* theme 'Yellow Pearl' – a song dating back to when Midge Ure was subbing in the Lizzy camp on lead guitar. This collaboration led to a very tidy sum being made by Ure. He was getting £350 each time it was played, enabling him to purchase a house for his troubles.

The promotional merry-go-round figured strongly in anticipation of this tour, with a littering of dates spread across the country. As Lizzy had done in their heyday, these dates were used to get the band tighter and more familiar with the material before embarking on foreign sands for further testimony. In early June, Philip dropped in on BP Fallon to discuss the forthcoming tour and, among other things, the success of 'Yellow Pearl'. Wearing a Huey Lewis t-shirt, he had this to confess to the Beep:

Huey recorded one of my songs from the *Solo In Soho* album. He did me a favour; I gave him a plug. I know him from when he used to play with Clover. Brother Huey, I call him – a great harmonica player. With 'Yellow Pearl', the people from *Top Of The Pops* – the producer of the show – really liked the song and approached me about writing the new theme music for the show. So we were in the studio and asking, 'Well, what do you want? What type of song are you looking for?' and he went, 'Something like 'Yellow Pearl''. So I just said, 'Well, why don't you use 'Yellow Pearl'?' and he said, 'Good idea.' When I first recorded it, there were no drums. They decided to release it as a single, so we added drums to it. We got Rusty Egan in from Visage, and he played drums on it. We released it and it went nowhere. When *Top Of The Pops* decided to use it as the theme music, they released it again. So, if at first, you don't have a hit, release it again. We did a remix of it again. The final mix is the best: it doesn't have the girls at the start. It was on that album *Action Traxs*. So it has made me a fortune – every time I see *Top Of The Pops*, the cash register in my head starts ringing.

When BP Fallon asked how much of a royalty Phil actually made from its use, he was characteristically coy: 'About 2p. I don't know; I wish I'd written the theme tune to *Coronation Street*.'

For the Irish tour, 12 of the scheduled 13 dates were played, with the penultimate show at the Maysfield Leisure Centre in Belfast being cancelled. Philip assembled a strong bunch of musicians intent on proving their worth and their virtuosity. Gus Isidore slotted in on guitar; bass was handled by Motor City man Jerome Rimson, drums by the boldly persuasive Robbie Brennan, keyboard duties subtly rendered by Trevor Knight (who also played with support Auto Da Fé), with the Lizzy liaison rounded out by tour musical director Darren Wharton, also on keyboards.

RTÉ had approached Philip a few months earlier about producing a documentary on his career. His relationship with the national broadcaster was fairly solid. During the promotional whirlwind for the *Johnny The Fox* album in late 1976, he'd filmed a two-part segment for a show called *The Man And His Music*. Though it was for a Thin Lizzy record, he appeared alone, singing live over a selection of backing tracks. He'd also worked with producer David Heffernan, in conjunction with promoting the compilation album *The Adventures Of Thin Lizzy*, guesting with the entire band on the *6 Five Live* show. So when it was brought to Philip's attention that it might be a good time to sit him down and document his career, he was receptive and set aside some time in the spring. Philip's segments were filmed at his residence in Richmond, and portions of the band at work were shot in his home studio at the end of his back garden.

The documentary shoot revealed some interesting stories. Philip being a huge Manchester United supporter, took to buying some shares in the club, and one clip shows the certificate proudly being displayed behind him.

Though his bad habits were cornering him, he looked remarkably well, with his hair shorn short for the first time in years. The pencil moustache was carved over his upper lip *à la* Rudolph Valentino and Errol Flynn, but it's the sequences in the recording studio that hit hard. Philip's constant grappling with his nose, his glazed eyes and his nasal tone told it all. Further down the road, his need for sustenance to get through a schedule became even harder to watch.

The production was filmed over several days in London, with further filming at the now-demolished SFX Hall off O'Connell Street in Dublin. The film crew didn't shoot the entire performance there, but the available footage highlights the regard and affection Phil's fellow Dubliners had for him. The documentary's opening sequence has him back in Leighlin Road in Crumlin, with children playing on the roadside. Philip, with his familiar hunch, strolls by the blissfully unaware youngsters. It was the perfect introduction to the documentary, which was titled *Renegade: The Philip Lynott Story*. Produced and presented by David Heffernan, it's one of the few in-depth documentaries that exist which feature Philip talking at length about his past and attempting to come to terms with his present. Heffernan recalls the shoot:

> His garage was converted into a studio, and as part of the shoot, 'the boys', as he called them, came around to rehearse. Snowy, Scott, Darren and Philip were there, but Downey wasn't in on that shoot. The SFX footage in the documentary was used for the final shot of the *Renegade* project. He was playing 'Dear Miss Lonely Hearts', which I thought was a great pop song. That gig was effectively a workout for him. I saw what was probably the foetus of Grand Slam.

The solo band was often dubbed the Philip Lynott Soul Band – a name that irked bassist Jerome Rimson a little with its black overtones. It's unknown whether Philip was bothered as long as the punters were showing up and enjoying the gig. It was, after all, an attempt to put Thin Lizzy on the back burner and show that he had more depth in his artillery than he was given credit for. At the urging of Jim Fitzpatrick and others, Phil was trying to explore his musical roots and embrace those influences that were new. Drummer Robbie Brennan offers his take on this period in his life:

> He was interested in Tom Waits and Prince around the solo tour time. The first time I heard Prince was from Philo because he bought his first album. He was also going through this black thing. He wanted to do

something that represented the fact that he was black. He was messing around with reggae and rap music. He was really into a lot of different types of music, and that's what really amazed me because he was known for his heavier material. He wanted to explore being black. We threw in the odd Lizzy song during the Irish tour, but it was mostly solo stuff. He wasn't attracting big crowds, and a lot of the audience kept shouting for Lizzy stuff. He had this other side, which he thought might be able to provide him with another outlet for these songs.

Once the short Irish tour was complete, Philip resumed his usual quick-stop visits home to Glen Corr to see his family. He continued to keep antisocial hours, working in the studio, though the aim and intended destinations of the various recordings were unknown. His second solo album wasn't yet released, so the tour was used to highlight a song as a taster for the new album. The song was called 'Together' and spoke of his attempts to communicate his true feelings to his wife and children. What he communicated effortlessly in song, he seemed to be incapable of doing in person. 'Together' was completed during the first few days of June, with Midge Ure producing. However, Chris Tsangardies and Owen Davies also worked on the track in London a short time before its release. Phil took the demo to a Dublin radio station to meet BP Fallon to promote the single's release and the upcoming tour:

I was in the studio, as I wanted to lay down a demo of the song. I'd been checking out Irish Studios I've been in – Windmill Lane Studios, and I was in Lombard this particular time. I had a few musicians over, and I was laying down 'Together' as a demo to take back to the powers that be in England, and if they liked it, they'd give me the money to finish it and make the single. (Paul) Brady was passing through the studio, and I asked him if he'd help out with some backing vocals; he did some ad-lib lines as well. It was just one of those things, and Robbie Brennan was about, and he played on it. It has Darren on keys, Jerome Rimson on some bass, myself on vocal and bass and Midge Ure doing everything else. I did a dance mix – tired of going to dances and not really being able to dance to it, like I really wanted to make a dance record. I've done a 12" mix, like a dub mix, heavy on the bass drum and bass guitar, which I really like.

The song is very much of its time, but the telling confession on the demo reveals a startling admission that the trust in his marriage was shot to pieces. Philip's conscience was far from clean as he continued to play the field on the road and out of sight, and he foretells the doom that is shadowing his marriage:

I'm so lonely without her
Together we were stronger
But now no longer are we together
God forbid if I should never see my children
Oh God forbid if she ever changed their name

The lyrics were substantially amended for the released track, putting a heavier emphasis on the hopes he had for his marriage rather than the sorrow that was suffocating his mindset on the demo.

So in times of pain, Philip retreated to his music, never availing confidantes to help him through his problems. He self-medicated with writing, recording and unhealthy social pursuits. Many unfinished songs emerged from this period, but others were reworked and included on his new solo album, which was due for release in September. Lizzy – who had just two albums left to deliver to fulfil their recording obligation to Vertigo – was due to convene in Eel Pie Studios in London.

As the autumn of 1982 kicked into gear, it brought a vacillating conflict in Phil's personal and professional direction. He had brought Phonogram critical success and financial rewards: a tricky duo to deliver in the industry. As the release of his new solo album was delayed to make space for the *Renegade* album in late 1981, Philip had time to record more material. While the second solo album could've, in theory, been released in 1981, the additional music recorded altered the original downbeat mood. Tracks were replaced, which changed the album's feel and tone, much to the displeasure of some involved. When interviewed later, Phil said, 'The album was real manic-depressive at one stage, and I had a very fatalistic outlook at the time.'

On one occasion, Philip ran over his predicament with long-time friend Jim Fitzpatrick, who recalls:

Walking along Burrow Beach with him while he played the album for me on a Walkman with old-fashioned headphones, I was blown away by what I heard and couldn't believe that the record company didn't like it. I realised from our conversation that Philip was up to his neck in trouble. He couldn't take the rejection nor the crap that went with it. The record company wanted 'The Boys Are Back In Town' part 40, while Philip wanted to be a bluesy Jack Kerouac.

Given the chart assassination afforded Lizzy's *Renegade* album, the record label was very wary of investing further in Philip Lynott as a solo artist. Also, with the merely mild success of 'Together' on the Irish charts and the complete lack of acknowledgement in the UK listings, Philip found himself adrift and commercially unsure when it came to promoting his latest solo effort. Though he knew the score prior to the release of the album – which was now called *The Philip Lynott Album* – the lengths to which the record company would stoop to sabotage its success eluded even him. He never made a video for the 'Together' single, as finance for it was refused. When it came time to make a video for the album's third single, it too was refused a budget. But soon something very special was to happen through another collaboration with RTÉ – an opportunity to make a video for a song called 'Old Town'. This piece of work was to be the one he became best remembered for.

The late Bob Collins, who produced *Renegade: The Philip Lynott Story* for RTÉ, was an industrious and imaginative producer of young people's programmes in the early 1980s, including *Anything Goes,* presented by David Heffernan. That show used to tackle issues while entertaining and informing people. It was Collins' driving spirit which led to the idea of producing one or two pop videos every month. There were four producers/ directors on the programme, one of whom was energetic talent Conor McAnally, who later went on to do *MT USA* and *Space Station Videos* for RTÉ. Producer/director Gerry Gregg recalls the origins of what became the production of the 'Old Town' video:

My recollection was that Dave (Heffernan) came into the office with Bob and said that Phil was coming home and that he had a new song called 'Old Town'. For some reason – I don't know why – his record company weren't willing to finance a video, which was a common practice for promoting a major artist at the time. Some of the biggest directors in film had started dabbling with music videos, probably culminating with John Landis on Michael Jackson's 'Thriller' video. There was a backstory to the whole thing that I wasn't made aware of, but I did find it strange that he was coming to us. It was certainly good box office for the show, and probably good box office for him if it went well. I remember Dave saying that we need to think about how we're going to do this and how we can't just shoot the song and do any old thing. So, I listened to the song a few times, and I felt we had to bring him out onto the street and shoot it.

Numerous meetings were organised, and ideas were presented to Philip in the weeks leading up to the shoot. In one of the last meetings before commencement, Heffernan and Gregg met Philip in a pub off Baggot Street in Dublin to present the formulated sequences. Gregg continues:

Because Dublin was known as the old town, it made sense to shoot this video on location in the town that Philip loved so well. In the early 80s, Dublin was down on its luck, and he was an exotic flower in a drab city at that time. He was very receptive to our suggestions, and I have to say it was made known to us that if he didn't like something, he simply wouldn't have done it. But I do remember him being very interested in our ideas, and once he was here, he just went with the flow. He used to say, 'I like the vibe of all this.' And so we sorted out everything for the shoot, which was to last two days with him on set and a further two days for editing.

The shoot was done by a small crew on a minuscule budget. Aside from Gregg and his PA (who sorted out shooting permits), there was cameraman Ken Murphy and sound engineers for the playback as Philip mimed. Logistically, the shoot was surprisingly straightforward. The very first shot done for the video just happened to be the opening sequence at the Ha'penny Bridge. Gregg:

It was a very hard scene to shoot because we had a big master shot of him walking over the bridge and then a long-range shot as he was leaning on the structure. There was traffic going by and punters trying to cross the bridge, which led to mayhem at times. After that though, we did find great rhythm in the other locations. Considering the weather conditions, it was very rare that he was hanging around for longer than 20 minutes before we started on the next shot.

Actress Fiona MacAnna was cast as the love interest in the piece. With long, flowing blonde hair, her key scenes were shot at Ha'penny Bridge and Liberty Hall, where a split-screen sequence features Philip on the Liffey River. The Liberty Hall sequence was significant in that the production needed an image that spelt big business. The required view of height and firm perspective were essential, with a lot of input from set designers to make sure the shot was perfect and the impression captured was what was intended. As the split-screen sequence was edited – with Philip on the Liffey and Fiona in the office – the parts of Dublin being filmed were instantly recognisable. Producer David Heffernan was present for much of the shooting: 'Philip had hit on the idea of evoking Dublin, so when you look at the video promo, you had to know that the song carried a certain romance. It was about somebody who knew that the game was up, which I think could be used as a metaphor for Philip's thoughts at this time.'

As the video cuts to just Philip on a ferry on the Liffey, we finally see the vulnerable spirit that was often prevalent in Thin Lizzy songs. Alone – if only in his thoughts – he turns to meet the camera, unfolding the emotion in his artistic armoury. To say the least, it was lustily lensed. No other piece of film captures him as truthfully as this. Gregg picks up the story:

> He had the ability to look inside the lens and reach out to somebody. You can't script that, nor can you say, 'I want you to look inside the lens and look vulnerable' – well, you certainly couldn't with *him* (laughing), not with a guy like Phil anyway. It was a very dirty morning that we were shooting on, and it was a tough environment, but he did it well. Whatever was happening in his career, there was a sense of 'There's life in the old dog yet' about the shoot.

As this section comes to a close, the most famous sequence of all unfurls. When it was suggested that Philip should walk down Grafton Street, the wild man of rock 'n' roll was initially reluctant. During a dinner break, the entire background of the sequence was discussed. His nerves receded somewhat when his pal Gus Curtis agreed to walk alongside him, off camera, to help him feel at ease. Gregg: 'On Grafton Street – which was done on the hoof – we just said to him, 'Walk down Grafton Street, and we'll do a few shots and see how it goes.' You can see it in the Grafton Street sequence where people are acknowledging him; you can see the affection they had for him – 'Ah, there's Phil.' Their reactions tell how they saw him. There was an element of the Paul McGrath thing about Phil: he's different, but he's one of ours. I think that's a general feeling about Phil to this day.' The Grafton Street sequence best captured Philip's mischievousness and how the public perceived him. It's impossible not to link him to the magic that makes up Grafton Street, its characters being the primary ingredient. He *was* one of its characters.

With the Grafton Street sequence filmed, the crew shut up shop for the day, with the next sequence planned to take place in the Long Hall Bar on George's Street the following morning. The production team had secured the use of the pub for a nominal figure, but if they went overtime, they were liable to cover the projected figure the pub would take in from paying customers. Philip was due on set at 8:30 am, and it was Gus Curtis' counsel that got him there on time. The crew arrived sometime earlier, setting up the shot, before Philip walked in looking very much the worse for wear.

It quickly became apparent that to make the best of Philip, the team had to work fast. He missed his cues on occasion. And though he was enjoying himself, it was obvious he was under pressure. Sitting at the bar and looking beside the lens amplified the despair in the lyric. The tired look apparent at the Long Hall Bar was in complete contrast to the sequence shot earlier on the Liffey. Philip is seen again on the ferry after the Long Hall Bar segment, but this time, he's going across to the middle of the Liffey, and that was another unusual perspective for most Dubliners. Gregg: 'The only people who would've traditionally seen that were the dockers going across. We shot that down where the O2 arena is now. We caught Philip in silhouette on the long shot with the distinctive hair, and it made for a great scene.'

As the video moves forward, various sequences showing Philip miming the song are intercut with snapshots of Fiona in Liberty Hall, culminating in her atop the hall. Heffernan: 'I am particularly fond of the section where she bursts out laughing at the top of Liberty Hall. We had to put the promo together very quickly, and I was happy with the fact that Fiona reacted to Philip's on-camera charisma very well.'

By 11:30 that morning, Philip and crew had moved to the next location: Ballsbridge, in the Dublin 4 area. It's at this point in the song that Brian Downey's drums bring new life into 'Old Town'. Gerry Gregg recollects:

At the bandstand in Herbert Park, we decided to do some shots with him responding to the music for the instrumental part of the song. We also did a sequence of him singing and then clicking his fingers. It was great editing on the video, but Phil was very capable. He had the experience with miming because he'd done *Top Of The Pops* so often, and if that was live, then it was only one take, so he had to be good. We probably only did three takes at most of all sequences, except for the Ha'penny Bridge, which would've been six or seven takes. The whole shoot was fairly quick. He was happy as long as he was kept busy. Overall, for the entire shoot, if he was waiting around for 20 minutes in the cold weather at any given time, then that was a lot. I have to make it clear to you, as well – to us, he was a star. He didn't ask for anything, but we knew and he knew whatever he wanted, he'd get. In the end, he didn't ask for anything other than to enjoy triple brandies during lunch breaks.

Getting the appropriate shots in Herbert Park was tricky. Without a Steadicam, the planned circling shots required a deft touch from cameraman Ken Murphy. He speedily improvised by taping the camera to himself and walking around Philip, with the resulting cuts proving pivotal to the video's charm. Heffernan: 'Ken Murphy had shot *Strumpet City,* and he put on a different lens for effect. It was a very tricky thing to do, but Ken – a big burly man – was very dainty on his feet, and after a few tryouts, we got the scene.'

The sequences shot on both days were seamlessly stitched together to propel the song's narrative towards its climax. The power of the footage is punctuated perfectly by the piccolo trumpet flutters and J. Patrick Duffner's dynamic editing. The video concludes with Philip walking down the pier in Ringsend, down by the Poolbeg Power station. Gregg remembers fondly: 'I used to swim down around there as a kid. It was also a place we could shoot without interruption.'

With two days spent shooting and Philip's work completed, the production team returned to RTÉ with the footage. In all, five rolls of film were shot. RTE's facilities used a colour reversal process which prevented proper grading of the picture. So, instead, we sent the rushes over to a company in London to process them. They then returned it to us, and we began the editing process, which was done by Pat Duffner, who went on to work on a lot of Jim Sheridan's films. He was a freelance editor at the time and what a great talent he was.'

Once editing was complete, Philip was brought in to view the footage and gave it an overwhelming thumbs-up. With his new solo album finally ready for release and another solo tour booked for Europe, the 'Old Town' single was unleashed on the public. Despite its strong commercial leanings, the song failed to chart in the UK and Ireland but *did* make significant inroads across Europe.

The Philip Lynott Album followed 'Old Town' into obscurity. The album is made up of 11 tracks veering across the singer's emotional spectrum. 'Fatalistic Attitude' opens the album with an ominous and repetitive keyboard riff over a groove made up of Simmons drums and a regular drum kit. The downhearted spirit of the words is lessened by snippets of American evangelist radio shows as if to heighten the message, but it only muddies it further. It certainly stands as a curious opener and justifies Phil's interview comments about his state of mind during the recording of it.

'The Man's A Fool' follows it. Interviewed by Radio Copenhagen, Philip said, 'In these cynical times, this song is the story of a man who thinks the world can be saved, just by us being together and pulling together as one. But, of course, with the cynical attitude, that man would be a fool.' It is certainly a well-crafted and simple pop song. Fiachra Trench arranged the brass, as he had for Lizzy since *Vagabonds Of The Western World* back in 1973.

However, the album's unmistakable highlight is 'Old Town'. It was a collaborative effort written with ex-Rainbow man Jimmy Bain. Bain: 'The first time I played Phil the 'Old Town' changes on the keyboard, Darren was there too. He picked up the parts really fast. It only took Phil about an hour to get the idea to make it about Dublin, and by the end of the day, we had it all finished and ready to record the next day.'

Fiachra Trench, who arranged strings and brass for 'Old Town', recalls it as one of the last times he collaborated with Philip:

We had a long-standing working relationship, and I had also worked on his first solo album. I added strings to a song Phil wrote for his daughter called 'A Child's Lullaby', and it was just such a beautiful song, so I was more than happy to see what he had come up with. Phil was in the studio when I did the strings for 'Old Town'. I think we did it in Advision. We got John Wilbraham in to record the piccolo trumpet section, and as I remember, we had some time to spare, so we also added strings to a contemporary version of 'Dirty Old Town' that Phil recorded.

The album's lack of chart impact made it difficult to get any TV coverage, though Philip did many radio interviews, during which the inevitable comparisons with the first album arose. Here, he divulges his stance on the album:

It's a completely different set of tunes where some of the production is better, and some of the songs need to be judged individually. You can't really judge it as an album concept. I think I got about 60% of it right. One or two of them are a bit naff, but when it's good, I think it's excellent. Overall, I think it's better than the previous album, but then I'm biased, aren't I? It's hard because I really like *Solo In Soho* – songs like 'King's Call' and the title track. I wouldn't like to put the album down, as I think I'm maintaining a high standard.

The next two tracks to unravel are 'Cathleen' and 'Growing Up', both of which reflect an innate sense of romanticism. The former is a tribute to his second daughter, and the latter is a fictional story of how family life can fragment under the duress of unemployment, the trials of adolescence and the need for social identity. Philip had this to say:

I felt that if the album was going to have a title like *The Philip Lynott Album,* then it should definitely relate to me. I thought it was very important that the songs I write should reflect the events that are major in my life, and obviously, having children is a major event. So, when I wrote 'Sarah' and then Cathleen arrived, I just thought, I'll have to write a song for her. So if I have lots of children, I'm going to have lots of songs (laughing).

'Growing Up' features Mel Collins on saxophone and Philip's cousin Monica on backing vocals. In many ways, it's another unexpected slice of his life that he was prepared to put down on vinyl. Yes, there was always a sensitivity to his writing, but with this song, he chose to deliver an honest reflection of his changing life as a father. It is quite possibly one of his most openhearted songs, telling as it does about not only the trials of an infant but the tribulations he experienced as a father. Mel Collins had this to say:

The best scenario for me would be to work with Phil and the band in a live situation rehearsing the songs together, but it didn't happen like that, unfortunately. I was brought in later on when all the backing tracks had been laid down. He gave me a tape to listen to, and we arranged for me to come back the following week after our first meeting. He was really full of enthusiasm and jumping around in the control room with ideas for this and for that, which is great and gives you motivation. As far as I remember, we didn't spend a huge amount of time with my overdubs; it would've been two or three takes at most. He was a sweetheart to work with, and there were no big dramas in the studio, unlike some sessions I did at the time.

'Little Bit Of Water' followed and was one of the earliest songs written for the album. It was first documented as being part of the Compass Point sessions from January 1981 with Kit Woolven. His recollections of the visits to the Bahamas and the staff are not without humour:

We had this guy Benji as a tape op, who was very, very funny. He used to insist on running the tape machine. It had a very loose atmosphere out there. Part of the Bahamas thing was that if a foreign company set up a business there, you had to employ 80% local staff. That meant, at the recording studio which Chris Blackwell owned, for every two Europeans out there, he had to have eight locals, and he had to find them all jobs. Every time you add another person, he has another five people to stick on your payroll. We were using an MCI 24-track recording. On a lot of the recording machines back then, you had to press play and record together to get it to go into record. But on an MCI machine, the record button has a shield around the outside of it, so you can hit it, but you have to hit it bang on the middle and you only have to hit that button. Benji used to dance all the time when the band would play, and if you have a drop-in coming up and you just need to do this overdub, and when you need to drop something in, I'd usually grab the remote for the tape machine, but Benji would say 'No man, no man, this is my job.' So while he was dancing away, he'd rush up to the tape machine and hit the button to drop in the overdub, be it a guitar piece or vocal, and he missed the fucking button every single time. It looked great with him dancing in the studio, but was totally ineffectual.

The available demo is very close to the final cut, though it lacks some overdubs. Lynott: 'I played Irish harp on that. I thought, if there's gonna be a harp on it, let it be an Irish harp.' In truth, it's one of the album's lesser efforts, and though it appeared on the record's original submission, it smarts of a song in search of a destination for its melody.

Of the final three cuts, 'Ode To Liberty (The Protest Song)' is an overlooked gem, with the vocals buried right down in the mix, contributing cleverly to the almost drowsy atmosphere. An alternative version exists in the recording archive, with Scott Gorham playing lead guitar. It was Philip and Bain's second and final collaboration on the album. Bain recalls:

It was one of my very average tunes, which Phil thought was great. I thought he was nuts, but after Mark Knopfler's guitar and Phil's vocals, I was sold on it. You could play something to him that you kind of thought was really mediocre, you'd just be pissing around, but he would pick up on things. That's what really happened with 'Ode To Liberty'. He loved it, and it became a song through his development of it. He could make these things happen.

Mark Knopfler made a return, having previously played on 'King's Call' from *Solo In Soho*, and it must be said that his contribution was again totally in sync with the mood and message of the song. Knopfler's ability to punctuate the vocal was right on the money. Knopfler recalls his participation: 'It was just a song that he wanted me to play on, same as the last solo album. I was in New York at the time, but Phil sent the tape over, and I worked on the song in New York and then mixed it with Neil Dorfsman and sent it back to London.' It was a major coup for Philip to have Knopfler again in the credits, as his and his band Dire Straits' profile was beginning to go global. During another interview, Philip said 'I was really drunk at about five in the morning when I did the vocal. The lyrics are intense, and Mark Knopfler put some excellent guitar on it.'

The penultimate 'Gino' is another stain on what could've otherwise been an interesting and more cohesive album. Its experimental, underdeveloped backbone is jarring in its laziness. Again, Philip returned to incorporating snippets from American religious radio programmes. The basic feel of the song is quite funky, allowing Jerome Rimson to demonstrate his abilities, but the shallow development is all too plain to see.

The album closes with 'Don't Talk About Me Baby', which was first developed by Thin Lizzy but later discarded until Philip decided to resuscitate it for the solo album. The most startling aspect is how the song was originally conceived, very much in the Thin Lizzy mould of duel-harmony guitars. Most of the Lizzy version was thrown out, except for the bass line and various verse lines. The demo was built around the title 'It's Going Wrong' and later 'Silly Willy'. 'It's Going Wrong' was a prime example of a very promising track that Philip somehow lost direction with. The catchy chorus is packed with what we came to expect from him, though he perhaps thought it was out of sync with the rest of the album and subsequently dumbed it down. If anything, the song, as it originally stood, matched the fatalistic attitude he readily admitted to. The curious thing about *The Philip Lynott Album* is that it carries the scars of the wounds that originated this fatalistic attitude. These original lines from 'It's Going Wrong' illustrate this:

I wanna jump, I wanna scream
I wanna shout, I wanna leave
Leave you here, leave you here
Just like I did yesterday

Hopping and jumping and squeezing and lying and loving and leaving
it out
I wanna jump I wanna scream
I wanna tell you my dreams
It's going wrong, it's going wrong and that's my song
It's going wrong, it's going wrong and that's my song
Play my song

Multiple versions of the song exist, all with a better focus than the final version. Chris Squire of Yes also recorded a version of the song with Philip, under the title 'Silly Willy', along with another song.

Of the 11 tracks that made the cut, it's interesting to note the quality of those Philip chose to omit – 'Somebody Else's Dream', 'Hate', 'Song For Jimmy', 'Beat Of The Drum', 'Someone Out To Get Ya', Mystery, 'Dirty Old Town', 'I've Heard Lately' and others. A different album lies in wait should it receive a deluxe or box-set treatment in the future.

During the period the album was released, a solo tour in Europe was booked to take him through October. This was on top of the solo dates completed the previous June and July in Ireland. It was leading up to this period that Philip discussed the future of Thin Lizzy with his management. While no announcements were made before Christmas, he'd spent as much time touring solo as he had with Lizzy during 1982. Also, Thin Lizzy's bank account needed a major overhaul. The commercial failure of *Renegade* lingered, and with the rumour mill running amok, Philip reconvened at Eel Pie in Twickenham to record the final Thin Lizzy studio album.

Guitarist Snowy White played his last gig with Lizzy on 1 August at the Castlebar Music Festival in Ireland, having become disillusioned with Philip's lack of commitment to the band. White departed, leaving behind the 'Renegade' track – a song that can stand alongside the greatest the band ever produced. White:

Any band has a natural lifespan. There comes a time when you're just repeating yourself. Maybe it was that time for Thin Lizzy; I don't really know. When you try to do something a bit different, you risk losing all the old fans, so it's easy to get stuck in just repeating the formula. Phil was the leader and had the image, and there was a lot resting on his shoulders. He did well, considering all the pressure on him. In my opinion, he was really great at what he was, which was being the frontman for Thin Lizzy. But ultimately he succumbed to trying to be a celebrity instead of a musician. Maybe that was part of the problem. I felt that he wasn't part of a band any more; he was trying to be a solo artist. Nothing wrong with that, but I didn't want to be involved in it.

The band's final recording sessions commenced in November under the stewardship of producer Chris Tsangarides, assisted by Andrew Warwick and Chris Ludwinski, whose introduction to the upcoming sessions went like this:

The first person who walked through the door before the band came into the studio was Andy Warwick, who introduced himself as Chris' assistant. I said, 'I'm Chris and I was gonna assist', but he quickly said, 'Don't worry, there's going to be loads of work for both of us to do.' So we cracked on and shook hands, and the next thing he said to me was, 'Do you fancy a joint?' and I said, 'No thanks, I don't smoke.' He just laughed and said, 'You will by the time this album is over.' It was great fun.

Chapter 7: Sometimes, Guilt Overcomes!

It was just another night out in London town when Philip and his entourage arrived at the recently-opened Camden Palace venue in the lead-up to Christmas 1982. Previously known as the Music Machine, it was located at a busy junction on the corner of Camden High Street opposite the Mornington Crescent underground station. It was also the last place Bon Scott from AC/DC was seen drinking before his unfortunate death. Back then, Camden was a grotty destination, but the charm of the venue always enticed a crowd. The Camden Palace had opened its doors earlier that year and was run by Steve Strange and Rusty Egan of Visage fame. It quickly became one of the top nightspots in showbiz circles. It was here that Philip was introduced to rising r&b artist Junior Giscombe, who that year had a monster hit with 'Mama Used To Say'. His impressive desire to mix different musical genres was not lost on the man with whom he'd struck up a conversation. This unorthodox combo was seriously considering working together, but both had contractual obligations to fulfil before their liaison could be cemented. Philip was in rehearsal for the recently announced Thin Lizzy farewell tour, and Junior was about to fly stateside for recording commitments. Junior recalls their initial exchange:

> When we met, he told me he was going to leave the Lizzy thing. I remember turning and saying to him, 'Why are you coming to me? You could go to anybody, Phil', and he laughed and said, ''Cause I like what you do, Junior.' I never forgot that.

The pair agreed to meet at Philip's house once both their commitments were fulfilled to see if their notions for material could amount to something commercially viable. Their first recordings were done at the Lynott home studio, where he'd upgraded his 8-track to a 16-track, and it was the perfect setting to develop the smattering of ideas they had. But it was with some trepidation that Junior approached the sessions, as he'd been informed through the grapevine about Philip being 'difficult to work with.' Giscombe: 'I would have to say that working with Phil did present its issues. Before meeting him, I was told and heard all kinds of things about him. But with me, I found a very warm, considerate man. Our work together reflects a time in his life when he wanted to show another side of his personality. The lyrics of the songs we wrote show that.'

At the beginning of 1983, Thin Lizzy announced that their new album would be their last. Philip confessed on Dutch radio: 'After Christmas, we had a band meeting, and everybody decided to call it a day. I was very reluctant, but if nobody wants to stay on the ship, then… let her sink. But I knew I'd be blamed anyway. In a certain way, I am to blame because I was the leader and I was supposed to keep things together, and I didn't, so I failed. It suited me for the band to stay together.'

In truth, disbanding was the only option. Thin Lizzy was no longer financially viable. Initial ticket sales for the album tour were patchy, so the PR machine licked its invidious intentions into shape and corralled public nostalgia: the tour was advertised as their farewell. The remaining unsold tickets were snapped up, and the band set about playing to packed venues for their last hurrah. When their last live assault concluded in September 1983, Philip never led the frontline for Thin Lizzy again.

Lead guitarist John Sykes' introduction to the band did much to energise a jaded unit. It was at the behest of producer Chris Tsangarides that Sykes came on board, and though his youthful hunger was a welcome shot in the arm, it also coated the final songs recorded with Philip at the helm with a heavy-metal fever. It was a furious fever, indicative of the early '80s when playing faster than the eye could follow or the mind could fathom ousted the intricate melodic structures previously established by Thin Lizzy.

Perhaps the wish to evolve their sound came too late, but given the batch of songs being readied for the album, it was a worrisome road for Philip to be on. The lyrical inconsistencies on the last Lizzy releases were never more audible than on their farewell album, *Thunder And Lightning*. Except for a few highlights, the album is the least emotionally driven of their entire catalogue. Routine and rote, nevertheless, it peaked at number four in the UK and allowed the band to finish on a high note and wipe clean the commercial blemish it had afforded itself with the prior project *Renegade*.

Philip tried to enlist Jim Fitzpatrick to produce artwork for the new album. Fitzpatrick:

I never did get around to finishing the *Thunder And Lightning* cover. I wouldn't even consider doing it now unless I got paid a lot of money. The concept for that was one of the best I had come up with, and if it's not used for its original purpose, there isn't any point in finishing it. I could see in the roughs that it was going to be one of the best, and really, that's where it's always at – in the roughs, where the initial concepts come together – and the rest is then just developing it. *Thunder And Lightning* was a better rough than those of *Chinatown* and *Black Rose*. It was the perfect rough. The fact that Philip liked it meant nothing. If the record company didn't like it, then that was the end of it.

Industry changes also seem to have played their part when it came to budget cuts, marketing twists and the subsequent impact on bands such as Lizzy. Sleeve designer Andrew Prewett offers his insight:

Record companies were constantly seeking to keep up with trends and reinvigorate old ones. It was a rapidly changing world, and market trends fluctuated like all products. Adding variable mixes of the same material was, in my opinion, a desperate indicator of this: it just increased all production costs. Cutbacks in the companies did not help, as good people were moving on, and their input was lost. The income in the industry quickly declined, and the *night of the long knives* became a reality, with each record company and its departments waiting for the call to be told who was next. Telephone lines buzzed as news spread between companies.

The breakup of Thin Lizzy affected all members in different ways. For Philip, it seemed immeasurable, particularly when we saw how it all played out. With his marriage also about to enter the same uncontrollable waters, he was left to ponder the after-effects of his choices. Just 18 months earlier, he'd confessed to Gay Byrne on RTÉ's *Late Late Show* that, because he was now a father, his wild ways were behind him. His carefully constructed lies no doubt allowed him to live the life of the rocker. But the lies, as deep as they were, dug in and allowed a toxic coterie of people to take advantage of him and his celebrity. While well-intentioned people were kept at bay, the rot was granted access to all areas. Philip's heavy abuse of all kinds of drugs was having a telling effect on the man he used to be. Jim Fitzpatrick:

It wasn't just me that was shut out. Frankie Murray was shut out; everybody was shut out. The people who chose to ignore this usage were the people he depended on, ya know. Myself and Frankie tried to point this out to him. I'd always refer to Frank as the one person that Philip trusted above all else. There were many people like myself, Gus

Curtis and others that were close to him – but for Frank to be shut out, I found extraordinary. He was very pained by that. The reason he shut him out was to make sure that he didn't find out about the drug use because he would've gone nuts, as I did.

The band released three singles from the album: 'Cold Sweat', the title track and 'The Sun Goes Down'. Only two made the top 40. Not a single penny was spent on making videos – the band couldn't convince their record company to finance them. Footage shot by RTÉ at Lizzy's farewell concerts in Dublin was utilised for the 'Thunder And Lightning' single. This was an agreement struck by Philip. The lack of support for marketing was telling, but it was a battle that Philip had fought when he first started, and now he was here again, as he confessed on *The Late Late Show*:

In Ireland, there's an awful lot of talent, and there's an awful lot of people stopping that talent from getting through. Okay, in the last couple of years, it's opened up a bit, but even so, you still have to go to London if you're in any way talented at all. That's a very harsh decision to make when you're a young man – to leave home, family and country. It's happened to all Irish artists, and I'm not just talking about the rock scene. You name any great Irish writer, and most of the time, they've had to leave the country. I hate that smallmindedness where they won't put that extra couple of bob into an Irish act, but they would for a foreign act. For example, we were with a record company that had Demis Roussos on it, right? At the time, we weren't well known. We had a hit in 1973 with 'Whiskey In The Jar', and the next hit we had was in 1976. So, around 1975, everybody thought, 'They've had their day, they've come and gone', ya know? I'd seen thousands of pounds spent on this fella Demis Roussos – a big fat Greek fella, right? – a good singer. I was handed 50 pounds and told to promote our record. It was that type of mentality that drove me crazy, and that type of mentality that made me go to England, even though I loved Ireland.

Just before the commencement of the final Lizzy tour, Philip returned to Dublin to help out a band whose demos he'd been given by Johnny Lappin and Deke O'Brien of Scoff Records. The band were called The Resistors – a band borne from the ashes of Noise Boys, and which featured Tim McStay on vocals. The band had built a significant local following but never quite managed to achieve a breakthrough. McStay recalls how Philip came aboard:

To begin with, it meant a lot getting the deal with Scoff Records, as we needed finance for recording and also distribution, which I think Scoff levered through CBS. Philo heard our demos, liked what he heard and asked if he could produce a track called 'Steel My Love'. The original arrangement differed from what Philo did with it, and though we were happy with the outcome, in the end, we struggled to see that as our sound. When we tried to reproduce it live, it was hard to get that sound.

'Steel My Love' was the B-side to 'That's It', coincidentally produced by friend and collaborator Jerome Rimson. Though McStay describes Philip as being 'meticulous and not too pushy' in his role as producer, McStay was happy to see that band suggestions were taken onboard as the track was cut: 'He seemed to be into the 'Yellow Pearl' sound, and he carried a blue electronic drum machine with him and liked what it did through a mixing desk. For 'Steel My Love', he wanted the rhythm track to be very repetitive and exact, so he built everything around that. He was also quite intense about the vocal takes, as well. To my memory, he played supplementary bass on the final mix, as he wanted to add certain sound

Time was running out on the session, and it was agreed that Phil would take the track back to London to mix it at Abbey Road. Philip did accept a fee for the work he did on the song. McStay never again m Philip, as once the track was mixed in England, Philip sent it back to Sc Records. One thing sticks in McStay's memory: 'I saw him one day walk down Grafton Street with his little daughter on his shoulders. Being tall as he was, and then adding the height of his daughter to that, m a lovely sight. People were just charmed as he strolled down – the p dad, it seemed to me. You just got the feeling he was home and pe loved him being a Dubliner.'

The Resistors were one of several bands that Philip and Jerome Ri assisted. Blue Russia was another band that the pair produced at Lon Blue Russia drummer Noel McMurray had this to say about one sessions:

The single was titled 'Russian Around' and it dealt with the feelin the arms race, nukes and the general fear that we were – are the road to blowing ourselves to Kingdom Come. The credit for not actually shown on the cover for the single because the sing remixed before release, and the cover was based on the original m did an all-nighter at Lombard Studios, and Philo did some awesom to the drum production, which gave it the live power we were looking to reflect.

It was on one of these many occasions that Philip bumped into his old Orphanage colleague Joe Staunton: 'I remember doing a recording session over in Lombard Studios, and my son was about four years of age and I had him with me. It was the first time that my son Paul met a coloured person. Phil was just going in, and I had finished my session, and Phil said, 'Jesus Joe, is that your young fella?' and I said, 'Yeah.' Paul was very shy, and Phil lifted him up and stuffed five quid in his hand – Paul still remembers that. It was a nice moment and a nice recollection for him to have of a very kind man.'

As Philip was obliged to complete his commitments to Lizzy's touring schedule for much of the first six months of 1983, it left little time to consider working on new material, but some work was done. Once this final Lizzy tour was complete, he would be left without a record deal, so there wouldn't even be an outlet for any newly written work to be pushed into the marketplace. With this in mind, he decided to continue his pursuit of production work with bands such as Auto Da Fé and others on the Irish music scene. He made a brief appearance in the Auto Da Fé video 'Man of Mine', which was made by the same team that lensed 'Old Town' the previous year.

Just as the bulk of Lizzy's dates came to a close, he was presented with an option to put a solo band together and tour Sweden in July and August before reconvening with Lizzy for their final dates. The one serious issue at hand was that the record company didn't present a solo option for him to record once the commitment to Lizzy was complete. Seldom discussed and only highlighted, the negotiations that fulfilled Thin Lizzy's contractual obligation album to their record company weren't played out in a way that would give Philip any leverage. In his heart and soul, he knew the reasons why, but acceptance wasn't on the preferred menu. Before he knew what was happening, the music industry collectively decided to drop him and leave him marooned on the margins, like an aged whore. He couldn't catch a break. Tours could be booked and money made, but the security most needed by a musician – that of a record contract – was something Philip would fumble with for the remainder of his career and Junior Giscombe:

I fully understand how management saw him; I really don't. I think more about – you don't need to switch; if you stick with this, you'll be fine. So it was more about keeping him in a particular place, as opposed to him stretching and you backing that stretch. I don't believe that they did that. To criticise his management would be wrong of me because I don't know enough about them to do that. But what I do know is that in his switch to move forward ... it's very strange, that one. You have to wonder what was going on. An artist of that calibre – you're saying you couldn't find him a home? I don't believe that.

Philip still drew a big crowd in Scandinavia; therefore, the offer of doing a summer tour there was hard to resist. He put together another version of his solo band, dubbing the five-piece The Three Musketeers. They played much the same songs as on the previous solo tours, with the odd Lizzy song thrown in to appease audiences. Interestingly, they also unfolded some songs that never made the Lizzy cut, such as 'A Night In The Life Of A Blues Singer' and 'Look In These Eyes' prominently featured in the set. Curiously, John Sykes' playing added to the presentation of the solo material, neither over-playing his axe nor being over-intrusive. Once Sykes laid off the metallic fuel, he showed he could adapt, certainly on the solo material. He later showed such playing on the unpublished track they co-wrote – 'Samantha' – rumoured to be written in tribute to Jimmy Bain's daughter, who was Philip's godchild.

Once the solo dates were fulfilled, attention turned to Thin Lizzy's final appearance in front of an English audience, headlining Reading in August 1983 before wrapping up with some German dates at the beginning of September. Thin Lizzy's final performance with Philip took place in Nuremberg, Germany, with a crowd estimated at over 30,000.

In between studio bouts with Junior, Philip and his management convinced the record label to accept a live recording from the Lizzy farewell tour as their contractual obligation album. With his solo obligation to Phonogram now complete, Philip was without a publishing deal by the end of the year. The live album that was released a month after their final dates – *Life: Live* – proved to be a disaster, as engineer Will Reid Dick explains:

Life: Live was a fiasco. He did a lot of the mixes on that. My biggest problem with the album was that I couldn't get a commitment from anyone. The management called me and said, 'Can you help us out with this and try to pull it together?'. It was a situation of me getting there at noon and Phil would arrive at ten that night. I couldn't really get through anything until he did turn up. So, for the most part, I was fighting a losing battle.

Reid Dick's association with Philip went back several years, but shortly before this period, even *he* was taken aback when he saw the condition Philip was getting himself in:

I remember being in LA with John Alcock. I can't remember what record I was working on, but I was staying in Laurel Canyon with this girl, and the phone rang. Who should it be but Big Charlie (Phil's roadie), who explained that they had tracked me down and that Phil was in town and looking to meet up. So, over the phone, Phil asked if I might come and meet him at his hotel to discuss working on the new Lizzy album. I ended up leaving and driving down to where they were staying, but by the time I arrived, Phil was fast asleep after popping a couple of Quaaludes, and there was no talking to him. He couldn't even speak, and the possibility never really came up again after that.

A quiet farewell at the airport upon their return to England saw the Thin Lizzy members disperse with the promise to keep in touch. There were no emotional goodbyes, just relief for some members. Some used the space to try to get their lives back on track, and others kept working. That the legacy of Thin Lizzy would be consigned to the corridors of music's past seemed fitting at the time. However, as time has told, it didn't quite work out that way.

Chapter 8: The Lady Loves To Dance

Once the Lizzy tour was finally over, Philip was free to link up again with Junior Giscombe. The creatively fruitful relationship they built over the next couple of years is a curious oddity. Of all the tracks they worked on, it was 'The Lady Loves To Dance' – the first one they demoed – that stands apart as having the strongest commercial leaning. Junior:

'The Lady Loves To Dance' was one of those songs. He was messing around in his studio with his bass, singing the part. We just wrote it there and then, if you get what I'm saying. It was done within five minutes. It was one of those real happy, up – let's mix these different styles together and see what we get. 'The Lady Loves To Dance' to me should've been a single – it should've been huge. That was him after Lizzy. That was him making his statement, moving forward.

The earliest known demo of it – put together in Philip's home studio – has him playing acoustic guitar and bass while Junior plays keyboards, with both of them programming the drum machine. The first demo runs to just over four minutes, with many of the words making it to the final version recorded later at Good Earth Studios. Another song preliminarily titled 'Time And Again' was also worked on in these first writing sessions. It was a song they would return to regularly over the next 18 months.

In November, two sessions were booked with Tony Visconti at Good Earth, where Philip and Junior recorded 'The Lady Loves To Dance'. They took the basic demo and employed a string of session musicians. Graham Broad – who had worked frequently with Trevor Horn – played drums. On keyboards was Robin Smith, who was the session keyboard player at Good Earth: 'I remember working with Phil, Junior and Tony on the track. I had a long working relationship with Tony and later had success with Junior on the song 'Oh Louise'. The thing I do remember was how lovely Phil was. He was really excited about everything, and they seemed to end up with hundreds of bass guitar overdubs.'

Philip wasn't the only bass player on the track, as engineer Bryan Evans confirmed: 'The track evolved in the recording process, starting much like the demo but then changing with each added part. Derek Bramble (Tony's first-call session player at the time) played some bass, but I'm pretty sure it was a late addition which influenced the funkier approach of the mix.' Evans started as a trainee at Majestic Studios, a one-time cinema.

Once the cinema closed, the balcony area was converted into a recording studio and christened Majestic Studios. The Sex Pistols and David Bowie recorded there. However, Evans was keen to work at a higher level and kept in touch with various studios until a vacancy arose at Good Earth:

> I met Chris Porter, then Tony Visconti and Diane, and we seemed to hit it off, and I went to work there. Later, I became studio manager/chief engineer when Chris left. When I went to work there, it was a family atmosphere, with staff, regular musicians and ex-staff members who liked to bring sessions back there. We encouraged each other to do the best in our roles and felt supported in our mutual goal to take care of our clients and to output great records. This altered a bit later when Tony decided he wanted to change direction and brought in people with a different agenda.

'The Lady Loves To Dance' represented Evans' only direct involvement in recording with Philip and Junior, though he was acting in the capacity of studio manager when Philip and Gary Moore came in to finish work on 'Out In The Fields' in early 1985. Evans:

> My impression was that, yes, they welcomed input to improve the track and were also willing to experiment, perhaps aware they would need a strong, unique sound to take their collaborations further. I'd say they were looking for that input from their producer, and Tony was very much in the driving seat, though Junior and Phil were right there, too. Often, Tony could appear to be just working methodically but then suggest something or arrange parts that took the session in an unexpected direction – a case in point being the funkiness of 'The Lady Loves To Dance'.

Though John Sykes was in the studio with Philip and Junior, it had yet to be decided if there was a need for a lead-guitar break: 'I remember it was a very long session with John Sykes there for hours waiting to play, and I think, after a while, Phil didn't like the bass, and Derek Bramble played it. But we all knew Phil's was the one.

With Philip and Junior affiliated with Phonogram, there was no obligation on the part of the record company to release the finished song. Junior takes up the story:

> They couldn't see our point of view, so it made sense to them at that time to squash the project and not allow it to be heard. We fought for it,

but because of the mentality of the time, they weren't going to see it as a project. It was on for him, as it was for me. It was for him a movement away from Lizzy, moving into that whole 'This is me' and I don't believe that they got that. I think if they did get it, they would've released it. It's a great song. 'The Lady Loves To Dance' is a finished article. I would've thought they would've released it 'cause it was Phil, not because it was me.

With the establishment of MTV a couple of years prior, the issue of black artists getting a fair shake of coverage was called into question. MTV's Mark Goodman interviewed David Bowie in 1983 when he was on the promotional trail for his *Let's Dance* album. Bowie: 'Having watched MTV over the past few months, I think it's a solid enterprise with a lot going for it. I'm floored by the fact that there are so few black artists featured on MTV. Why is that?'. Goodman's response in the face of a fair and just criticism from Bowie was botched at best: 'We have to try and do what we think not only New York and Los Angeles will appreciate, but also Poughkeepsie or the Midwest – pick some town in the Midwest that would be scared to death by Prince, which we're playing, or a string of other black faces. We have to play the type of music the entire country would like.'

By the time MTV launched, Thin Lizzy had a bank of videos available for use. They were state-of-the-art productions. The band had worked with Bruce Gowers and David Mallet, who were both closely connected to Queen. MTV needed product for their channel, so bands that had made videos – particularly in the wake of Queen's 'Bohemian Rhapsody' – with the specific creation of a video to promote a single was to become commonplace. It also sired the opportunity to create a new stream of income. However, Lizzy never became a familiar face on MTV despite a slew of available videos. Scott Gorham:

MTV wouldn't play any type of video because we had a black guy up front. A black in a rock band wasn't right back then. They didn't know how to explain it, and then, Christ, he's Irish. I didn't get it, and I still don't. I mean, what's to get? It was a fucking rock 'n' roll band. Back then, it was a big issue. MTV wouldn't put a blackface on TV. It wasn't until a few years after he (Philip) died that this situation became apparent to me.

These were very real obstacles that artists of this time had to face, and it was under that cloud that Philip and Junior continued their collaboration.

But it didn't stop them, and it's a pity that the material wasn't developed further. Had the single at least been released and the floodgates allowed to be left ajar, who knows what impact it might've had? There were a substantial amount of musicians involved in getting the backing tracks together, as Bryan Evans confirms:

It was a matter of just putting down what Phil and Junior had as a demo to begin with – which was a programmed LinnDrum, bass, guide vocals, etc. I was trying to pay attention to the fine-tuning of tempo, key and structure. It's possible that the guitar went down at this point, too. Once the initial stages were agreed upon, we started on the real drums with Graham, who suggested putting down bass drum, snare, hi-hat and cymbals in one pass. Then he overdubbed his Simmons toms, emphasising accents and busily doing fills. This already excited us in the control room, as it transformed the feel of the track to be much more vibey and up. At this point, we recorded the keyboard part, with Robin building on and responding to the new feel.

Evans recalls Visconti's dissatisfaction once the backing tracks were complete and guide vocals were laid down on 'The Lady Loves To Dance': 'I think, at this point, Tony realised the guitar part was too much in a routine rock style, and removed it, muting-out unnecessary bits, and may have had me help him fly-in parts repetitively. This was what we did before sampling, using a tape machine to put parts where they hadn't originally been played.'

The final day was kept to complete the vocals. Philip and Junior then recorded their respective parts at the same time while facing each other in the studio. There's no doubt it added to the upbeat and fun nature of the track, as they vocally sparred for the object of their affection in the song. In some ways, the vocal interplay was reminiscent of Paul McCartney and Michael Jackson's hit duet the year before: 'The Girl Is Mine'. Giscombe:

We had agreed to do it that way because it would add to the excitement of the track, and it was cool. We had some overdubs to do, but we captured the vibe vocally. Phil didn't feel he had nailed it, so he did go back and forth during the vocal session. Considering 'The Lady Loves To Dance' was the first thing we actually wrote together from the beginning to both of us it had to be the first single, as it got the balance right. I found it was a very natural thing for me to work with Phil. For instance, if

I came up with a line or a verse, and if it felt right, he was very receptive to my input, and it stayed. There were other things that made him a great artist, though – a really great writer – because what I remember most was Phil's vocal timing. He taught me how to half-time melodies in different tempos, what women liked about a lyric, and how best to express them. There was a certain organic quality in his approach that appealed to me.

But the sessions were not without incident. At one stage, Philip became frustrated with recording some of his vocals. The first couple of days had run smoothly, finishing up mid-evening. But on vocal day, an unexpected visitor arrived, as Evans recalls: It was the only negative aspect of the time, as towards the end of the vocal session, some guy who I never saw – only heard him referred to as the witch doctor – called to see Phil, and after the visit, Phil was a different personality, insisting on endlessly doing vocal takes when most agreed he had nailed it many times over.'

Once the track was finished, Tony Visconti mixed it: 'I remember that the stereo toms tracks were recorded out-of-phase, which is something I had to fix in the mix. The whole song was built around Phil's signature chorused bass sound and plectrum playing. Though there are other musicians on the track, Phil was by that time pretty efficient at making his own keyboard sounds – something he didn't do much for Thin Lizzy, but mainly for his solo work.' This was indeed the last time that Philip worked with Kit Woolven and Tony Visconti.

The sessions yielded 7" and 12" versions of the track, with the hope of securing a release the following year. But record-label reception was lukewarm. Junior:

It was such a shame for both of us that Polygram, at the time, refused it. When we presented it, they refused it and we were both a bit taken aback 'cause it wasn't that the song wasn't good enough, and neither one wanted to go into the colour issue. But we couldn't see why they couldn't understand it or see it the way we did in terms of ... when you're in a band and you decide to move away from a band, you struggle for a few years 'cause you try to find *you* after being within a unit for so long. You think about the unit and what you're doing, and you're not really thinking about you as the individual. So here was a chance to come away from the band thing, work with people that aren't within a band, or even if they are within a band, who are individuals who will listen to where I'm coming from and try things with it. It takes time to find the right people to come around and have around you. He managed – and this is the thing for me that people don't fully grasp with Phil – he managed to understand this industry so well in terms of how to write songs that would touch people that he could work with someone like myself and teach me how to write a song; how to touch. He was a teacher as well as a musician, but they tried to make out he was just this and that. He had so much more, and that was the thing that hurt me the most – that nobody saw it. Sometimes, people want to align things with money as opposed to with art, and Phil was about art as much as he was about money. He was about art, and he understood it.

In today's marketplace, Record Store Day seems like an ideal avenue to finally issue the song, one of the few finished pieces of music that Philip completed after the cessation of Thin Lizzy. However, the failure in getting the song released didn't stop the duo from continuing to work together, and in total, they worked on six tracks, including 'Time And Again', 'He Fell Like A Soldier' and 'Breakdown'.

By the end of 1983, Thin Lizzy was over, as was Philip's marriage. His first instinct was to form another band, to keep working.

Chapter 9: Waiting Just To Catch Your Eye

The dress rehearsal for the next phase of his career may well have been the summer break from Lizzy's farewell tour in 1983 with the Three Musketeers in Scandinavia or – as David Heffernan previously mentioned – as early as the 1982 solo tour of Ireland featuring Jerome Rimson and Robbie Brennan. What *is* certain is that by the end of 1983, Thin Lizzy was gone. Caroline would soon follow, taking the children with her.

The instinct to form another band proved to have dire consequences. Conversations took place, and a new band, created after the recent solo tours, included Brian Downey, John Sykes and Mark Stanway. However, a short time after the first series of rehearsals, John Sykes defected to Whitesnake. Philip's relationship with Sykes had become close after the latter joined Thin Lizzy for their final fling with the charts on the *Thunder And Lightning* album. His departure from the new band was the first blow. Later, Philip confessed, 'I was a bit sick and disillusioned when Sykesy left, and I even considered joining a well-known band.'

Jimmy Bain turned him onto a guitarist named Laurence Archer during the Wild Horses period, and Philip's enthusiasm returned: 'I liked Laurence's playing so much that I decided to stick with the band, and we prepared for a tour of Ireland.' Archer takes up the story:

I got a call from Mark Stanway. Previously, I had toured with Magnum, and around this time, Mark had been touring with Phil across Europe on a solo deal, I think. He asked if I'd be interested in getting together with Phil to form a new band. Then Phil rang, sussing me out, and before I knew what was happening, there was a limousine outside my front door. Now, I had just got back from a cycling holiday and had cut all my hair, and here I was, standing in my tracksuit, watching this limousine pull up outside. Shortly, I was in Stringfellows, feeling like a right prick when I was watching all these rockers walking by in their gear.

Following Sykes' departure, the new four-piece of Philip, Brian, Laurence and Mark began to map out their ideas for the band, and by the middle of December 1983, the first demos were put to tape at Gary Numan's Rock City Studio at Shepperton. Engineer Martin Adam worked on the long day (and night) session: 'I had a good time. I remember on the day that Phil was being a bit *dependent*, for want of a better word, which is really sad. But when he actually sat down next to me behind the desk and sang those songs ('Nineteen', 'Sisters Of Mercy', 'Crime Rate'), I can remember it. I've done a lot of sessions over the years, but I can actually remember that day. I remember the songs, and that's not usual for me.

Of the songs that received attention in the session with Adam, 'Nineteen' and 'Sisters Of Mercy' were at a more advanced stage. The first attempt at 'Crime Rate' was a tortured affair. Philip delivered his jaded guide vocal over the skeletal backing track, amusing himself along the way when coming in too soon on one of the lines before leaving out an exasperated expletive. Instead of being out front, he propped himself up at the desk to sing once he eventually returned to the control room. Adam:

> I seem to remember there was a bit of tension because Phil had left the control room before doing his vocals. He was up in the office, faffing around with whatever he was doing, and I was ready to go home. It's a terrible thing to admit right now, but that was how I felt at the time. But he came back in and he blew me away. He was incredible and brilliant, so whatever he was on, it was working for him. It was almost a spiritual experience 'cause he really got in it, he was really going.

All things considered, Philip hadn't wasted much time since the final Thin Lizzy shows in September 1983. The first rehearsals for the new band took place at the local community hall in Howthbreak. New material had to be written and rehearsed while a debut in England was still in the distance. The plan was to break-in the new band on an Irish tour planned for spring 1984. The first clutch of songs was recorded before Christmas, and a considerable batch was to follow over the next year, culminating in November in what proved to be the band's final studio sessions with engineer Pete Buhlmann, again at Rock City in Shepperton.

Philip also continued to record at his home studio with Junior Giscombe, despite the label not wanting to release 'The Lady Loves To Dance'. That Philip was dabbling in collaborations outside the new band was very telling. He undertook a variety of other recording commitments throughout 1984. He was hedging his bets as always, waiting for one of his ongoing projects to catch the eye of A&R executives in England.

The imminent launch of a new band kept his name in the mind of the public, but privately, he faced the very serious challenge of a failing marriage. The debilitating drug habit he'd endured for the better part of a decade was *also* in the foreground. He looked and sounded different. Weight gain hadn't helped his appearance. Also, his breathing in interviews sounded laboured, while his personal choices had also wreaked havoc on his voice, as was evident throughout the final Lizzy albums. Yet he still chose to march on.

With Philip having been the chief lyricist in Lizzy, and also releasing two poetry books to that point, there was media talk of a book deal. It was set to be a series of anecdotes about life in the music industry. Philip: 'I've drafted the details for 13 short stories, which – although they'll be based on my own experience in the music business – will be classified as fiction. I do want to become a writer, but I know I'll have to discipline myself because now that I actually have to sit down and write the book, I keep putting it off.'

Once the Christmas period passed and 1984 began, it was back to the task at hand, with Philip frequently flitting between London and Dublin, prioritising deals and charting his intent with his new band. He'd retained CMO to manage this new project, but he no longer had the day-to-day support from Chris O'Donnell. Support came from a man named John Salter. Following on from the experience of John Sykes' departure, another blow was just around the corner. Laurence Archer – Sykes' replacement – recalls the impact of drummer Brian Downey's decision to quit the new band:

After breakfast, I'd stroll up to Howth. We had the back line and PA set up in the local community hall. I would get there at about ten and play about. Brian and Mark wouldn't be too far behind, then Phil at about 11 or 12 or sometimes not at all. I think this was when doubt set in for Brian. We would rehearse hard for about six hours and then hit the pub. Phil was in good spirits, but I think he was under the influence at that period. Strangely, though, apart from the timekeeping, the band was sounding really good as a four-piece, and Phil was together enough at rehearsals to make it work. Unfortunately, a couple of missed rehearsals and Phil being the worse-for-wear on a couple of occasions was too much for Brian. I think he didn't need it in his life at that point. For me, I was devastated it didn't work out. I loved Brian's playing, and he was a large part of the reason for doing it in the first place. He was such a nice guy, too. I can't imagine it being anything but a sharp piece of reality for Phil when Brian went.

Downey's concern, aside from inconsistent rehearsals, also included the planned setlist. There was none to speak of in the early weeks of 1984. Everyone brought what they had to the table when it came to new songs.

Downey's concern was dismissed by Philip, as they were always going to be obligated to play a certain quota of Lizzy songs to satiate the audience. So, as it stood for the upcoming Irish dates, the plan was to conveniently litter portions of Lizzy and slices of the solo work amongst the relatively scant new material to cushion out the set.

However, as February came around, keyboardist Mark Stanway found himself obligated to complete some live shows with Magnum, who were without a label in the autumn of 1983. A privately funded tour was planned to try to acquire a new deal for the band, but due to illness, band songwriter Tony Clarkin was unable to participate. This paved the way for Laurence Archer to complete the tour with Stanway. While all of this was happening, Philip and Downey were on the sidelines, waiting to recommence rehearsals for the upcoming Irish tour. By the following month, Stanway and Archer resumed band activities in Ireland. Rehearsals moved from Howth into the city centre, where the band took up residence at McGonagle's, previously known as the Crystal Ballroom. Thin Lizzy's original manager, Terry O'Neill, ran the place during this period.

A review of the early setlists from the new band's debut tour confirms Downey's concerns and backs up at least one of his reasons for opting out of the new project. In late April – only days before the commencement of the tour – Downey's replacement was found. His name was Robbie Brennan: 'I had one rehearsal, and the gig went ahead the next day. His supporters just wanted the heavy stuff off him, but he was trying to get a few new angles into the equation to make a clean break from Lizzy. At the same time, he was very determined to press ahead with it. The only trouble was that he was doing lots of drugs at the time.' Philip's relationship with Brennan dates back to the Skid Row days in Dublin. Brennan had also been a member of Philip's solo touring band in Ireland in 1982, as well as being the drummer for Auto de Fe, the support band on the solo tour of Ireland. Brennan: 'I always liked him. He was a great fella to go for a drink with. Again, people always recognised him, but he was used to it and he didn't mind it once they didn't hassle him. At an odd time, he might have to tell someone to fuck off and leave him alone if they were messing, but generally, people said, 'Howya Phil, how's it goin', what are ya up to?', and then left him alone.'

Soon after the Irish tour, Brennan made the move to London, living with Philip in his family home for about seven months. As time passed, he became aware of Philip's broad interest in other genres of music and, in lighter moments, enjoyed playing cricket in the back garden with band members, friends and even Philip's daughters Sarah and Cathleen. Brennan: 'I enjoyed his solo material because I hadn't realised he was so interested in other music – reggae, funk and highly-melodic pop tunes – and I was delighted with it, 'cause some of the songs were nice and funky, and I prefer this style of drumming.'

One look at the setlist for the first few gigs tells its own story, and therefore, littered throughout are solo hits such as 'Yellow Pearl' and 'Dear Miss Lonely Hearts', distastefully shacked up alongside new cuts like 'Nineteen' and 'Crime Rate'. The early medley featuring 'A Whiter Shade Of Pale' is welded onto the Lizzy outtake 'A Night In The Life Of A Blues Singer', though this wasn't to last long. The band eventually decided to morph 'A Whiter Shade Of Pale' with Dylan's 'Like A Rolling Stone' to superb effect.

With all the talk of the new band for Philip, deciding on a name was beginning to be a lethargic pursuit. Taking the lead from another new song provisionally titled 'Slam Anthem' – which was performed on the Irish Tour of April and May 1984 – a new chapter was about to begin. Laurence Archer remembers chatting with Philip at his house in Kew while sitting on the stairs: 'He seemed to be sold on this Slam idea, which later transposed to Grand Slam.' The band was billed as Grand Slam very early in the tour and even featured promotional materials, with Brian Downey still showing as a featured member. These images soon tailed off, and promoters began using images of only Philip. In many cases throughout the tour, 'Phil Lynott's Grand Slam' was featured prominently, or even 'Phil Lynott's New Thin Lizzy.'

In an interview with Dave Fanning on RTÉ radio, Philip provided some insight into the new band, which revealed a second guitarist had also joined. Doishe Nagle was drafted in before Brennan joined. Philip:

Mark Stanway on keyboards – he was with Magnum, who I didn't particularly like. He had a lot of class with his keyboards. He's a very good contemporary player, very much a feel player. Doishe Nagle – initially when Doishe came to the band, he wanted a lead guitar gig, but I was adamant that this band would not be based on a dual lead as Lizzy was. I asked if he was willing to play rhythm and concentrate on guitar techniques like Andy Summers. He's such a good singer, bass player and songwriter. Archer is the one all the pressure is on – the 21-year-old whizz-kid guitar player who has to take on the legend of the other guitar players I've played with. I've worked with a few guitar players in my time, and, of course, there's the big bad wolf himself: myself. Robbie, well, we met in Skid Row. Robbie's such a feel player; done stuff on solo tours and Auto de Fe. He was the most obvious guy to think of after Brian decided he didn't want the gig. At the moment, we're using my reputation to get some publicity. When you come and see the band, it'll become fairly obvious that they're all very talented people.

The low-key tour was met with mixed opinions in the press, as so much Lizzy material was evident in the set. Philip:

When we started last week, the first date, we were doing 60% Lizzy songs and 40% Grand Slam. Now, within five dates, we're doing 80% Grand Slam and 20% Lizzy, so if you wanna hear Lizzy tunes, you better hurry up and come and see us (laughing). The response has been great. Last night was really good, which is why I'm acting all confident now. Everyone's working so hard, and this is our day off, and we're in the studio putting down more of the new stuff. It's really good fun for me. When I did the solo stuff, it was like, it was just doing something different to being in Lizzy. This is like bread and butter to me. It's far more dedicated and far more theory involved in the music.

Philip had written and co-written songs with Laurence Archer and Mark Stanway, such as 'Nineteen', 'Sisters Of Mercy', 'Slam Anthem' and 'Crime Rate' – songs that were works in progress by the time they were debuted in front of a live audience. Given the short time they spent to come up with material that reflected their direction, it's interesting to note that the aggression Philip had gravitated to on the last Lizzy album was still present, but now he added some atmospheric dimensions, with a heavy emphasis on Stanway's keyboard playing: particularly on 'Slam Anthem'. The songs revealed the versatility and influence that each member brought to the group. On the flip side of this evident versatility was a new band playing the field with multiple genres. Just what type of band were Grand Slam to be? That question was never really answered for the duration of their lifespan. As with Lizzy, Philip wrote the majority of the lyrics, continuing to write his life story in song.

By the time the band concluded the Irish tour – which took in 13 dates, with the penultimate gig at the SFX in Dublin – only five of the 13 songs played were new material – quite a long way shy of the radio claim made by Philip. Any attendees imbibed their fill of some Lizzy, such as 'Whiskey

In The Jar', 'Sarah' and even 'Parisienne Walkways'. Many more gigs were done in the larger pubs around the country. Writer Tony Clayton-Lea – who interviewed Philip at work in Lombard Studios for a *Hot Press* feature – bore witness to a gig at a venue in Co. Dublin, as he recalls:

I saw them in a pub in Balbriggan. Now clearly, Phil Lynott, in any band format in the early to mid-'80s playing a pub in Balbriggan, was a kind of step down from what he used to be doing. That said, there was a sense from chatting with him that this was the next part of the game plan. He certainly had no problem going around the smaller towns of Ireland creating what he only hoped would've been a kind of crack unit of a live rock band. That's the reason why he embarked on that smallish Irish tour. But certainly, the gig in the pub in Balbriggan was not good. I didn't like it. I thought they were really sloppy. He played two or three Lizzy songs. The venue was stuffed. Not to play Lizzy's songs would've been out of character and, maybe, unwise. The band themselves were very, very heavy-handed – almost kind of like metal, like not very good hair metal.

Soon after the dates in Ireland concluded, the media reported on another crushing blow for Philip. His marriage to Caroline made unfortunate headlines. The tabloids jumped on the news, pasting their pages with tales of heartache and woe in celebrity land. Caroline was quoted on the marriage breakdown: 'There's a whole list of reasons. We thought it best to sort out our lives separately. Phil and I are both going through a period of change, but it's certainly not the end of our marriage.' The separation agreement dictated that Phil's mother, Philomena, be present when he took the children every second weekend. Refusing to resolve his personal problems, Philip kept his head down and kept working with Grand Slam. He would later open up about his lifestyle and choices in the media, but only on his own terms. And even then, the picture painted was one of convenience rather than truth.

Prior to the English tour, Grand Slam rehearsed at E-zee Hire Studios in London. Bill Cayley – one-time road manager for Thin Lizzy – was running the place. Roughly a year later, Cayley was to hook Philip up with E-zee engineer Maurice Mulligan to record demos in preparation for a planned new album.

The first two dates of the planned Grand Slam UK tour (Newcastle's Mayfair and Victoria Hall in Hanley) were cancelled at short notice, though a warm-up gig in Northampton *did* go ahead, with an eye on the all-important Marquee debut to the industry planned for 30 and 31 May. But those were also cancelled, and the band regrouped for the rescheduled dates a couple of weeks later. In between the move from Ireland to England and gearing up for a nationwide tour, the band needed to make sure their setlist was in order. A recurrence of the Irish tour setlist wouldn't do them any favours. In fact, on 1 May, before travelling for one of the Irish dates, the band completed a short session at Lombard, recording a new song called 'Military Man'. An undated session from the archive shows Phil working on several songs around this post-Lizzy/early-Grand Slam period – songs which in some cases had most certainly working titles – 'Paddy Rap', 'Time And Again' (with Junior), 'Robbo's' (with drums), 'Military Man' and 'Harlem'. A Lombard engineer during this period was Pat Fenning. He oversaw sessions of Lizzy, Grand Slam, and solo ideas Philip wanted to document. Fenning:

> The first time was when Phil was putting 'Thunder And Lightning' together. I didn't do too much on that except clean up after a bunch of rock stars. There were just too many people in the control room; you couldn't get in. After that, though, he came in as a producer for a few bands. There was one from Howth, I don't recall their name (Clann Eadair), but they had a residency at some place in Howth, and met up with Phil there. I was really impressed. He took what I would've called an average trad band and gave them a really great sound, and showed them how to arrange and make their music present itself. After that, I worked mainly with him on his Grand Slam band.

With the band having settled in London – mainly at Philip's home – given the breakdown of his marriage and the empty house, recording sessions began aplenty. However, having a recording studio – while basic – at the end of your garden didn't always yield the results needed. By the time of their debut at the all-important showcase gig at the Marquee on Wardour Street, the band had seven original songs to show off out of a 12-song-strong set. Stanway:

> There were many songs being worked on by Phil, myself and Laurence … 'Sisters Of Mercy' was one of the first Grand Slam songs, which was written by Phil and myself. The song 'Nineteen' was one of Phil's; 'Military Man' was a song that Phil and I wrote. Later down the line, Laurence wrote 'Dedication' and 'Can't Get Away' with Phil, and I also wrote 'Slam Anthem', with Phil writing the lyrics.

According to Stanway, 'Crime Rate' was the only Grand Slam song with creative input from John Sykes prior to his departure to Whitesnake. One jarring change to the majority of the Grand Slam material was a lack of heavy emphasis on Philip's chorused bass. Stanway: 'We tended to use less chorus on Phil's bass, as it seemed that we were getting tuning discrepancies with the keyboards.'

From the first batch of songs, it was hard to identify a potential single. 'Crime Rate' – as it reveals its drizzled, dank and utterly bleak tale of murder, didn't quite fit the mould. 'Slam Anthem' – experimental and excessive – also falls short. 'Nineteen' probably came closest, as would prove to be the case the following year, but it too sounds routine and generic. While 'Sisters Of Mercy' yields insightful lyrics, its arrangement is chaotic. The alternating tones and moods in the song don't quite gel, and in their attempt to advance the song, a lot of the early gravitas is lost.

Mama oh Mama, this is your boy
In this life that you gave me there is sadness, there is no joy
I am weary, I am lost and overcome
In my sadness, my anger, my squalor
Oh Mama oh Mama, what went wrong?
Help me

Though Philip's relationship with his mother was deeply rooted, there were times in his life when his actions towards women were highly questionable. Some consider his upbringing as a source of upheaval for him in later life. His distrust of the opposite sex became even more pronounced as he came to the end of his life. Robbie Brennan:

Personally, I think he had more in his head about his family than he had about the black thing – I think he had come to terms with that. At an odd time, if we were travelling down the country, there might be a bit of a strange reaction. I think he hadn't quite resolved his relationship with his mother. I still think he had misgivings about having to live with his grandmother when he was a child, and his attitude toward women, in general, was iffy. He probably needed to have a chat with her over a period of years and sort out things. A lot of this stuff is in hindsight now.

Many of his lyrics throughout the Grand Slam period are tinged with loneliness that spotlights this inner conflict which for so long he vigorously kept under wraps. Lizzy's songs – no matter the era – were never about pleading for help. There was adventure and misadventure; there was love lost and lust found; there was street poetry propped up by carnal urges and tales of the outsider looking inward. The Philip Lynott who wrote lyrics for Grand Slam material was very different. Free of the Lizzy legend, his confessions in song allowed a deeper insight into his misguided ideals. Robbie Brennan:

> He was a very sociable fella, but he did have his black moods. And I think, when it came to it, with Caroline, he was a bit irrational. His thinking was a bit, ah – maybe it was because he wanted to be the macho man or whatever. I thought he didn't treat her very well sometimes. He took the separation very hard 'cause he adored his kids. At the same time, he didn't act like a very responsible father.

As Philip's private life continued on unsteady ground, it bled into his Grand Slam lyrics, evinced above in one of the many recorded versions of 'Sisters Of Mercy'. However, one of the few things worth noting around this time is that his voice appeared to have recovered somewhat since the final Lizzy tour, though singing in lower keys now seemed to be a constant. Grand Slam members and others keeping pace with Philip in this period attest that his energy levels, when working, worked as hard as ever. In some respects, starting all over again, living and breathing the energy of a new band, helped him. In a band situation, his focus could be goaded – but alone, he floundered. Drunken sessions in his garden studio yielded little of merit. He was also never unaware that he was the star of the show, and making it work in his favour became second nature. On a break from rehearsals before their London debut, Philip chatted with writer Mark Putterford:

> I don't feel I have any God-given right to success because of what I've done before. I want Grand Slam to be successful for itself, and not because it's Phil Lynott's band. I wouldn't want any band to be a cheap imitation of Thin Lizzy, and I'm trying to make sure that this band isn't built around me. There is gonna be a comparison because I do lead the band, but as much as you can say that Mick Jagger is the Stones, you can't say that Keith Richards isn't the Stones as well. So, as much as you could say that I was Thin Lizzy, you can't say that the kids didn't also come to see some of the best lead guitarists around. Anyway, one of my

aims for the band is to feature Laurence because I've worked with some of the best lead guitarists around, and he's potentially as good as any of them.

There were other record label offers on the table in England, including the allure of forming Blackmail with his friends Jerome Rimson and Gus Isidore. Blackmail was their concept, though, in the end, Philip decided not to pursue the idea. Just how two bass players and a lead guitarist were going to figure a way forward, is unknown, as the band never became more than a conversation. What *is* certain, is that the second solo album is poorer for not featuring the songs he worked on with both musicians. 'I Heard Lately' with Rimson is a seductive funk triumph, even in its incomplete state. Philip worked on it multiple times and sang multiple alternative lyrics, trying to find the right fit. One verse was co-opted for the final Lizzy album track 'This Is The One'. Rimson: 'We did it on the 8-track at 184 Kew. Phil walked in one day and heard it and just went, 'You know what you need to do there?' – 'cause it had a kind of jazzy overtone, and he changed the hook line to 'Have you heard lately', and he turned it into this jazzy thing. Parts of it were brilliant and parts of it were throwaway.'

Meanwhile, Isidore's 'Someone Out To Get Ya' was a monster hit lurking in the wings and is far more complete than the Rimson collaboration. Multiple versions exist, and it's no surprise that Philip revisited it in 1985 to record what would be his final vocal attempt. Isidore: 'Phil had a lot more to offer than just the Lizzy thing, which to this day is still great. Being the romantic he was, he had a more sensitive and subtle side to his nature, which you can hear on both his solo albums.'

Jeff Wayne of *The War Of The Worlds* was also back on the horizon, trying to form a touring version of the show. It was one of many propositions to consider in the summer of 1984 – coincidentally around the same time Grand Slam were launched in the UK. Wayne:

We were trying to get a stage show going, and I had held talks with Richard Burton about doing something, and he was committed to the idea. Technology – even at that time – wasn't great in that we were guaranteed a spectacular light show, but there was the possibility of problems. What *was* around at this point was Mike The Talking Head, which was an interactive 3D computer-animated head. So, if we could reach an agreement with Richard – which we did – then he would sit for us and we could use this effect in the show. I was also working with Richard on a TV special for an American network, where he was going to read the works of Dylan Thomas, and I was to score it. We worked for a couple of days, and then he said he was going to Switzerland for a short holiday, and we were due to reconvene upon his return. This, of course, didn't happen, as he passed away during that holiday, and that pretty much left my dad and me devastated. After this, I stepped back from *The War Of The Worlds*. I had acquired the rights to use this talking-head technology, and after Richard's death, I gave the rights back, and it was Dave Clarke who was the benefactor of that, as he used this technology in his musical *Time*.

It could have been an interesting challenge for Philip had the project come together, but without a doubt, it would've been the death knell for Grand Slam. The high energy levels required for such a tour may well have been the jolt that Philip could've benefited from to reorganise his life. Often when the band were recording, Philip wasn't present but would arrive later to overdub his vocals. Various inside sources over the years questioned his true commitment to the band when he seemed to be organising other deals for himself, be they book deals or otherwise. The issue of even getting Philip to rehearsals wasn't the biggest problem in an increasingly crazy picture. Brennan: 'The bigger problem was not getting him to do detours on the way to rehearsal. We would be there at the given time with the gear set up, and Philip might turn up, but not after getting what he was looking for on that earlier detour. Most of us weren't innocent either, but we would still be on time. Most of us partook in what was on offer but to a much lesser degree than him.'

Grand Slam slowly gained a reputation as a wild band of desperadoes on the London music scene. In many ways, it echoed the gang mentality that was prevalent within Thin Lizzy, but because Grand Slam were only together for a short period, they never quite generated the charm that oozed from Lizzy. After the June debut at the Marquee, Grand Slam interspersed their live gigs with short blocks of recording time in various studios and started to generate a solid catalogue of songs. Just as they'd done in Ireland, and with time at a premium, they often recorded during the day before gigging that night. Having Philip's home studio at their disposal was an obvious benefit to quickly document ideas as they came, and as a few bandmates were living there, it was logical to use the facilities at their fingertips.

The initial burst of UK shows found them in Sheffield, Middleborough, Worthing and Nottingham, amongst a host of gigs in the greater London area. An undated session from the archive shows work on a series of tracks such as 'Harlem', 'She Tries' and 'Military Man'. The same songs were frequently re-recorded as the band tried to bring them to fruition. Also of note regarding these sessions is the lack of information about the location or engineer involved, which may indicate sessions that took place at the home studio.

By the middle of July, the band had completed the first round of shows before some downtime allowed them to recharge and get another batch of material down on tape. Grand Slam was using their audiences as a soundboard for songs. To that point, none had been developed to their fullest potential, and they only would be should a suitable record deal be forthcoming. The problem was that Philip's reputation as a hellraiser had started to go against the band's chances of securing a record deal. He saw little correlation between his past exploits and the difficulty in convincing a record company to take a chance on his new band, Archer:

The drawback with Phil and the forward motion of the band was the press and the drugs and Phil's reputation within the industry. It seemed we could not get over the stigma of drugs, etc., with the major record companies. As a product, we had loads of interest and admiration from industry people, but no one would stick their neck on the line. Also, whatever is said, people would have prefixed ideas, and for Phil to move on from Lizzy totally was always going to be difficult in other people's eyes. Although we all – including Phil – had the belief that it would make it as big if not bigger than Lizzy as a stand-alone product. We will never know.

Equally, it wasn't helpful when the band held preliminary interest at EMI, only for that curiosity to quickly abate when the head of A&R – a guy who once worked as a journalist – was knocked out by Philip. Needless to say, that was EMI out of the picture. It was going to have to be the take-no-prisoners motto invoked by Philip to try to continue the pursuit and maintain interest in the band. After the latest round of disinterest from record labels, the band resumed recording at the home studio.

The 14 August saw Archer and Philip at work on a selection of tracks, including 'Can't Get Away', 'Blackmail', 'New Rap' and 'Sweet Thing'. While the latter two songs are listed in his recording archive as tracks he worked on, they have yet to be heard by the wider public. It is conceivable that

'Sweet Thing' is a cover of the Van Morrison classic. In the recording archive, the song titled 'I Still Want You Back' was not yet listed as a working title for 'Can't Get Away', and was listed as being recorded in early September, along with multiple versions of a song called 'Gay Boys' which features input from Archer and 'John': quite possibly John Sykes. By 27 September, 'I Still Want You Back' had been dropped as a title, and the song was recorded as 'Can't Get Away'. Other song titles worked on on 27 September were 'Breakdown', 'Jimmy Don't Call' and 'Philip's Keyboard Track'.

As with any mutation in musical trends as time passes, it's especially tricky to identify any particular Grand Slam track that might've potentially troubled chart compilers. Duran Duran, Wham!, Spandau Ballet, Culture Club and others were fighting a commercial wave to reach the pinnacle of the UK and international charts. It may also be unfair to compare songs that were works-in-progress with songs that were being released commercially and becoming hits. But the matter remains – just what common thread throughout the Grand Slam material might've best represented them to a record-buying public. Jeremy Nagle of Driveshaft played on most of the Irish support gigs and offers some insight:

This was my first time meeting Phil. He was always someone I admired. To this day, I think he was the best rock singer/bass player and songwriter ever. It was a real thrill. Well, their material was melodic heavy rock, as you would expect. Among their songs, 'Nineteen' really stood out as their best song and riff in my opinion! I remember them playing the theme from *Top Of The Pops,* which Phil had written, and a few Lizzy songs. Everyone in the world loved Thin Lizzy, so that was hard to follow – it must've been hard to break away from that. He was an icon! Phil's voice was amazing, like musical Guinness! his writing was truly inspired, and his type of bass-playing was perfect for rock. But let's face it, everyone will remember Phil for Thin Lizzy.

Mark Stanway: 'We had no intention of erasing the Lizzy dynasty. The only conscious thing was more apparent keyboards than Lizzy used to use and less of a constriction on the material. Any style of musical form would be considered, whereas I think Lizzy tended to stick to a more tried-and-tested formula.'

So, Grand Slam – no matter the effort – continued to musically hobble in the shadow of Thin Lizzy and limp behind the preconceived notions of their leading man. Philip was typecast in many respects, but he was also his own casting agent. He'd created a definite identity, as Lizzy's commercially successful trajectory rose exponentially after 'The Boys Are Back In Town' became a hit. He enjoyed the spotlight that came with success. He was seduced by the temporary glow and perhaps felt he'd worked hard enough to indulge himself, given he'd been in the business since he was a teenager. When Lizzy ceased, rather than being left on the sidelines, his instinct was to push ahead rather than sit back and consider. 'He didn't want to fade out', as Jerome Rimson confirmed in *The Rocker*: the documentary directed by the late Shay Healy.

By this point, Philip was mixing his drugs, taking Belushis, as they were known, or speedballs, as they are more commonly known today: a concoction that has killed many over the years. He frequently combined heroin and cocaine, injecting it into his toes, thereby avoiding telltale marks on his arms. He was willing to go to whatever lengths necessary to keep his growing addiction a secret from his closest friends and family. But everybody in the music industry knew what Philip liked, and some preyed on this to get into his inner circle, plying him with drugs of every variety. Unsavoury types never stopped coming to his house – deliveries from dealers trying to keep the party going, even when he tried to clean up his act. It isn't commonly reported, but he did make genuine attempts to remove the heavy drug use from his life. He certainly wasn't oblivious to his growing dependency and knew he was in trouble. The irony of it all is his protective behaviour of other people – some new to the business – where he asked them to heed his warning and not get involved in drug use.

Had he the right people around him, he might've taken the time off that he needed to address the problems in his personal life and returned with a clear mind, some fresh ideas and the hunger to work to the level he had done in the heady days of Thin Lizzy. It would be wrong to say that the right people weren't available to help – they were. Jim Fitzpatrick pleaded his case, as did Frank Murray, Gary Moore and others. Phil just needed to acknowledge it himself. It's difficult to even determine if he ever realised he wasn't bulletproof. The late Philip Chevron on the downward trajectory of Philip's private life:

> When I spoke to Phil, he spoke lovingly about himself as a family man, but in truth, he was just constructing another mythology which he thought would help him to live his increasingly difficult life. Philip was his own worst enemy. He never let people love him enough to be able to tell him

how things really were. When he needed help, he didn't know whom to ask. And, in truth, I think he had us all believing in the myth, too.

But Grand Slam wasn't dead in the water just yet. Considering they'd only been a working unit for ten months or so, a further slew of gigs was booked, and more material was recorded. The showcase June Marquee gigs hadn't landed the fast deal hoped for, and while it was a disappointment, they ploughed on, wrote, and focused on another industry showcase in December. Between Grand Slam commitments, Philip also found time to continue his collaboration with the traditional Irish group Clann Eadair.

September saw the release of the single 'A Tribute To Sandy Denny', on which Philip sang the lead vocal. It was to serve as a taster for the album to follow, which Philip was to produce. Sessions were done *ad hoc* between 1982 and 1985 in Ireland and at Philip's home. Other tracks recorded featured vocalists from the group, such as Siobhan Moore and Brendan 'Bull' Harding. But as time moved on, a decision was made to make the planned album entirely instrumental except for 'A Tribute To Sandy Denny'.

Whenever Phil was back at home, he frequently jumped in with the band on sessions held at the local pubs of Howth. Leo Rickard: 'There were a couple of songs that Phil was doing with Grand Slam. I can only remember the name of one of them – it was 'Sisters Of Mercy'. He would do a couple of verses, and we would do an instrumental break in the middle with a jig in the key of G. Jerome Rimson on bass/keyboards and Doishe Nagle on lead guitar would also accompany him.'

Phil also found time to guest on numerous TV shows throughout the year, though his appearance on *TV-Am* on ITV in Britain was – to say the least – ill-advised. He hadn't yet come to the conclusion that he needed help, though it is visible he was in deep trouble. He confessed the following:

The frightening thing about heroin is that it is very enjoyable to take. It cuts off reality if you've got a lot of problems. It would be so easy for me to just jump up on television and say, 'Hey, this is the pits, don't do it.' The thing that's never put across on television very well is how enjoyable it can be. Now, I never got to the stage where I became so addicted to it that my body physically craved it. But mentally, that battle will continue for the rest of my life.

It was as revealing a quote as he ever gave.

Work continued on songs like 'Breakdown', 'Gay Boys', 'Dedication' and 'Can't Get Away', all dispersing the band's potential commercial attributes. 'Breakdown' was rewired from the original concept developed with Junior Giscombe, who wasn't aware that Philip co-opted the track for Grand Slam: 'I think 'Breakdown' was one of those tracks that we both had an affinity to in terms of its lyrical content and where we were going with it. That he continued to play it with his band and stuff, really does touch me. I never knew that. I did not know that. Wow.'

A curious entry in the home recording archive dated 13 September 1984 involves the Belle Stars. Their self-titled album released the previous year was in part produced by Peter Collins, with whom Philip would shortly be working himself. The archive shows tracks such as 'He Fell Like A Soldier', 'Breakdown', 'Hard Times' and 'Slam' as having backing vocals added by the group or possibly Jennie Matthias alone. Another session during December at his home studio shows additional work was done on 'Breakdown'.

Between the final batch of sessions with Grand Slam in the studio and on stage, Philip was reacquainted with his old Lizzy mate Gary Moore and was a special guest on his latest tour, playing two or three songs each night he appeared, loving the warmth of the arena spotlight that came his way as a result. Moore's return to Ireland to tour as a solo artist also involved the making of a documentary, later titled *Emerald Aisles*, directed by Phil Tuckett. For eight years, he was the director for all of Moore's film projects and recalls Philip as 'one of my favourite people that I've met in my 45-year career as a documentary filmmaker.' The backstage banter featuring the pair at work and play acts as a cleanser for how they parted ways just five years earlier when Moore was touring with Lizzy in America. It's a documentary that merits revisiting and re-issue.

Grand Slam was back on the road throughout October and November but paused for additional studio work in Shepperton at Rock City – incidentally, where their first demos were recorded. The sessions dated 15 November are the last that Grand Slam officially completed with engineer Pete Buhlmann. The tracks that received work were 'Gay Boys' and 'Can't Get Away', while 'Military Man' got another coating, having been reworked several times throughout the year.

The final half dozen gigs in December were not meant to be the end. Philip knew he was going to be recording with Gary Moore in the new year and on several other sessions organised by management. Conversations needed to take place. Headway was limited, and no major deal was forthcoming for the band. Robbie Brennan: 'We were put on hold. The talk at the time was that he was offered money to put a version of Lizzy back together, which he may or may not have done. We never found out.'

And so, quietly, Grand Slam was put on the shelf despite a serious investment throughout the past year. That the band were recording demos to bait record labels with just weeks before they essentially folded spoke volumes about the insecure life of a musician. What the next tide would bring Philip while Grand Slam was quietly scuttled ranged the breadth of the spectrum.

Chapter 10: Hard Times

In the early 1980s, when engineer Martin Giles started work at Wave Studios, it occupied a four-storey corner building on Hoxton Square in London's East End. Studio One was on the ground floor – a 24-track studio that housed a decent-sized live room, which could facilitate a large group of musicians at one time. A second studio was situated with the same floor footprint one flight up, but the focus of Studio Two was more on tracking live bands. Later when studio owner Peter Ind opened the Bass Clef club in the basement, tie lines were installed from the stage to both studios, ensuring the recording of live shows was done with ease. While the studios continued to be used separately for sessions during the day and evening, friction was often at hand when a band was tearing the club to pieces while musicians were trying to record in the studio.

Philip worked at Wave during 1983 and 1985, though the recordings he made there have never been released. The first sessions took place shortly before Thin Lizzy's final UK gig at the Reading Festival in August 1983. The initial stint at Wave yielded a song provisionally called 'Time And Time Again', or 'Time And Again' as it has become known. The song was among a batch that Philip recorded with Junior Giscombe, as previously mentioned. Wave offered reasonable rates for musicians either recording demos for major labels or masters for independents and smaller labels. A series of sessions were booked for Philip during the summer of 1985 in the hopes of securing a new publishing deal. Martin Giles recalls the sessions: 'It was just Phil turning up with tapes in hand. I don't remember anyone else being there, except I think someone turned up at some point to overdub something for a while. For a lot of the time, Phil sat at the piano trying out parts, working on lyrics, and we recorded some vocals too.'

During the last of these summer sessions, two songs received work, provisionally titled 'Hard Times' and 'Still Thinking Of You'. While Philip would often work at his home studio, he just as frequently used recording studios around London. Engineering his own sessions at home was a non-starter anyway, as he couldn't be in two places at once unless Tim Martin was on hand on a visit from Dublin. Martin handled the majority of Phil's technical support in Dublin and was also the recording engineer on the road with Grand Slam when they toured Ireland.

The two songs above have found their way into the world courtesy of various streaming platforms. While both sound low in audio quality, the spirit of the songs is easy to identify, and they are very much Philip Lynott in 1985, enduring hard times professionally and personally. Within six months of making the recordings at Wave, Philip was dead.

These later songs created at Wave and in other sessions in London throughout 1985 are very revealing; softer and often laced with heartbreaking honesty. Also, the hard edge evident in the image was betrayed by the eyes hiding behind the shades in interviews and betrayed further by the lyrics he wrote during the post-Lizzy period. His creativity hadn't totally run dry, but few UK A&R men – if any – were pasting 'Wanted' posters bearing his image across the industry. On a home recording of 'Hard Times', he wearily sings:

Bad Days
Hey Mister, is there nobody to praise?
Sad eyes
Hey mister, I wear my disguise
Nobody waves
She says 'You crazy fool'
She says lost and alone
I said 'Don't you get weary, don't leave me alone'
Hard times

Philip had braved tough terrain since the early days of Lizzy, and their failure to elevate themselves to the level of the Stones or Beatles *did* bear down. The collective aim of Thin Lizzy was high, and that it tapered at crucial times in their career was a scar only time and reflection could make visible. By the last year of his life, Philip was perceived as a bygone figure from an age in music that was seen as cold and no longer relevant. New trends had pushed him to the side. He also no longer had the moorings of a band situation to keep him focused, nor did he have the immediate security of his family. He was alone in his Mock Tudor house in Richmond. While others passed through to party he continued with the next batch of strangers that came knocking. His personal choices ensured his eventual outcome. Plenty of friends and family pleaded their case about how Philip was living his life – to no avail. When bereft of direction, often the fox broke out the bottle.

Still, options were on the horizon beyond the now-inactive Grand Slam. In early October 1984, Philip linked up with Huey Lewis, who was due to play the Marquee in London. They jammed with Bryan Adams and Nick Lowe, and another seed was set in place. Huey Lewis and The News had broken through in America with their album *Sports*, and while an unknown quantity in England, Lewis had some free time in his schedule the following January to tangle with Philip for what turned out to be the last time they worked together.

Philip was no longer a major earner for his management company, CMO. Over the years, and on his recommendations, they took on artists that *did* become major money spinners, such as Ultravox. So, while Ultravox and other CMO-managed bands were filling the coffers, it left little space for Philip. It can't be said he did much to help himself, either. CMO may have been built on the money that Thin Lizzy generated. And to survive, they needed to sign acts that could get into the charts. With Thin Lizzy gone, his discipline wavering and his writing worrisome, simple commerce dictated who received the most support. There's no doubt that this was a catastrophic blow to his creative breath and a deathly pill that he was forced to swallow.

The Grand Slam project was all but dead, though no publicity statements were issued during January. He had agreed in principle to work with his fellow soldier of fortune Gary Moore on a song he was developing called 'Out In The Fields'. But before they met to discuss it, Philip was due to fly stateside to meet up with Huey Lewis and The News. Philip had arranged to take Grand Slam guitarist Laurence Archer with him to the sessions, the plan being to record several songs.

With some downtime on his hands before travelling to America, sessions convened at his home studio with some members of Clann Éadair, a trad band Philip had befriended some years earlier. The band consisted of Leo Rickard (pipes), Tina McLoughlin (recorder, whistle), Pearse 'Snowy' McLoughlin (concertina), Colly Moore (fiddle), Brendan Harding (mandolin), Davey Mooney (guitar) and Paul McLoughlin (flute). Clann Éadair formed in late 1979 in Howth. The group regularly played at two pubs in the area – the Pier House and the Cock Tavern – on Sunday mornings and afternoons. It was at a Cock Tavern gig that some group members first met him. Uileann-pipes player Leo Rickard recalls:

He had just bought Glen Corr on the Burrow Road in Sutton, so he began frequenting the local hostelries in Howth. After a few months, he suggested that we should record an album and that he would help us to achieve it. Phil was very generous, and he financed the recording of the album in what was then Lombard Studios. Around that time, we secured a Sunday morning residency in the Royal Hotel in Howth, and any time

Phil was home from touring with Thin Lizzy or his other projects in England, he would always appear with us in the Royal Hotel. So we had good times there and I have fond memories of it.

The album with Clann Éadair was a work in progress from the time the group met him until his death. He could only work with the group intermittently, as he still had obligations with Lizzy and later to his solo work. Most of the recording was done at Lombard with engineer Tim Martin. On some occasions, plans were dashed entirely when he was unable to return to Dublin. Tina McLoughlin:

Phil liked the band and had offered to support us and finance an album. None of us had money, so we were over the moon with that. I then would get the odd phone call in West Cork to come up to Dublin, as Phil was due to come home from a tour and we should start recording. I think I made a few trips all the way up to Dublin from West Cork, only to be told that Phil wasn't coming home yet. I think we waited nine months before we actually started recording. But it kept us excited about it. Sometimes, I wondered, though, whether this was going to happen at all.

Despite several false starts, sessions commenced, paid for by Philip, as agreed. Up to 13 tracks were recorded to varying degrees of completion over four years, and the sessions at his home studio in Richmond in January 1985 represent their final collaborations.

During those final sessions, they recorded the track 'The Frieze Breeches'. On a relatively unproductive day and quite late in the evening, they once more found themselves ensconced in the back garden studio. Rickard explains: 'The studio was well insulated for sound. It was small, so we were crammed in a bit, but it was fun to be there. I can still see Phil with one foot up on a chair, with the bass strapped on and operating the recording machine and drum machine all at the same time while we were doing the 'Frieze Breeches' track. It was fun and a nice memory to have. We finished the sessions at 5:30 am and went into the kitchen in the house and ate a whole tub of banana ice cream between the four of us.'

The Clann Éadair was only one of many projects that took his interest. He constantly spread his time across a multitude of projects that were quietly fermenting in the background. He was asked to work on the film soundtrack for the provisionally titled *Soldiers Of Destiny* by producer/

director Maurice O'Callaghan. The film was released as *Broken Harvest* several years later but without input from Philip. O'Callaghan's initial pitch to Philip was for a song about the Irish War of Independence. Unknown to O'Callaghan, one of the final songs Philip demoed at home was titled 'Revolution', shortly before he took ill. As with many recordings from this period, it remains unfinished and unreleased.

On 14 January, *Supporters Club* magazine reported that Laurence Archer flew to San Francisco, minus Philip. He began work on the backing tracks immediately with Lewis' band The News. A combination of issues prevented Philip from flying out – principally visa problems. Multiple arrests for drug-related issues had begun to hamper his ability to travel. However, when those issues were eventually resolved, he flew out to San Francisco, but valuable time had been lost.

Lewis and his band had only come off the road on 11 January after extensive touring throughout 1984 and were committed to another American tour to take them from 3 February through to April, so this short window was shrunken even further by Philip's inability to organise himself enough to get on a plane on-time to help salvage his career. Lewis had also been tapped to perform on the American charity single 'We Are The World', recorded in the final week of January. So, if Philip arrived somewhere between 21 and 24 January, it gave Lewis very little time to extract the performance he still believed Philip could deliver. Philip arrived just over a week later than planned, and though he sang on 'Still Alive' and 'Can't Get Away', neither was considered complete. The two tracks were later used to bait record companies to secure Philip a solo deal, but it wasn't just those songs alone that were pivotal in extracting a contract for Philip. Archer felt his original graft was being exploited, with his creativity being used to secure a record deal for something he wasn't guaranteed to be part of. The pursuit of a deal, by now, was not in favour of Grand Slam but in propelling his career as a solo artist. This wasn't what Archer signed on for. The sessions with Lewis And The News would not be Philip's final fling with America.

He returned from America in February and immediately began preparing to record 'Out In The Fields' with Gary Moore. This anti-war song was soon paired with the older Grand Slam number 'Military Man'. The pair also recorded an updated version of 'Still In Love With You'. Moore and Lynott's professional and personal relationship was the stuff of legend. The tumultuous racket that the pair caused often led to strong commercial results, such as 'Parisienne Walkways' – the top-ten hit that every aspiring mirror-in-the-bedroom guitarist wanted to copy.

Written and demoed by Moore in late 1984, 'Out In The Fields' was to be Philip's swan song in the upper echelons of the UK charts. The song's anti-war theme resonated strongly with men who grew up on opposing sides of the Irish border. Lynott's commercial instincts kicked up a gear upon hearing the demo, and ultimately, he was pleased to be putting his name on it. During March, the pair shot a video for the song along with drummer Charlie Morgan: 'I was in the studio both when Phil was doing his vocals and bass, and also when Gary was putting down his parts. Some parts of the promo video were done at Eel Pie studios, and others at a North London Studio (Air Studios). We did quite a lot of promotional work for the single and usually had about five or six songs together to play at the various shows.'

Philip used the late Bill Graham of Ireland's *Hot Press* magazine as father confessor in regard to working with Moore on the record: 'When Gary said he wanted to work with me, it could've been one of two things – like the old-pals trick, like this is a good financial thing to do, or like this is a good gimmick reason.' Later in the interview – from which Phil departed early for a dental appointment, he added, 'The funny thing is that I've shown the video to some of my black friends in England, and they went more for the aspect that I was black and from the south, and he was white and from the north.'

Neil Carter – guitarist with Moore around this time – also toured with the pair in promotion of the single. Here, he discusses the Moore/Lynott dynamic:

Phil and Gary were a volatile mix at times. But by then, Gary was a much calmer man and gained more patience as he got older and was more successful. Even in the years I worked with him, there was a great change, and he was better to be around as time went on. Therefore, he and Phil could get on with things on a more equal footing, as Gary had established himself as a solo artist by that point, which also made him stronger. So much rubbish gets in the way of a friendship when you work in that highly-charged rock environment, and there is a lot of childish behaviour. I think that in 1985, all that had passed, and they could enjoy what they did together.

Old *compadre* Tony Platt was the engineer on 'Out In The Fields', 'Military Man' and 'Still In Love With You'. Demo work on 'Out In The Fields' was initially done at a small studio in Camden, London, and the pair also worked at the home studio. Platt:

The sessions I worked on with Phil were always great, always enjoyable. We would just get on with the work, really. I think what we had was a complete vocal. I'm pretty certain we had complete vocals from both of them for the song. The songs were written, and they sang them live before they were recorded, so a lot of the stuff was sorted out during rehearsals. I didn't do the final mix, so I don't know what was left on the tape, but my recollection is that there were more bits of vocals than were used at the end of the day.

The cover sleeve for the single was worked on by Bill Smith in March and April. Smith remembers:

I was at the photo session for the single, which was done at the time of the video. Very often, ideas from single sleeves and albums would be used as a basis for video shoots. I would also come up with ideas for videos, and since working with The Jam, I have directed video shoots for a lot of artists we also designed for, such as Van Morrison, Mike Oldfield and King Crimson. Sadly, apart from meeting Phil at the photo session and video, I never had much to do with him. I did, however, become Gary's art director/designer for all subsequent releases, pretty much until his sad death.

'Out In The Fields' was released in May 1985 and peaked at number five on the UK singles chart: a career-high for both Philip and Moore in the UK. Incidentally, two of the highest-peaking UK singles in his *resumé* were not written by him – the other being the perennial Lizzy favourite 'Whiskey In The Jar'.

One of the many promotional stopovers that the pair endured was a Belgian TV show. Existing backstage footage of the show highlights acts such as Marillion, Matt Bianco and others playing football, with Philip making Spiderman strides, complete with cowboy boots on, as Fish of Marillion recalls: 'No one would go near him for fear of being mangled. About 20 minutes into the game, the band Matt Bianco got a call, and they went on stage pissed as farts, in green stained suits: it was wild.'

Reinvigorated by the single's European success, Philip began plotting outlines for his new solo album by booking time in a variety of London studios. Feeling confident in the material he'd been working on at home, it was the logical next move, as vibes were positive that a new solo deal was in the offing via Polydor. While in Belgium, Philip met David

Knopfler again, who'd only recently left Dire Straits. The pair agreed to try writing together when both were back home from promotional duties. Knopfler recollects:

> It was at the TV show in Belgium where he very generously – and probably disingenuously, after seeing me out of the side of his eye – said loudly in his inimitable Irish brogue to an assembled throng of attentive journalists: 'Of course, I always thought David Knopfler was the best thing about Dire Straits. Ah, there you are, David, come on over here!' and proceeded to put his arm around my shoulder and steer me to the gaggle of writers to try and let some of the attention he was getting be shared. Very illustrative of how Phil was with *all* his friends, I think.

Physically, Philip was in poor shape throughout the promotional duties for 'Out In The Fields'. Record-company indifference since the demise of Lizzy hadn't helped, but neither had he helped himself. His inability to get Grand Slam off the ground wounded him deeply, and the slow build in acquiring a new recording contract had been grinding him down. There was also the upcoming Live Aid extravaganza, for which he had yet to receive a call from either Saints Geldof or Ure asking him to perform.

One of the final promotional appearances for 'Out In The Fields' was a slot on *ECT* – a UK music programme fronted by the mighty Bailey Brothers, Mick and Dez. Moore – flanked by Philip, Neil Carter and Charlie Morgan – performed 'Out In The Fields', 'Military Man' and 'Still In Love With You'. It was heartbreaking to see his spiralling health decline as he struggled to get through the short set. Carter: 'We did a few light rehearsals in London, and I remember vividly going to Bermans & Nathans (one of London's premier costume hire companies) to get the jackets, which had been used in *Zulu*, I think. These TV shows are generally a long, drawn-out process, and Phil was very poorly with pneumonia. That day we did *ECT*, he found breathing difficult. I'm only sad that the version of 'Still in Love With You' didn't survive, as it was a cracker.'

Philip approached the Bailey Brothers after rehearsals were complete, and looking bloated and short of breath, he asked if he could borrow a dressing room to lie down before going on stage. Dez Bailey:

> We gave up our room for Phil, and at that point, I turned 'round to Mick and said, 'He ain't gonna be here for much longer' – meaning that the drugs would take him down. To his credit, he thanked us and did a corking version

of 'Out In The Fields'. Phil came back up to our dressing room, thanked us, hung out for a while and had some pics with us. Guitarist John Sykes also popped in and had some pics with us as well. Phil seemed positive about the future. I think being back with Gary and on TV gave him a lift. The song was doing well in the charts, and it could've kick-started his career again.

With the promotional fanfare for 'Out In The Fields' complete, Moore returned to working on the rest of the album. But Philip received a major blow when he wasn't invited to perform at Live Aid, even though the idea for the concert was hatched by his two old friends Midge Ure and Bob Geldof, and very few black acts were performing at Wembley Stadium on 13 July 1985. Feeling marginalised, Philip went into a deeper sense of confusion about his career. He was now someone in need of support with his career, and he *had* played his part in helping others advance theirs, particularly The Boomtown Rats. Robbie Brennan:

Any Irish band that came to London were always invited down to the house for drinks. Philip was nice like that. He always tried to get Irish bands a support slot. In 1977-78, he offered the band I was in at the time – Stepaside – the support. At the time, a lot of bands had to buy their way onto tours. Philip came back to us and said, 'You can have it for nothing. We'll give you a few quid for your bed and board.' He did the same with a band called The Vipers. He did it with all the Irish bands.

Chalkie Davies has strong views on the snub from Live Aid:

I'm one of the people who is still very angry that Lizzy wasn't asked to do Live Aid. Thin Lizzy should've been part of the bigger purpose of Live Aid. If there was a band that shouldn't have played Live Aid, it was The Boomtown Rats, who performed purely and simply because Charles and Di were there. They weren't really a group who should've been on that stage, in my opinion. The groups that did best that day were U2 and Queen. If Lizzy had played, I think you would've added Philip to that list. I think, if Lizzy had played, it would've had a much bigger long-term effect, and I think that Geldof and Ure were wrong not to pick them. I also think that it was probably tough for Philip to accept that.

Philip made an appearance at the RTÉ studios in Dublin during coverage of the Live Aid concert, having flown back to Ireland on the afternoon of 13

July. His appearance drew gasps from fellow panellists in the RTÉ studios. Author Damian Corless, who was the last Irish journalist to interview Philip before his death, was present in the studio when Philip arrived:

> He basically turned up at the studios and I remember being absolutely shocked at how ill he looked. He sat down for a chat on a panel that was changing every few minutes. He was bloated and slurring and his eyes were glazed. I can still vividly recall setting eyes on him that day and letting out a gasp of shock.

He even spent time on the phones accepting donations from the public. He was interviewed briefly and confessed, 'I'd love to be up there playing, but because I haven't got a band and stuff like that, obviously, it's impossible. But I feel jealous when I watch it now.' The following night, he joined Clann Éadair for a gig at the Royal Standard in Dublin, which was used to generate funds for the Live Aid cause.

One of my biggest regrets is that I never asked him to put Thin Lizzy together again for Live Aid,' admits Midge Ure in his autobiography, *If I Was*. 'Why that never struck Geldof or me, I don't know, but not for a nanosecond did it cross my mind. I don't like to think what went through Phil's mind with two of his best mates putting the whole thing together and we never asked him to do it. I'd seen him that year, and by then, he was bloated and out of condition; perhaps subconsciously, I knew it was too late.

Philip hid his disappointment at being excluded from Live Aid relatively well, knowing that if he came out to slag off the venture, he'd come off the worst for it. Just before the global event was staged, he contacted his old friend and Lizzy guitar tech Bill Cayley, who now managed Ezee Hire Studios in London. Philip was a familiar face at the studio, having rehearsed Grand Slam there the previous year. There, he linked up with engineer Maurice Mulligan on numerous occasions throughout the summer and autumn of 1985. In June, the pair worked on 'Hard Times'. He made multiple demos at his home studio in Richmond before he decided to work on the song in the more professional confines of Ezee Hire.

But it wasn't just new material he was working on, as he had frequently revisited and updated works in progress over the prior two years. Between studio spurts with Mulligan at Ezee Hire, he also worked at Wave Studios, as previously mentioned. Martin Giles: 'Phil was quiet and gentlemanly throughout – no leather-clad hellraiser when he was writing. He did always have his pocket flask with him, and occasionally took a swig, offering me the flask once or twice. I hadn't met him before the sessions, and I'm sure these recordings were demos. I don't think they were intended to be released.'

By this point, Philip had slipped so far down the pecking order in the music industry that, by the summer of 1985, he was without a publishing deal. His friend and frequent collaborator, Jerome Rimson, takes up the story:

> I remember having a conversation with Phil after Lizzy had crashed, and it was sort of like the story told by Sammy Davis Jr. about Frank Sinatra – suddenly, my greatest hero was walking around lost. Phil Lynott could not get a publishing deal, and no record company would touch him, partially because his writing wasn't up to scratch, and everyone knew about his habits. While Phil was trying to get Grand Slam together, the problem was that everybody was indulging in the same thing, so not enough was getting done. Phil was getting depressed to a greater degree. It was a very strange time because he would change his mind about things in a flash.

The highs from the recent public acclaim appeared to be barely enough to sustain Philip through the lows of not appearing on Live Aid. The major issue of not having a publishing deal was what brought about the sessions with engineer Maurice Mulligan:

> I think the sessions were booked and organised by Fay Woolven to set up a new publishing deal. To be honest, I had completely forgotten about the 'Hard Times' recording, as it was never a prize winner in my mind, although it was the first thing that we did, and it cemented our relationship through a couple of incidents. I do have a copy of it somewhere, along with a couple of other more robust songs, including the original recording of 'Nineteen', which was used as the basis for the Paul Hardcastle-produced sessions, which lost a lot of the spirit.

The sessions mainly consisted of Mulligan and Lynott working together, the latter programming an Oberheim drum machine, though there were also a few external guitar players involved, such as Gus Isidore. The material was all recorded in a very piecemeal manner, partially because Philip had scored the studio time for free through his friendship with studio manager Bill Caley. He would bring over some tapes of ideas from time to time, and the pair would work these up into finished tracks, with Philip working on vocal ideas. Mulligan recalls: 'He had a really clear idea of how he wanted to deliver them and in a most unusual but constructive way.' The fun part for Mulligan was always mixing them, and that was how their brief friendship developed:

> We never started working until mid-late afternoon. And when we were ready to try some mixes out, I'd set up the board while he went up to the White Horse to order the drinks. After a couple, we'd return to the studio to finish the mix, which meant he sat at one end of the giant MCI board, and I'd pilot the other end and grouping. His end consisted of a couple of vocal channels and his bass guitar on channels 1-4, which meant I had to repatch everything so he could sit at that end and sneak the levels up and down, and this is where a lot of the mutual respect and friendship came from.

In his lighter moments, Philip was never one to waste an opportunity to wind someone up. A couple of days into the first session, Mulligan turned up for work, and Bill Caley called him into his office, complaining that he and his partner were not amused by being woken up in the middle of the night by random calls from Philip. Mulligan recalls:

> It turns out that he called Bill to ask where I had come from and had a rant about the fact that no one had ever had the nerve to tell him to turn the bass down! This all came from a comment I'd made during the last mix, which went along the lines of 'Don't you think the bass is a bit loud, mate?'. Although he agreed at the time, and it was all taken lightly, he decided to wind Bill up with this when he got back home from the Limelight Club much later. When I got into Bill's office, it was all very acrimonious, and I was given the usual 'Do you realise who you were talking to' speech for a few minutes until Bill couldn't hold a straight face any longer. He then went on to explain that this was his way of getting back at me for having his sleep interrupted and that the main reason behind the phone call was that if I was confident enough to do that (tell Lynott his bass was too loud), I was more than confident and competent to do the rest of the sessions whenever he came into the studio!

Intermittently over the coming weeks and months, Philip would appear at the studio, and the pair would work on whatever track he was developing. There were background noises, which were an attempt by his management (particularly Philip's point of contact in the office, John Salter) to secure a new recording deal. In the afterglow of his recent chart success with Gary Moore, and also the promise shown by the tracks recorded with Huey Lewis and the News, rumours were emerging and eventually confirmed when Polydor Records expressed an interest in releasing a new Philip Lynott product. Robbie Dennis was a product manager at Polydor, and when Philip's name as a new signing came up at a staff meeting, Dennis found himself raising his arm in request to work on the project. It was to him that Philip delivered a bunch of demos outlining the direction he was working towards. The tape contained about ten songs with 'Sisters Of Mercy', 'Breakdown' and 'Harlem' among them: songs originally played with Grand Slam. To clarify, the record deal was for Philip as a solo artist and didn't contain any reference to Grand Slam being signed. Philip *did* converse with keyboard player Mark Stanway, who'd since moved on to pastures new: 'The fact that there didn't seem to be any light at the end of the tunnel and that we hadn't secured a recording deal made me want to return to a reformed Magnum, where there were good prospects. I had given Grand Slam my best efforts, and unfortunately, it never really happened.'

Before Philip took a family holiday in August, details of his Polydor contract were finalised. However, there were going to be challenges to overcome before this deal could be fulfilled. Recording the album wasn't a straightforward deal as long-time Lizzy archivist Paul Mauger confirms:

> They wanted three singles before committing to record the album. So, the album depended on the success of the planned singles, the first of which was 'Nineteen'. Philip's hands were tied because if the next two singles released were hits, he then had to have the album ready for release by the autumn of 1986, with Huey Lewis involved in the production of it. Huey's star was on the ascent during this time, so it was going to be virtually impossible for Philip to make the whole thing work.

By this time, he had an impressive quantity of material in various stages of development. 'Christmas Song' (a working title] had been worked on at Compass Point Studio during the visit in April and May 1978. He revisited the track at Odyssey Studio sometime in 1981, re-wrote the lyric, changed the arrangement and retitled it 'Catholic Charm'. It's unknown if more work was done on the song after this, but it *was* considered for inclusion on his second solo album and was worked on during those sessions. That Philip revisited the track three years after its initial recording wasn't at all unusual for him. Often, lyrics in his notebooks went unused for years until they found a home.

He also recorded a series of demos with Jerome Rimson at the home studio, that were worked on in July 1980 at Good Earth. A series of four demos exist, one of which – 'You're So Cheeky' – Philip later lifted a riff from to write 'Together': the lead single from his second solo album. 'The Great Escape' was another song they recorded, though Philip did not contribute to the writing. At his home studio in late 1982, he worked up the duet 'Living In Ecstasy' with Steve Strange, and the track was dubbed at Polygram Studios the following April.

Another song with Junior Giscombe emerged in 1985 and was titled 'What's The Matter?'. It has that Marvin Gaye vibe to it and certainly would've been a strong contender for inclusion on any album Phil was considering. 'Partner In Crime' was also recorded as a duet with Mark Stanway's wife, Mo Birch, though it was actually an early attempt at what later became 'Hard Times'. So much was lifted from 'Partner In Crime' to form 'Hard Times', that the songs cannot be looked at as separate tracks. That Philip and Junior were unable to convince a record label to release their collaboration 'The Lady Loves To Dance', still wrangled, and it's a testament to both that they continued their work together despite not knowing if anything might happen. Junior:

My management at that time was very happy because I was able to move into a new sphere of music and was able to write, produce and do things like that and be successful. In doing that, it opens up loads of other doors for you. So my management was really really happy, and I know at the beginning, I know Phil's management was very happy. They were very much up for it as well. But I think once Phil played them 'The Lady Loves To Dance', I think everybody got cold feet. It was very strange. I don't think they believed it was gonna come out that good. I know that sounds strange. I think they feared its success more than being successful and how it left Phil. I think that was their fear at that time. We enjoyed writing together and were going to write some more to try to get it out somewhere else. Being signed to Polygram meant that it wasn't going to be easy. The problem for them was the combination of who we were and the music had nothing to do with their decision. On 'He Fell Like A

Soldier', Phil had a lot of that in his head but knew what he was after out of that song. I added to the melody and lyric on that one. 'What's The Matter?' and 'Time And Time Again' were working titles that we liked. We started both of them together, but they were then written while we were apart and changed around when we got back together.

There was also the reverberant 'Someone's Out To Get Ya' – a song Lynott and guitarist Gus Isidore had been developing since late 1981. On 11 January the following year, serious inroads were made on the song, with the pair working through until 14 January with Paul Thomas and Kevin Maloney engineering at Windmill Lane Studios in Dublin. The song was returned to again during the summer of 1985 when Isidore visited Philip at his home studio in Richmond. It was a sinewy slice of rock 'n' roll with a very Hendrixian feel, though, disappointingly, it remains unreleased. Multiple versions of it exist in Philip's archive, with some that could be considered to be in a finished state. Isidore:

I wrote the music for 'Someone's Out To Get Ya' in 1980, and the first studio recordingwas when Jerome and I hooked up with Phil in Dublin at Windmill Lane Studios in 1982. I played Phil the riff, and he liked it and quickly ran into the vocal booth and did an impromptu vocal take. Subsequently, I re-recorded it, both with Third Man and Blackmail. Phil was always intrigued by Blackmail, and it was Jerome's and my dream to have Phil front that band. I would just put it down to bad timing, which is why it didn't happen. The industry at that time was not ready for a full-on black rock band on this side of the water. Shortly after, Living Colour emerged, and it seemed there was only room for one act of that kind at the time. The record company loved us but didn't know how to promote us. What could've been is anyone's guess. The early 80s was a strange period in the industry, trying to find its feet and direction.

When Isidore and Rimson were trying to get Blackmail off the ground, they had a tentative deal with RCA, as Rimson recalls:

We were rehearsing Blackmail at Ezee Hire at the same time that Lynott was rehearsing Grand Slam, and we were burying them, and he knew it. He used to laugh at us when he'd pop out for a bit, and what I and Isidore were trying to do was convince Phil he should come with us. What we were doing was going to be nowhere near Lizzy. I think he was a bit confused at this point because I think he wanted to take a bite off this thing, but he was going through a few traumas, as well as egos coming into play.

There was also 'Freedom Comes' from this era – one of the heavier efforts from Philip during this late period. Producer John Alcock: 'Great track. It could've been made into a really good track with a bit of tweaking. I hear in my mind a really tough arrangement, like earlier Rage Against The Machine.'

While on holiday with his family, Philip played one of his last live shows at a club called Cuba, though the performance is not remembered well, as the makeshift band took to the stage at about 4 am Sean O'Connor – guitarist and lead vocalist of Dublin band The Lookalikes – was flown out for the gig, along with his Grand Slam cohorts Doish Nagle and Robbie Brennan. O'Connor:

Philip, body-wise, was pretty much shot by this stage. Robbie on drums, Doish on rhythm guitar, Philip playing bass, me on lead guitar, and a guy – I don't even know why he was there – named Justin from Julian Lennon's band, but he didn't know any of the songs. Myself and Doish were brought out specifically for the gig. I got a call one day from a guy called Maurice Boland who was involved with the club. He introduced himself and said Philip was there on holiday, so he told me that he'd asked Philip to play a gig in his club and that he'd agreed to do it as long as either I or Gary Moore could play guitar. So I kind of laughed and asked, 'Why can't Gary do it?.' He told me he was tied up with recording, so I said, 'Aw, grand.' So, he told me it was just going to be one night but that he'd give me an apartment for a week to make a holiday of it. But, he made a mess of booking the flights, from what I can recall, and we couldn't take the flight that was intended. Now, I had Philip's bass and a couple of other things. I spoke with a supervisor at the airport, and I explained the problem, and he worked out a way of getting us over there, which in the end was about four flights instead of taking a simple flight to Marbella. We arrived about an hour before the gig.

The scene O'Connor encountered on arrival was an uneasy one, and with a hint of trepidation in his voice, he confesses:

The Philip that I met was not the Philip that I knew. He was bloated and very cranky, which he never was with me, I have to say. He was always very nice to me and treated me very well. Now, it wasn't just me he was cranky with; it was everyone. He seemed to be in a very aggressive mood. Anyway, we barely had time to plug into the amp before we were playing. We sat down fairly quickly to work out a setlist, and I knew most of the Lizzy stuff. Robbie knew the songs, Doish thought he knew more than he actually did and Justin was just told to stand over there. We played 'Dancing In The Moonlight', 'The Boys Are Back In Town' and 'The Rocker': mainly the popular Lizzy songs. The gig was packed, but it wasn't all that great.

Upon his return to England, Philip commenced further sessions at Ezee Hire with Maurice Mulligan. The engineer recalls Lynott's vocal recording methods at this time:

Instead of getting the most expensive-looking valve microphone out and faffing around for *that sound*, he just used to ask me to set up a bog standard Shure 58. This was fair enough in a lot of respects, but it was where we would put the thing that was really different. There was a sound-trap space about 3" wide between the control room and the main studio playroom, created by a couple of sets of oversized French windows. His decision was to get the 58 set up in the gap between the doors because it was closer to getting back into the control room and it did actually sound just right. All I had to do really was set up the input again, give a little tweak to the EQ, and bung it through an ancient DBX box for some compression. Perfect!

Alternating between the confines of professional studios and his 16-track home studio, Philip met with John Sykes before the latter departed for new Whitesnake sessions. They completed the backing track for a song called 'Samantha' – not to be confused with 'Sweet Samantha', a demo he made in 1981 at Odyssey Studios with Kit Woolven engineering. Philip also put a vocal on the track. Soon after Sykes' departure, new record label Polydor requested a single for release as a taster for his planned third solo album. Though still in the early stages, Philip chose to rework a song he initially trialled with Grand Slam, called 'Nineteen'. During this period, he also met with Maurice Mulligan, with whom he'd been developing the track beyond what Grand Slam had done. Mulligan: I remember he said that the original guitar tracks for 'Nineteen' had been recorded by David Knopfler prior to us starting work on the song, but those takes were never used. I'm fairly certain the guitar tracks that left the studio were recorded by Gus Isidore, but I might be wrong. He only came to the studio a couple of times to do his parts, and I never saw him again.'

Philip's choice of song for single release had been erratic even before Thin Lizzy split up and opting for 'Nineteen' further evinced a concerning pattern. To choose a track previously used to bait record companies while he was a member of Grand Slam is an oddity, as the band had failed to secure interest or a record deal. And he had some strong tunes in the barrel; 'Someone Out To Get Ya' would have been an ideal choice, showing the public that he could still rock it out with the best that the current climate had to offer. It rocked dark and grim with some clever lyrical development since it was first put to tape in 1981. By the time he finished his last pass at singing the song, the lyrics adopted a strong autobiographical feel, far more than they did when the original idea was conceived:

You're down to the breadline, living from day to day,
You've been left on the sidelines, somehow it all slipped away.
You're like a wolf howling at the moon and you're the leader of the pack,
You gotta get away real soon, gotta get 'em off your back
There's always someone out to get ya.

With Mulligan and Caley, Philip went to see the young band FM, who also worked out of Ezee. Mulligan:

They were supporting some big US outfit which I really can't remember. Before the gig, we quietly popped into a back room at the pub next door, but he (Philip) was spotted, and soon enough, he became swamped with well-meaning and adoring fans. Given his status, he duly signed and chatted before Bill announced that we should go into the gig: he'd seen this over the years. Once we got in and found a quiet row down the side of the venue, all was good until, one by one, heads started to turn – he was hard to miss, after all – and folks started to move in on the poor bugger from the rows in front. After a while, this all became too much, and he made some apologies to me and Bill, then exited quickly through the stage door. What stuck with me really, and unsurprisingly, was the fact that although he obviously relished the adoration and platitudes thrown at him, it was obvious that he had a more personal side which really needed space to spend quietly with friends, and this was one of those. The following day, everything was back to normal, with a simple apology for leaving early – lovely man.

Due to securing the deal with Polydor and being asked to come up with a single fairly quickly, a planned writing experiment with David Knopfler never came to pass, as he explains:

We were going to get together and see if we could write together – I think it must've been around the time of the Notting Hill Carnival in 1985 – because Phil had suggested we set up our gear and then go to the carnival, have a few beers and play hooky, which kind of amused me since we would've been paying for the rehearsal room ourselves, and who was going to be short-changed or notice we were missing but ourselves? Then something came up – possibly the birth of my son, or maybe it was the beginning of his heading downhill into the pneumonia that would kill him a few months later. But in any event, for some reason or another, we needed to reschedule, and, of course, by January, he was dead.

Around this time, Philip also opened his home to Lizzy fan Jalle Savquist, who had attended a couple of the Three Musketeers gigs that Philip did with his solo band during the summer of 1983. Jalle was a member of the Thin Lizzy fan club, which by 1985 had ceased and was updated as The Philip Lynott Appreciation Society. Savquist remembers:

I went with Sue and Linda from the fan club out to Phil's house in Richmond at the beginning of September 1985, and we had a nice afternoon there together. Phil was very tired after a late session the night before with Rick Parfitt, but he was very friendly and openhearted about his life and future plans. He was depressed but spoke about some of his hopes for the future – for instance, about the fact that John Sykes had just left to join Whitesnake; Scott Gorham wanted to reform Thin Lizzy; Robbo living nearby on a barge; the new guitarist he'd found in Huey Lucas; missing Sweden, and how depressed he was about both Thin Lizzy and Grand Slam breaking up.

Soon after Rick Parfitt's death on 24 December 2016, a series of tracks emerged online featuring vocals from Philip. They were very much works in progress, and some familiar couplets appeared in the tracks. Philip's recycling of ideas for lyrics never ceased. The tracks included 'My Father's

Son', 'She Got Class' and 'Bad Boy'. There was certainly potential in them, but they do sound very much like the product of a short time spent together working.

Having chosen to record 'Nineteen' as his comeback single, Philip's management set him up with the then hot producer Paul Hardcastle, who was just coming off having a massive hit single with a song called – coincidentally – '19'. He was no doubt keen to associate with an artist whose star was rising. The pair worked at Roundhouse Studios in Chalk Farm in London. Hardcastle:

> I spent a couple of weeks working on the 'Nineteen' record with Phil. I'd have to say it was a great buzz listening to the ideas he was coming up with and then working up the song within the context of our union. It all came about as a result of our management – at the time, Chris Morrison was still looking after Phil through CMO, and the guy who managed me – Simon Fuller – also happened to be connected to the office. It was their idea to get us to come up with something. The song did suggest teen angst, and Phil related to that sensation. It was while we were in the studio that the notion of trying to get a motorbike sound on the track came about. We soon walked out of the studio and down the street to the nearest bike shop. Phil casually walked up to the assistant and enquired about borrowing a bike for an hour. The assistant never recognised him at first, but when Phil explained the situation to him, the poor guy behind the counter ... he just shrivelled up. Though Phil laughed at the whole episode, I have seen other stars in that position get really sticky about that kind of thing. Phil would refuse to take offence. So we got the bike into the studio and set everything up. The engineers didn't know what to think, but Phil was having a laugh. All I expected was a minute or two of revving it up, but Phil just sat on the bike for about ten minutes, revving her like crazy. By this point, the studio was filling up and the place was in chaos. Everyone had to clear out, but Phil just sat back, looking on hilariously at the disorder he'd partaken in and executed in true Lynott style whilst nearly suffocating in carbon monoxide. After we played back the recording, we realised that it wasn't in time, and Phil wasn't too keen on the clarity. I sampled a bit of the rev and played it in time, and he was delighted with the result so much that he left it in the final cut.

For the re-recording of 'Nineteen', Philip decided to plunder some verses from the unreleased 'Bad Is Bad' that Lizzy had recorded during the *Renegade* sessions. The specific sections he adapted to the lyric of 'Nineteen' were those used in the rap toward the fade-out. Multiple versions of 'Nineteen' were produced, while on the extended version, he siphoned a verse from the Grand Slam song 'Harlem'. I asked Mark Stanway for his thoughts on his decision to use 'Nineteen' as his comeback single: 'Interesting, but also maybe a little desperate – meant in the nicest way.'

Even during this late period, Robbo – who now lived a short distance from Philip – regularly called on his old friend and tried to rally him. Numerous friends would often drop by and jam in his home studio, and on many occasions, these jams were recorded. Another possible outlet for Philip was a band that included Robbo and Philthy Animal Taylor from Motörhead. Robbo:

I remember we went from my place in Richmond, up to Phil's – me and Philthy Animal. He's got his drum kit in the back of his Golf GTI 'cause Phil wanted to put together a three-piece with me and Philthy. So, we drove in, and he had the studio out the back, so Philthy was setting up his kit and sitting there waiting with the sticks, and Phil wasn't even there. I went into the house and knocked on the bedroom door, took a peek in, and there was shit everywhere. By now, I realise he's not up to it, so I have to go down and tell Philthy Animal. I told him, and he's fuming, still sitting there with his sticks. About 20 minutes later, he stuck his drum kit in the back of the car and took off. Philthy was hugely disappointed because he was a huge fan of Lizzy. That was the end of that band.

If the band had gotten off the ground, producer Tony Platt was waiting in the wings and had been doing quite a lot of work with Robbo during this period. Platt was unfamiliar with Philip's solo work for the most part but was very interested in the combination if they could ever get it together. Platt:

Towards the end, I was aware of his solo work because, by then, I was involved with Brian (Robertson), and at that stage, Brian stayed fairly close to Phil right up to the end. My wife and I used to stay with Brian and Chrissie Wood for Christmas. We'd done it for a couple of Christmases, and we got there that particular Christmas, and nobody was there. We thought, 'Have we got this wrong?.' That was when Brian had to go down to the house because Phil was in a really bad way. So Brian was one of the last people to be there with Phil. I was sort of aware of those things, and Brian was always trying to get something happening to try to help focus Phil and give him something that would stop him from pushing the self-destruct button. So we talked about how that might happen, but nothing ever came to fruition because there was always something that would get in the way of it. I would've loved to have done it; it would've been great, but it would've been really difficult. Lizzy was over and done with by then, and there was no more mileage in it, so it would've been a different thing entirely.

Guitarist Robin George was recruited to contribute to 'Nineteen' and soon ended up writing some new material with Philip. He recorded a demo for a song called 'Revolution' at his home studio around this time with George and later again with a guitarist named Steve Johnson. Multiple versions exist, with the lyric and music in various stages of development. After 'Nineteen' was recorded, Philip guested with Gary Moore again on three dates toward the end of September, silencing once and for all the notion that he wouldn't have been able to perform at Live Aid due to his physical condition. Without a doubt, he shouldn't have been anywhere near a stage performing, but instead, he should have been proactively addressing his health problems.

Philip asked Hardcastle to experiment with the track, and the result was the dub mix. He also pitched the idea of including 'A Night In The Life Of A Blues Singer' on the 12". The song was worked on by a multitude of engineers and became something of an ongoing joke, as Kit Woolven recalls:

That song used to keep rearing its ugly head for years and years. Gary did a blinding solo in one session. It was one of those songs that would just never go away. I can remember it note-for-note. In those 'What should we do now?' moments, Phil would say 'What about 'Night In The Life'?', and we'd be like 'Christ, let's see what we can do with it this time.' I don't think it was actually ever finished. Gary was really the guy that brought the song to life, with the chromatic scale as well as the riff. In some ways, it would be hard to put a solo onto that chromatic style, but Gary could do anything, and he did.

Soon after the 'Nineteen' sessions, Philip reconvened with producer/ director Maurice O'Callaghan to discuss 'Soldiers Of Destiny' at his home in Richmond, but there was also an additional project to propose. An Irish writer named Dermot O'Donovan had written a book titled 'Silas Rat' and O'Callaghan had co-written a song of the same name, which was going to be used to promote the book. Incidentally, the illustrations for the book were done by Tim Booth, the originator of the Thin Lizzy logo and a long-standing friend. When O'Callaghan visited Philip's home, he was greeted by engineer Tim Martin over on a visit from Ireland:

I do recall that meeting Phil before noon wasn't the best thing to do. Prior to the meeting, I did discuss a few things on the phone with him, particularly *Silas Rat*. He agreed to do *Silas Rat* for a token amount, something like £100, as a gesture of goodwill. His main interest was really the movie. I gave him the demo scenes we had shot, using music from the film of a few years previous called *The Long Riders*. We did run into problems with *Silas Rat,* as his record company didn't want him to use his voice on the track. So Tim Martin took the tracks to Lombard Studios in Dublin and re-dubbed the song. I also had plans to direct a music video for it, for which Phil agreed to appear, but this was planned for early in the new year.

Once it couldn't be sidestepped that Philip wasn't to use his voice for the song, another Irishman was brought on board to help finish the vocals that Philip had recorded. His name was Freddie White. He remembers:

The idea was to release it for Christmas, but it got delayed and then Philo died and the whole thing was put on hold. We made the video, though. An all-night shoot in Captain America's on Grafton Street in Dublin. About 50 small kids and myself dressed as rats. Absolute torture! The song sort of escaped as opposed to getting released with anything like a purpose behind it. Philo was one of a kind; at least, that's how I regard him.

In October, Philip flew to Ireland to make what turned out to be his final Irish TV appearance on *Space Station Videos*. His appearance aired just two weeks later and showed him bleary-eyed and bloated – the sheen from his recent chart success with Gary Moore on 'Out In The Fields' and a new record deal with Polydor was nowhere to be found. He filmed his segment on 23 October and was the final guest on the six-episode show. *Space Station Videos* was a concept show filtered from the imaginations of producers Conor McAnally and Bill Hughes: '*Desert Island Discs* turned into video', recalls Hughes. Each guest would choose a selection of videos to play, but eventually, securing video rights became so much of a burden that after the first season, no further shows were produced. Bill Hughes recalls Philip's participation:

> Phil pulled up on the day of the shoot and got out of the back of the car, and he was pretty wasted. On the day, he told me he wasn't going to do the show unless I sent somebody to the Dockers Pub to get him a Jack Daniels and Coke – a large Jack Daniels and Coke, preferably a triple. That's what he wanted, or he wasn't going to give the interview. I was like, 'Phil, you're already after ...', but he said, 'I'm not fucking doing it, man, unless you get me a Jack Daniels. It's only in the Dockers, and I know them there, so if you tell them it's for me, they'll be grand.' The show's runner went around, got the drink and came back. So Phil started to sip that, calmed down and got into it. As I said, he was already buzzing when he arrived.

The crew filmed for a couple of hours, and Philip earned the then-tidy fee of around £1,000 for his appearance. Luckily for the other guests, it was a Favoured Nations contract, so each guest got the same fee as had been negotiated for Philip's, much to the chagrin of the notoriously tight-fisted *RTÉ*. Producer Conor McAnally says, 'Phil had been through a pretty rough patch leading up to that time. He struck us as pretty vulnerable but determined to get back on track. I remember he was very close to his mum at the time and spoke about her a lot on the day.'

The shooting wasn't without its hilarious moments when Philip would get flustered and the crew had to keep retaking, as he would lose his train of thought, even up to the point of disagreeing with his own music-video choices. This could've led to problems, as he'd already chosen the videos prior to shooting, which the production team then sought clearance on, so any changes he tried to make had to be carefully dismissed. Hughes: 'I really wish I had the outtakes from *Space Station Videos*. My memory of the shoot with Phil is that we could've made an amazing programme about him after he passed. He cracked up laughing at his own jokes, and then he started contradicting himself on camera, and then he'd laugh at the absurdity of him contradicting himself, and it was all there on tape, but we don't have the footage, sadly.'

The said footage does actually exist, but the format it was recorded on is long out of date. The show was shot on videotape, which at the time was the height of sophistication. The problem with videotape was that it didn't hold the images – they bled, colours faded, and the tape would fall to pieces if not kept in the right environment. The footage was put into storage, and if anything was to be done with it in terms of transfer, it would require expensive expertise and equipment, with no guarantee of a successful outcome:

I didn't work with Phil prior to the show, but I had met him socially loads of times. I had met him out in Howth, at receptions, record launches, movie premieres and different parties. I'd also met him at different nightclubs in Dublin – The Pink Elephant and Lord John's – and I have to say, he was wild. He was always wild, always mad. He was always ... ahh ... well, you knew he was always buzzed as well, and you knew it wasn't alcohol. You'd meet him at the Bailey on a Saturday, and he'd have the leather coat and the jeans, the whole thing, and he'd just be ... you knew that he was talking to you, but you also knew he was nodding along to some track that was in his head. He wasn't fully engaged with you; he was different, and he was extremely different on so many levels. It was also his height, his colour, his hair, his dress sense, his addiction to leather coats ... it was like he was forever in these flowing leather coats, and he would arrive at the place, and everybody would just turn around because it was Phil Lynott, and it wasn't because he was a superstar. It was because he was 'Yer man', he was a character. It wasn't awe; it was 'Oh, Jaysus, there he is.' He was also unpredictable, and people didn't know what he was going to get up to.'

There are thousands of acres of desert to explore within a relatively short driving distance of the city of Los Angeles, and on Halloween night, Philip arrived in America for the last time to film what would turn out to be his last video.

The following day, the cast and small crew endured searing heat while filming new single 'Nineteen' in the desert outside Los Angeles. The director, Clive Richardson, had already worked out the sequences to be filmed back in London and he was anxious to ensure the shoot moved along at a brisk pace due to budget restrictions. The first shots were as they appear in the final edit of the video, and once completed, the cast and crew leave for the more comfortable confines of an indoor location, namely 'the bar scene'.

In the early 1980s, Richardson was working for Chase Films and got to know Chips Chipperfield, who happened to be 'big friends with everybody at Polydor'. Richardson had worked with Marillion and Tears for Fears by this time and very soon found himself meeting Phil to discuss the possibility of working together. Richardson: 'I got a call and I went to see Phil at a place. It was at this big type of Mock Tudor house. It was obvious that nobody was living there really but I met him there. There were a couple of big jukeboxes in it and stuff and we had a chat about it there. I think there may have been problems between him and the record company but I don't know the full story there. It was all this thing about him being a solo act now. I don't really know if that was being organised and whether they (the record label) agreed with it or were into it.

The shoot was done over three days, with Richardson and his partner leaving for America ahead of Philip, who remained in America after the shoot was completed. Richardson offers more background on the shoot:

Why we ended up filming in America, was because of the helmet laws, really. Phil obviously couldn't wear a helmet, and I think he was keen to go out there for some reason. It was obvious we needed bikes in the video because that was the soundtrack to it, really. We agreed with Polydor that Melissa, Phil and myself would go to LA to do it. Once out there, we hired a freelance producer who was really good. She brought in a cameraman and assistant, a sound guy with his assistant, and that was all we had. It was pretty basic really, in respect of the crew numbers. In terms of the small crew, that was how we got the agreement off Polydor if we could do it cheaply. I know there wasn't a lot of money around really for it. All of the gear for the shoot was hired in America. On the second day, we were in the car park. I have a feeling it might've been in the hotel car park where we were staying. It was totally guerrilla-type shooting, so, no permits or anything like that. Phil really enjoyed it, actually. He had a real good time.

There was still additional footage to film for the promo, as no guitar solo was shot in America. It was Richardson's understanding that more filming would be done on their return to England, but Philip had stayed in America, so editing commenced in the meantime. Philip spent his last night in America socialising with Jimmy Bain and others on Sunset Boulevard:

When I hooked up with Phil, I had just completed a three-month American tour with Dio, and he had been filming the 'Nineteen' video. We managed to go to the Rainbow Bar and Grill for some dinner and cocktails and he flew back to London the next day.

During the edit, Richardson received additional footage featuring the guitar solo which was then edited in. It is unknown if the additional footage was completed before or after the Los Angeles shoot. It is possible that a straight-to-camera performance of 'Nineteen' on a small sound stage in London exists, featuring Philip, George and an unknown drummer, somewhere in the archives of Polydor, as director Clive Richardson confirmed all materials were returned to the record label once the final product was delivered.

George: 'For the promotional video, I only appear in snatches, while Phil is obviously the primary focus of the shoot. Phil later told me that my main part was edited out because I made him look too rough. He was very apologetic about it, but that's just the way it went. We did a few promotional appearances for it, one of which was the *Razzmatazz* show in Newcastle with Kid Jensen hosting.' Richardson continues:

After I had finished editing it and it was sent back to the record company, there was no feedback at all. So, I don't know what was happening, really. I remember asking my producer Melissa at the time, and she couldn't find out anything either. So, I don't know what the story was beyond making the video. But then, I was doing other things as well at the time. A little later, we did get some feedback, so I do know they liked it, and I know that Phil liked it. I got that bit of feedback, but nothing further, really.

While Philip wasn't being directly handled by Chris Morrison at CMO as such anymore, he did occasionally have to get involved to rescue Philip from various scrapes. He was also only too aware of the support that Philip needed. Polydor A&R man Robbie Dennis:

Chris Morrison was pretty much the hands-on type of manager. For example, with the 'Nineteen' promotional video, he would've come to us with a storyboard that he or Phil had worked out for the song. Then he would've laid down all of the expenses involved, which would have to include airfares, food, hotels, cameramen, director, etc., and if we saw it as a viable option, the green light would be given. Back in the mid-'80s, you were probably looking at the budget for a single like 'Nineteen' as being between £30-50,000. Also, though Polydor signed Phil as an artist, we didn't own the material. We had the right to market, release and promote it. The only track delivered to us was 'Nineteen'.

'Nineteen' was released on 15 November 1985 and was Philip's last single issued in his lifetime. The reception afforded the single was unfortunate, and it stalled at 76 in the UK. Despite heavy promotion and several appearances on TV shows miming the track, it just didn't take off. According to producer Paul Hardcastle, one of the reasons was due to a printing error at the pressing plant that Polydor used. Hardcastle puts the blame at Polydor's feet: 'The sleeves got mixed up; the A-side and B-side got mixed up. People weren't listening to the song that we intended them to hear as a single. It did get a lot of airplay, though – Gary Davies, for one, gave it a lot of time on Radio 1. Primarily, I think his interest was in the rather odd combination of me and Phil.'

On his time working with Philip, Hardcastle says, 'Our relationship reached a certain point in a short space of time when he left me to handle the final mix, which I took as a great compliment. During the sessions for 'Nineteen', we might break for a game of pool, at which Phil used to hammer me constantly. By the end of sessions, we were both happy with the outcome and agreed to work again in the future.'

In an interview to promote 'Nineteen', Philip hooked up with his friend DJ Peter Antony. He spoke of the fun he had while making the video in the US, which featured Philip and a biker gang extolling the aggression of being nineteen. During the chat, Philip confessed, 'We were cruising down Hollywood Boulevard and Santa Monica Boulevard with the sounds blasting out of a truck and the spotlight on us, the bikers. Everybody was cheering us along the streets. The police let us go, and it was really fun.' The pair continued their chat, where Philip announced that more plans were in place to record with Gary Moore:

The thing is, me and Gary are probably gonna do another single in January. We're both heavily committed – me with my single and him promoting his album. When we last spoke, I jumped up with him at Hammersmith on 'Parisienne Walkways' and 'Out In The Fields', and I did Manchester as well, and that went a storm. When we spoke after the gigs, we said that we'd try and get another single together for January, which would coincide with … I'm going to try and bring out another single myself in January, and then I'm going to try and put a band together for March to coincide with the release of my album, 'cause hopefully I'll be finished my album and I should be on the road and have my album out for March. So, the next thing you might hear from me and Gary should be January.

The commercial failure of 'Nineteen' was a body blow. His attempts at getting his career back on track were constantly being compromised by his personal problems. In an interview with the *Coventry Evening Telegraph* on 3 December, Phil said the following:

I doubt I will ever get over the breakup. My marriage was breaking up at the same time, and I went through a period of drugs and drink. I would never encourage people to take drugs because they are really bad for you. This is from someone who was on the inside. No one can tell you anything when you are in that state, and yet, I landed back on my feet. My kids were my turning point. One day, I looked at my girls, and I wanted to share their future.

Philip was certainly not without some degree of awareness in respect of his choices. He was no fool. Just a year earlier, in an interview with Peter Marriot for the *Irish Evening Press*, he was also forthright in his admission of using heroin, if a little misleading in terms of his dabbling: 'I took it maybe two or three times, but I was never hooked on it … In the music business, it always seems available.' While he may have been fooling himself, others around him who at one time were close were somewhat surprised when they met him during this period. The Philip of the post-Lizzy period bore no relation to the man who'd rigorously climbed the mountain to mainstream success in the early-to-mid-'70s. The extent of his deception only became apparent to his mother while he lay in a hospital bed over Christmas, fighting for his life – seeing the condition of his feet, which he'd been injecting.

Time was running out when he rallied one more time shortly before Christmas to make what turned out to be his final UK TV appearance on *Razzmatazz*. The show was hosted by his old friend David Jensen. For the appearance, he requested the assistance of Brian Downey, whom he hadn't seen for quite some time. Robin George also made an appearance on the programme. Incidentally, Philip saw Junior Giscombe as their paths crossed for different commitments in the North of England. Giscombe:

> He had totally changed colour because of the amount of drugs he was taking at the time. He had blown up and got a lot heavier. We met one another as I was walking out and he was walking in, and he pulled my arm, pulled me to one side, and he said 'Look at me', and I said 'Oh Phil.' I'll never forget it. He said, 'Look at me'… and continued … 'Junior, ya know. It's just one of those things, and I was like, 'Oh mate. We've been on this for a long time, Phil; it's time.' 'I know, I know, I know' he said. He gave me his number and said, 'Ring me, ring me.' That was the last time I heard from or saw Phil. When I rang him up, I couldn't get him.

Just a few days before his last TV appearance, he was working in his home studio with guitarist Steve Johnson, where he sang on what is considered to be his final song: the unfinished and defiant 'People Get Ready (For The Revolution)'. Philip had begun the song with guitarist Robin George, and intermittently added to it in short bursts during the period of promoting 'Nineteen'. As the track developed, it was retitled 'Revolution', but it's impossible to say what it might've eventually become known as. More than one version exists, with alternative lyrics and arrangements.

> People get ready for the revolution
> People get ready for the overthrow
> Now, the time has come to use our guns
> The battle's over, the war is won

Philip also reworked 'No More' with Johnson during the final weeks of 1985, which had been played on the summer 1983 Three Musketeers tour, as well as being tried out by Grand Slam. Johnson recalls recording with Philip: 'When we worked on the songs, he would dive straight in there and put down a bass line, keyboard and guide vocal, and then he would let me fly on how the lead should be improvised.'

David Jensen – an early champion of Thin Lizzy on the radio – was also concerned for Philip's well-being and intimated that he should look after himself. After spending some time together backstage, they met again later that same evening: 'After the show, we met up at the airport, as we were all flying back to London. We talked for a while, and he told me he was cleaning up his act, but he didn't look very well. He was talking about his children and how he wanted to be around for them, and then he took all these little gifts and cards from his bag, which were for their Christmas presents. He spoke fairly positively, expressed no regrets, and we wished each other well.'

After filming the *Razzmatazz* Christmas Special, Philip immediately returned to London and attended management's yuletide celebration, where he was photographed looking spirited, to say the least, dressing smartly. Philip's mother was due to spend Christmas with him in London with the agreement that he would return to Ireland to celebrate the new year. She arrived about a week before Christmas day in preparation for the festivities. The terms of his separation agreement with Caroline dictated that Philomena was to be present when Philip had the children under his supervision. By this time, Philip and Caroline had been separated for around 18 months. Since the period of their separation, from time to time, Caroline would spend the weekend at their London home, which was noted by Philip's mother in her memoir *My Boy*. It gave her some hope that all was not lost for their relationship. While the couple never actually divorced, unfortunately, the action taken by Caroline in removing herself and both children from the family home did little or nothing to deter Philip from his chosen path.

A few days before Christmas, Philip overdosed in his Richmond home. While he survived the overdose, the damage was immense. As outlined in *My Boy*, she returned to Philip's Richmond home with Sarah and Cathleen after attending a nativity play with Caroline and her family in Bath. While he rallied to spend some time with them by watching a film, he soon began to deteriorate. Thereafter, Philomena entertained the children while Philip returned to bed, showing no signs of improvement as Christmas Eve arrived. Later that night, Philomena phoned Dublin, and family friend Graham Cohen agreed to travel over to support her and Philip. Two doctors visited the house and administered medicines, but there was no improvement. A Christmas Day conversation between Philomena and Caroline resulted in a decision being made – Caroline drove from Bath to Richmond to collect him, and not knowing how serious his medical condition was, Philip was taken to a rehabilitation clinic. The invoice for the self-abuse inflicted over the past ten years was now falling due.

By the time he was admitted to hospital later on Christmas Day, he was slipping in and out of consciousness. The measure of drug abuse he'd inflicted upon himself led to multiple organ failure. He developed pneumonia and sepsis, and consequently, his weakened body couldn't fight the infection. For 11 days, he fought but succumbed on 4 January 1986, a matter of months after his 36th birthday.

The subsequent days were a blur for family and close friends. The man who sold himself as bulletproof was dead. As days turned to weeks, months and years, the gravity of his death lost little of its impact. The anger and frustration that was felt by those who knew him and had trouble comprehending his unnecessary demise at the young age of 36 eventually gave way to acceptance, but seldom, understanding. Photographer Denis O'Regan:

I felt that his death was inevitable because I knew of his drug problem and the fact that he was in the hospital. I was at home when I heard of his death and felt an unhinging sadness ... I remember him as a fun person who, for some reason, allowed drugs to get the better of him, not just ultimately but on a daily level. He was talented and amusing, demanding and loyal, arrogant but kind, and like Bowie, he knew when a trend was developing and took steps to take advantage of it. He liked to experiment and would have loved the digital age and the internet for what he could have done with it and how it could have satisfied his creative and demanding mind.

Philip was brought home on 10 January 1986 for the final time. His funeral took place the following day in Howth, Co. Dublin, a short distance from his family home in Glen Corr. Jim Fitzpatrick recalls a 'cold, black day' when he attended the funeral. While the funeral mass and burial were held in Dublin, a few days prior, a reception was held in Richmond. Fiachra Trench:

I witnessed something that gave me a tingle when I came out of the church in Richmond; not a tingle of joy, but something that so disgusted me. Caroline got into the car and there was a big crowd, and I remember the press pushing their cameras so far and obtrusively close to capture this woman in her grief. I recall going back home and being so angry at this intrusion ... okay, they were estranged. But this woman was, at one point, his wife and I had never seen such viciousness before.

Philip was buried in the St Polan's section of St Fintan's Cemetery. The grave was marked for a time with a temporary white cross, which made it somewhat comparable to that of a cowboy, only in this case, an emerald cowboy. In keeping with the regulations of the graveyard, a flat stone later replaced it featuring a design by Jim Fitzpatrick with the inscription, 'Go dtuga Dia suaimhneas de anam Roisin Dubh', which loosely translates to 'My God rest the soul of our Black Rose'. This was later replaced again after the death of Philomena. His grave site has since become a shrine for supporters the world over to come and pay their respects. In their droves, they arrive, leave notes and mementoes, light candles, and chat. Their shared admiration for the legacy of Lizzy and that of his work beyond the band corrals their conversation.

On the first anniversary of his death, Smiley Bolger began nourishing Philip's legacy by presenting what became an annual Vibe for Philo. In a conversation recalled by Smiley with Philip a few years before his death, he recalled his request to 'Do a vibe for me some time'. Bolger's industry didn't come up short and, like the music, provided a much-needed catharsis for all involved. The Vibes continued until 2023, but their echo continues, like Smiley's efforts and much like Philip's impact on people. The Vibes were strongly supported by Philomena over the years, and even at an advanced age, she would do her best to attend. Philomena Lynott died on 12 June 2019, aged 88. She is buried with her son beneath the hills of Howth in St. Fintan's Cemetery.

While Philomena was alive, she welcomed supporters from all over the world, invited them into her home, and watched as strangers gathered together. She created and gave this vital space to friendly strangers. Once she opened her heart to the love that people around the world had for Thin Lizzy and Philip, it aided in some small way in her grieving. Perhaps it helped everyone who came to visit.

In the aftermath of his death, Philomena moved into his home in Glen Corr as Caroline retreated to Bath in England to be nearer her parents. In the early nineties, Caroline began court proceedings to have Philomena removed from the property, which proved successful. In her book *My Boy*, Philomena commented that she felt the property should be retained until Philip and Caroline's children came of age to make up their own minds on what to do with the property. Eventually, Philomena had to vacate Glen Corr, whereupon it was put up for sale and promptly sold in the mid-90s. It remains to this day one of many stop-off points for any visitors looking to trace the footsteps of his life in Dublin.

As the 1990s wore on, various Thin Lizzy compilations appeared, including *Wild One*, and there was even a re-issue of the poetry books, *Philip* and *Songs For While I'm Away*, issued by Boxtree. There were also rumours of an impending box set, a career retrospective of his work. Robbie Dennis, Philip's Polydor support, recalls:

> Sometime in 1998, I sent copies of all the demos Phil had given to me to a guy in the States called Bill Levenson, who wanted to produce a historical document on Phil's solo work. These tapes were not masters, merely copies of what I had left in my collection. Bill spoke to Phil's manager, Chris Morrison, and got verbal approval for this proposed box set. He would go away and work on it and then present it to Morrison. For some reason, the project has never seen the light of day.

It's very likely that the original project concept was rinsed and recalibrated, as Bill Levenson was credited on the first considerable box set release of Thin Lizzy's music *Vagabonds, Kings, Warriors, Angels*, which eventually saw the light of day in 2001. The thirst for Thin Lizzy products hasn't gone away in recent years and has likely been kindled even further since the unveiling of the Philip Lynott statue in August 2005. Paul Daly was the Dublin artist responsible for what has become a hugely popular tourist site in the years since its unveiling. It's a remarkable piece of work, located on Harry Street in Dublin City Centre.

Thin Lizzy supporters continue to see the redistribution of the band's back catalogue in various formats. Studio albums received the deluxe edition dust-off, and box sets have frequently flowed, peaking with *Rock Legends*: a triumphant career retrospective. The *Live And Dangerous* set has also been re-released in an expanded format to include all the shows that Lizzy performances were culled from to build the album. It showcases an incendiary band at the peak of their heroic power. For an additional lap of honour, the album *Vagabonds Of The Western World* has also received the expanded-format release. The sets keep coming, and the supporters keep applauding. The latest box-set addition is *Thin Lizzy 1976*, showcasing the breakthrough albums *Jailbreak* and *Johnny The Fox* that consolidated the band's commercial viability and growing fanbase, featuring a series of unreleased diamonds hewn from the Lizzy vaults. Some thirsts just can't be quenched. In the right hands with the right concepts, perhaps more such sets will see release, specifically a re-examination of Philip's work beyond Thin Lizzy. We have yet to see a collected written work featuring his lyrics, which would provide important insight into his writing process as he often continuously reworked material up until the last minute while in the studio.

In life, rather than song, Philip is remembered by those who knew him as a reserved character. He was gently spoken and considerate of his friends and fully aware that his graft afforded him an enviable position. He helped his fellow musicians, who were starting out as his star was on the ascent, as they have recalled in this book. He remembered where and what he came from. Studded guitar belts and painted-on leathers were the act. Sometimes, the actor let slip the facade. Sometimes, the actor purposely rinsed the facade and that's how we can listen and digest this other character singing on *Solo In Soho* and *The Philip Lynott Album*. We can hear songs about the people that meant the most to him, about the city of Dublin and all its traditional allure. We can also hear the impact of his travels and how they affected him and his writing. We have the opportunity to hear the echo of his personal life experiences, the times before and during Thin Lizzy. They offer glimpses and, on occasion, answers to questions that could never be put to him due to his early death. His final writings do offer strong clues to where his musical future may have taken him. By all accounts, the experimental musical urges that were a constant from the beginning of his career still appeared to be firmly in place as he was plotting the next phase in 1985. Philip Lynott didn't have a third act, but the legacy he created as a solo artist and that of the leader of Thin Lizzy ensures that he and his bandmates will be spoken about for some time to come.

A Renegade that lost his way but is remembered still.

Coda: Don't Talk Behind My Back

Lizzy were such a funny band. On *Jailbreak*, their friendship was quite tight, and although they had ups and downs, they were all going in the same direction. By the time of *Johnny The Fox*, there were cracks appearing. Even then, Phil had this solo stuff at the back of his mind and once he reached a point where he could do it, that's what he would do.

He was the main songwriter and probably had a huge bunch of other material he wanted to experiment with. A bit like Pete Townshend, he kept stuff aside for his solo albums when (Townshend was) actively involved with The Who. I guess it must be difficult for songwriters; you've got your main thing going, which is your bread and butter, I suppose, but there's this burning desire inside of you that says you really want to have a go at this other stuff. Phil was always pretty professional. He knew where he was going and how he wanted to do it. Plus, he had the talent to back it up with.

I'm sure Phil would have found his way through if *Jailbreak* had been a flop and the band had to break up: he'd have found another way, I'm convinced of that. He was probably the most naturally talented person I've ever worked with.

Will Reid Dick

He was a star and exuded star quality. He wasn't someone who used Hai Karate aftershave, shall we say. But he was a star who was down on his luck. By the time he was working with us, he should've had the financial muscle that a major record label could provide behind him, but he didn't. If he had the support of his record company, then video shoots would've been comfortable affairs, but 'Old Town' certainly wasn't. We were all freezing our asses off, but we just got on with it. I remember at the end of the second day, him saying he wanted a lift to Lombard Studio, and we drove him down there, and he was meeting Luke Kelly. Now, Luke was working on something, but they obviously arranged to meet up. I left him there, and that was one of the last times I saw Luke alive. They obviously had a friendship and were setting up to do some damage that night.

Gerry Gregg

The first time I actually met Phil, was at the press conference in Dublin to launch the Dalymount Park gig that September. I found him

charming, but at that point, we did not speak for long. I can tell you that The Radiators were on that show because of Philip. He quietly insisted on us being on the show despite unspecified resistance from the promoter.
Phil Chevron

I guess they (Thin Lizzy) really were a rock 'n' roll band, almost in the same way as a band like The Doors that was right on the edge of everything ... the image of Thin Lizzy, you know, 'The Boys Are Back In Town' ... it's an outlaw image, let's face it. I think the whole thing went together. I think it's entirely possible the band could've been quite massive rather than just really, really big. Phil's bass playing and vocals were utterly unique. There isn't anybody that could ever play bass like Phil; there isn't anybody that could sing like Phil.
Tony Platt

Whenever things got tough, Phil always insisted I try to sort it out through Chris Morrison, and he would more often than not help iron out any problem we might have. I think Phil did this consciously, in order to keep our relationship at a somewhat-intact station. We believed in the band, and I think they had a pretty good idea of where we were coming from. To the last day of his life, we remained friends and never did fall out.
Frank Rodgers

After he died, I was speaking with my mother, and she told me that Phil used to ring her to let her know I was doing alright. He'd actually ring her every five or six weeks, and I never knew that until he was gone. I was never one of those guys who was always ringing home. I know I helped him out over the years as well, but that took me by surprise and it showed you the kind of guy he was.
Tex Read

I think he opened a huge amount of doors for young aspiring musicians to get out there and do it. He wrote a very nice type of almost soul music with a little touch of Irish in it. The Irish roots were there, as were his black roots, and it was a very interesting combination. There was a huge fusion of stuff going on. I think if Irish popular music is a mountain range, he might not be Everest, but he's definitely up there – certainly Kilimanjaro. I see his music as a formidable mountain range, and though I

don't know who Everest might be, Philip would certainly be a contender to be one of the more influential people of the last 50 years.
Tim Booth

I think the statue is a fitting tribute to Philip's memory and a nice addition to the street scenery in Dublin. He was an international ambassador for Ireland in the music industry, and without him, a lot of the doors he opened would remain closed to Irish music in general. Long may his memory be kept alive.
Sean O'Connor

... and a final word from Junior Giscombe ...

Phil was always honest with me. The man I knew would want to cover me, put himself in front of me. He was a teacher and my guide at a time of me wanting to learn how to approach melody timing at different speeds. His humour was dark and always had me in stitches. It was a privilege and a pleasure to have worked with him. He is still greatly missed.

Skid Row – 1969, A Tribute To Philip Lynott

Bumping over Sally's Bridge, heading for Leighlin Road
The windscreen wipers swishing away the torrential rain
And 'Albatross' playing on the radio

Phil's gran is away, he has the house to himself
So we can all party and it's not my turn to pay the taxi fare

Phil has plenty of bread – it was a good gig
CYMS Fairview – always goes well
It's a pity Brush's amp keeps breaking down
Scully nearly electrocuted me tonight
With that f'n Soldering iron

In the house ... 'Phil, what did you do with my Etta James LP?
You said you'd give it back to me months ago'
'Cool it Mick, don't be getting ratty, I told you –
I loaned it to Brian Downey'

Phil keeps telling jokes about Biafrans
The others think it's funny – I'm going to sleep – it's 4:30 am

Morning sees Philip ironing his jeans
And polishing his brown brogues – with black polish

You couldn't swing a cat in Phil's kitchen

Michael O'Flanagan

Further Notes And Sources

Eamon Carr Quote: Radiators From Space, *Sound City Beat* Inlet Notes.
Alan Sinclair Quote: *Evening Herald* Interview.
Brush Shiels Quote: *Irish Folk, Trad And Blues: A Secret History* by Colin Harper and Trevor Hodgett.
NME article 'A Peep into the Soul of Phil Lynott' by Chris Salewicz (10 September 1977)
Terry Woods Quote: *Hello Magazine* article by Yvonne McMahon.
Eric Wrixon quote: *Irish Folk, Trad And Blues: A Secret History* by Colin Harper and Trevor Hodgett.
Philip Quote: *The Sun* article by Bob Hart (10 June 1977).
Mail Online article by Jason O'Toole (31 July 2010).
Philip Quote: *Record Mirror* article (18 June 1977).
Philip Quote: *NME* article 'Ireland's Own' by Harry Doherty (1976).
Jim Fitzpatrick Combined Quote: *Hot Press* Yearbook article 'The Art of The Matter' by Jim Fitzpatrick (1991).
Philip Quotes: *NME* article by Chris Salewicz (1976) (precise date unknown).
Philip Quotes: *Record Mirror* article by Rosalind Russell (1977).
Caroline Crowther Quote: *The Rocker, Portrait of Phil Lynott* by Shay Healy (1995).
Philomena Lynott Quote: *My Boy* by Philomena Lynott and Jackie Hayden.
Various articles in *The Sun, Mail Online, Record Mirror, Hot Press, My Boy*.
BP Fallon Quote: *Sunday Independent* article 'My Friend Phil – A Tale of Wonder and Waste' by BP Fallon (9 February 1997).
Brian Downey Quote: *Hot Press* article (1979).
Tony Visconti Quote: BBC Documentary *Bad Reputation* (2011).
Article 'Solo in Soho – A Masterpiece' by Jorgen Holmstedt and Mats Pettersson (April 1980).
Philip Quote: BBC Radio One show *Rock On* by Trevor Dann.
Philip Quotes: *NME* article (1980).
Darren Wharton Quote: *Manchester Evening News* article 'Darren Made it with Lizzy' by Ray King (November 1980).
Philip Quote: *Record Mirror* article by John Shearlaw (25 October 1980).
Philip Quote: Radio Copenhagen (30 September 1982).
Philip Quote: Dutch Radio (1983).
Philip Quote: RTÉ *Late Late Show* (1981).

Noel McMurray Quote: Interview by James Taylor (*http://www.trcjt.ca/*) (23 October 2004).
Caroline Crowther Quote: *Daily Mirror* (May 1984).
Philip Quote: *Sunday Mail* article by Daniela Soave (28 July 1984).
Philip Quote: Dave Fanning Radio Show (1984).
Philip Quote: taken from an interview by Mark Putterford (1984).
Philip Quote: *Hot Press* article 'Across The Great Divide' by Bill Graham (7 June 1985).
Gary Moore Quote: *Hot Press* article 'Across The Great Divide' by Bill Graham (7 June 1985).
Midge Ure Quote: *If I Was... The Autobiography* by Midge Ure.
Robin George Quote: *Spirit Of The Black Rose* CD release sleeve notes.
Caroline Crowther quote: *The Sun* (21 May 1984).
Philip Quote: *Sunday Mail* (29 July 1984).
Philip Quote: *Oxford Mail* article by Ben Fenton (27 April 1984).
Philip Quote: *Coventry Evening Telegraph* article by Jim Taylor (3 December 1985).
Philip Quote: *Irish Evening Press* article by Peter Marriott (16 November 1984).

Would you like to write for Sonicbond Publishing?

At Sonicbond Publishing we are always on the look-out for authors,
particularly for our two main series:

On Track. Mixing fact with in depth analysis, the On Track series examines the
work of a particular musical artist or group. All genres are considered from easy
listening and jazz to 60s soul to 90s pop, via rock and metal.

On Screen. This series looks at the world of film and television. Subjects
considered include directors, actors and writers, as well as entire television and
film series. As with the On Track series, we balance fact with analysis.

While professional writing experience would, of course, be an advantage
the most important qualification is to have real enthusiasm and knowledge
of your subject. First-time authors are welcomed, but the ability to write
well in English is essential.

Sonicbond Publishing has distribution throughout Europe and North America,
and all books are also published in E-book form. Authors will be paid a
royalty based on sales of their book.

Further details are available from www.sonicbondpublishing.co.uk.
To contact us, complete the contact form there or
email info@sonicbondpublishing.co.uk